Practical Export Managemen

Practical Export Management

CHRIS J. NOONAN

London
GEORGE ALLEN & UNWIN
Boston   Sydney

George Allen & Unwin (Publishers) Ltd,
40 Museum Street, London WC1A 1LU, UK

George Allen & Unwin (Publishers) Ltd,
Park Lane, Hemel Hempstead, Herts HP2 4TE, UK

Allen & Unwin Inc,
Fifty Cross Street, Winchester, Mass 01890, USA

George Allen & Unwin Australia Pty Ltd,
8 Napier Street, North Sydney, NSW 2060, Australia

First published in 1985

British Library Cataloguing in Publication Data

Noonan, Chris J.
    Practical export management.
1. Export marketing—Great Britain
I. Title
658.8'48'0941   HF1009.5
ISBN 0-04-658246-0
ISBN 0-04-658247-9 Pbk

Library of Congress Cataloging in Publication Data

Noonan, Chris J.
    Practical export management.
Bibliography: p.
Includes index.
1. Exporting marketing—Management—Handbooks, manuals,
etc. 2. Export trading companies—Management—Handbooks,
manuals, etc. 3. Foreign trade promotion—Management—
Handbooks, manuals, etc. 4. Foreign trade regulation—
Handbooks, manuals, etc. I. Title.
HF1009.5.N662   1985   658.8'48   84–28223
ISBN 0-04-658246-0
ISBN 0-04-658247-9 (pbk.)

Set in 10 on 11 Times by Grove Graphics, Tring, Hertfordshire
and printed in Great Britain by Billing and Sons Ltd,
London and Worcester

Contents

PART TWO   PRICING, PACKAGING AND PROMOTIONAL CONSIDERATIONS

PART THREE   PROCEDURAL ASPECTS OF ADMINISTRATION AND DISTRIBUTION

PART FOUR   LEGAL AND REGULATORY CONSIDERATIONS

List of Examples

Foreword

Mr Noonan's book is well-named. He distils practical experience into words. His advice has the quality one associates with tips given by an old hand. He warns the novice against pitfalls, but he gives hints that the experienced man will not be ashamed to pick up.

If asked to pick out chapters that best illustrate the book's special characteristics I would suggest the chapters in Part V which describe alternative market development programmes. For example, I am not presently aware of any better treatment of that very necessary extension of normal selling, the granting of a licence.

I am flattered that Chris Noonan should have paid such heed to the sparse comments I had on his first manuscript and am sure that what is now laid before the reader will prove rewarding to the man who is up to his neck in the business of selling overseas just as much as to any student of export marketing and overseas trade.

D. N. ROYCE
Director-General, The Institute of Export.

Acknowledgements

The early drafts of this book were produced while I was living and working in the United States. The book was motivated by my awareness that many competent business managers were unfamiliar with the practice of export development and management, yet knew there was opportunity to be pursued and tapped. Friends such as Rollie Rierdon and Leo Culligan provided support services in tackling the project. Dr Lyle Sussman, of the University of Louisville, gave most useful comments on the style as it related to communicating effectively with the readers. My close friend, Dr Eric Hill, gave constant moral support over the year or so it took to get a workable draft together, as did Len Ogden, Jr. In London, David Royce, Director-General of the Institute of Export, provided a most useful commentary and review enabling me to improve on initial drafts. The other friends and associates who provided advice, comments or simply their invaluable support are too numerous to mention.

CHRIS J. NOONAN
LONDON, JAN. 1985

Introduction

The book's scope, purpose and target audience

Exporting and the general conduct of international trade require a far broader range of managerial skills and knowledge of a company's operations than do most positions in a company's management structure. Although the exporter may be seen by some as a generalist rather than a specialist, he does need specialist training and knowledge, which must go beyond knowledge of products and company operations to encompass international distribution and shipping, export documentation and payments, and the many legal and quasi-legal aspects of international trade.

The purpose of this book is to impart a sufficient level of understanding and knowledge to enable the reader to commence travelling and trading with a degree of confidence, or to enable senior executives to feel competent in discussions with colleagues and subordinates who have export responsibilities. It is compiled from personal experience gained over sixteen years of practical international business operations with major blue-chip multinational corporations.

The work is intended to offer, in a concise, informative and readable style, a guide to the practicalities of entering international markets, and an introduction to practical export management. It is not intended as a major reference work on the subject, but is designed to pull together the many facets of international business and exporting, summarizing under the various subject headings and sections the key elements of each subject that a practitioner and manager should be familiar with. It gives a broad coverage of the field of exporting and export management, going into greater depth on subjects particularly related to the practical side of export management and development. On the very technical and specialized legal and quasi-legal aspects (including carriage, insurance, protection of industrial property, and contracting) the interested reader is referred to the supplementary reading list at the end of the text. A number of these works definitely have a place in the professional exporter's library, but the senior executive less concerned with fine detail than with a broad understanding of the role, scope, development and management of export and international business operations should find this volume alone a sufficient guide to the subject.

There will be critics who feel that many comments or statements simplify the problems of exporting. I am certainly not trying to imply that we are dealing with a simple subject, but I do feel that exporting is no different from any other business discipline, and that the key to problem-solving is found in realistic assessment of situations and opportunities and forming an action plan. All too often managers have a tendency to make life more complicated and frustrating than it need be. In reality, all parties to a business transaction have an interest in trouble-free completion of commercial agreements and in finding mutually satisfactory resolution to problems.

This work should be of interest to:

- chief executives, sales and marketing directors and other senior line managers who want to understand export practice and management, and the role and contribution it can make in their organization;
- export managers who wish to consolidate their knowledge and experience and 'see the wood from the trees';
- other managers providing support services to an export department, such as warehouse, production, shipping and distribution, and finance and costing;
- students of lower-level export courses such as BEC and Institute of Export, or students of other basic business courses at college or university that deal with international business;
- businessmen attending short courses in export and international business related subjects at colleges or management training centres;
- management and clerical recruits to export departments;
- those in government service who provide export support services;
- bankers who specialize in international trade related matters and who wish to be better briefed on practical aspects of exporting.

The final chapter deals with some practical suggestions to assist senior executives in considering alternatives and developing a medium- or longer-range international strategy. It considers the structure, role and benefits of an internal committee to formulate strategy. I am aware that some chief executives and top managers of smaller companies will feel that they cannot formalize to the suggested degree, perhaps because of limited staffing levels; equally, in many medium to large companies the chief executives and directors may assume that such suggestions are not applicable, perhaps because they already have an active operating international business section, or they find it hard to coordinate a formal grouping. Whether a committee be formally structured, or a looser group be considered, I would still strongly urge chief executives of both smaller and larger companies to give serious consideration to this approach to develop a realistic formal international strategy and implement resultant plans and proposals. The positive sense of direction must come from the top; commitment must be demonstrated, rather than excuses accepted.

How to use the book

This work is intended to give breadth of coverage and introduce in one readable volume the subject of practical exporting and export management. The reader is therefore recommended to adopt the following system, depending on his/her own particular purpose and needs in reading or reviewing the subject:

- Read the book quickly from cover to cover, particularly noting the chapter summaries, to get a broad understanding of the subject matter and scope of the book. This may well be all that is needed by the non-specialist exporter, such as those in other support roles or senior executives.
- Those with specialist export involvement or responsibility should then re-read the book chapter by chapter. On any subject or chapter of special interest where additional depth of knowledge may be required, I would refer the reader to the recommended reading list at the end of the text, where books are listed under broad subject headings.
- Where examples, figures and tables appear, the export student or practitioner not already familiar with such systems or activity may benefit by creating his/her own examples. Familiarity comes with practice.
- It may be found very beneficial to produce your own summary of key points, or checklists relevant to your own needs.
- The book may also serve as an occasional reference point subsequently when problems arise in areas covered by the book.

Little attention has been given to the actual completion of the multiplicity of forms associated with exporting, because such coverage is really beyond the scope and purpose of this work, and is very effectively covered elsewhere, as in the booklets of the Simplification of International Trade Procedures Board (SITPRO) or similar works in the United States.

The interested reader can additionally supplement this work by including discussions with specialists such as shipping forwarders, bankers, international trade lawyers, and government export agencies, to expand on the knowledge base imparted in this book.

Desk research
- Analysis of export & import statistics
- Identifying rules and regulations
- Identifying potential representatives

Overseas contacts
- Introductory letters & questionnaires to potential representatives, trade associations, banks, government agencies
- Initial market visits to above contacts
- Contact reports for action and follow-up

Product marketing
- New/existing product opportunities
- Packaging for physical protection, regulation compliance, and market positioning
- Pricing and costing studies
- Advertising & promotion plans & budgets

Alternative sales systems
- Overseas branches & representatives
- Joint ventures
- Foreign subsidiaries
- Foreign licensing agreements
- Export management companies
- Other export agents

Insurance & distribution
–Delivery of goods to carriers
–Negotiation of freight rates
–Mechanics of shipping
–Carriage practice and laws
–Marine insurance policy
 negotiation
–Government insurance of
 exports

Legal obligations
–Contractual performance
–Export documentation &
 regulations
–Import documentation &
 regulations
–Dispute handling & arbitration
–Terminations

Export documentation
–Bills of lading
–Export licences &
 declarations
–Commercial invoices
–Insurance certificates
–Other requisite certification
 for product importation

EXPORT
MARKETING

EXPORT
ADMINISTRATION

Order processing
–Processing quote request &
 order enquiries
–Issue of pro forma invoices
–Scheduling production and
 distribution
–Monitoring progress from
 order receipt to payment
 receipt

Planning & monitoring performance
–Analysis of export shipments
–Market stock & sales reports
–Market shares
–Performance against budgets &
 plans
–Year-on-year performance
 comparisons

Finance & payment methods
–Drafts & letters of credit
–Internal financial resources
–Discounting drafts
–Loans and advances secured
 against firm orders
–Loans from export banks or
 agencies

PART ONE

IDENTIFYING INTERNATIONAL OPPORTUNITIES

1

Why Export?

One frequently hears or reads of comments, often from politicians, that the country needs to export more to improve the balance of payments. Rhetoric may imply that companies are not sufficiently aggressive in seeking international opportunities. Domestic companies, on the other hand, frequently complain that imports are killing their traditional home market for products and reducing employment opportunities and profits. Both commercial and political interests may join together in a plea for protection, including requests to impose or change import quotas, tariffs and other non-tariff barriers, or to put direct and indirect pressure on the exporting nation to reduce the trade imbalance voluntarily.

Historically, in countries and industries where protectionism has been a policy, it has been to protect fledgling or stagnant industries that would otherwise not be competitive and possibly simply have to cease production, or it has been designed to give a degree of protection to assist a domestic industry that is considered essential to the industrial base of the developing country, such as defence-related industries, heavy equipment producers, possibly even automobile assembly plants. The governmental objective here may be to enable the work force to acquire industrial skills and promote diversification and a gradual shift from an agrarian economy and lifestyle.

International businessmen, and many wiser members of the political and governmental circles, realise that protectionism is generally not a satisfactory solution to trade imbalances in today's environment of increased international economic interdependence and moral commitments to developing nations. Moreover, protectionism has often been cited as a cause of inefficiencies in management and production practices, including poorer quality control and higher prices, and reduced rates of technological innovation.

Exports benefit the exporter and the importer in the following three areas of concern: (a) political activity, (b) economic activity, and (c) social activity.

Politically, international trade is important in building permanent relationships, loyalties, dependencies and spheres of influence. The major western industrial powers, for example, want to use trade as a medium for extending their influence and countering what they may see as subversive elements opposed to the capitalistic lifestyle. Governments are usually concerned directly with two main areas of trade: those dealing with mass feeding (often through food aid programmes) in developing nations, and those dealing with technology, training and equipment related to defence or the ongoing supply of essential resources such as energy.

Economically, trade results in specialization and a cross-flow of goods and services from the country with the greatest economic advantage in production to the country with needs that cannot as efficiently be satisfied domestically. This is clearly evident in the case of commodities such as coffee, wine or oil, where specific climates or environments are needed to produce the products yet the taste or industrial need for these goods have resulted in enormous markets in the non-producing world. Levels of work-force skills and technology also vary to such an extent worldwide that, in general, traditional agrarian and non-industrial economies need an ever-increasing range of industrial products in exchange for their raw materials and commodity-oriented exports.

Socially, trade brings about change and progress by transferring skills, services and products from more advanced to less advanced economies. There are those who take the position that the less developed countries are better off and would be happier in the long term without the social change, pressures and problems considered to be associated with industrialization and consumer societies. In general, this is a minority view. The population of less advanced (developing) nations is more usually considered in contemporary thinking to have the right to develop and improve living standards, including health and education facilities. International trade has its role in contributing to the development of both peoples and nations.

Generally, therefore, if freer trade encourages better use of the world's resources, and if improvements in technology and product range and quality help advance the less developed nations by opening new opportunities and creating a greater international interdependence, perhaps reducing the belligerent threats to world peace, surely it should be encouraged.

Exporting benefits an individual country because it helps improve its own balance of payments and trade through increased foreign exchange earnings. Exports need not just be physical goods; they can equally beneficially include services such as banking, insurance, consultancy, technology transfer and training. Perhaps the greatest pressure on world trade since the Second World War has been the phenomenal rise in demand for energy resources – mainly oil – and the economic pressures this has placed on nations without domestic oil reserves to produce other goods and services needed in export markets in order to acquire the requisite foreign currency to pay for energy needs.

An individual company benefits from exports through increased plant utilization, which, in turn, gives more secure employment opportunities, better labour force morale and training, a better profit base to reward shareholders and employees, and the generation of more funds for reinvestment. Increased production and productivity add to the gross national product. Higher profits and employee earnings increase the tax base, enabling the local and central government to generate additional funds for those programmes it sees as politically, economically and socially desirable.

The individual company can often benefit by exporting at less than full cost, particularly where spare production capacity exists, because overheads can be spread over a greater volume of output; indeed, these overheads may already have been costed in to be recovered from the planned level of domestic sales. There is a positive benefit in marginally costing exports as long as the variable production costs associated with the export orders can be recovered, along with costs of distribution. If there is spare capacity in the plant, and the domestic market cannot for any reason be encouraged or manipulated to take more products, then seek export markets, either of standard home market products or of such export-modified products as can conveniently be produced on the home production line.

There will always be individuals in any organization who can see only the problems associated with handling export orders: payment, credit and currency problems, special packaging and labelling requirements, additional quality control, small production runs involving time-consuming changes and product modifications, and so on. The professional exporter has to liaise and mediate between all the departments involved in ensuring that the order is filled correctly and on time, and must motivate the less enthusiastic individuals involved in the project to contribute positively to the required effort. The export manager is responsible for finding the profitable export markets for his company's goods and services, for identifying other products his company could be producing to meet existing or new markets, and for increasing plant utilization with the least disruption to current business activity. The keys to success in exporting are flexibility and perseverance.

Summary

- International trade confers social, political and economic benefits in the exporting and importing nations at both the micro and macro levels.
- The exporting manufacturer benefits from utilization of spare capacity of plant and labour forces, with similar benefit to related suppliers of goods and services such as ingredients or raw materials, shipping, banking, insurance, and other support services.

- The exporting nation benefits from fuller employment, improved balance of international payments, higher gross national product levels, a broader tax base on income and profits with the related benefit on domestic social or infrastructure programmes, and greater international economic influence.
- The importing nation has a broader product base resulting from the provision of goods and services, with consequent increases in living standards and industrialization, including the acquisition and development of new skills.
- The use of new technology, plant and skills benefits the foreign company and worker through increased earning capacity, expanded employment base, rising standards of living, and diversification of economic opportunities.
- International trade facilitates a more optimal use of the world's resources.

2

Preliminary Desk Research

Now that you have considered that there may be opportunities for your company outside the home market, the next step is to start identifying and quantifying the opportunities.

Overseas travel is expensive, so as much preliminary work as possible should be done from the home base − the desk research. Here you can consider what types of information and what sources might be available that would help you in forming a preliminary view of where to concentrate your efforts.

You may think that the whole world is your oyster, but in reality comprehensive desk research will normally narrow your interest to a manageable number of markets where other knowledge (e.g. home market experience) suggests that you have the best chance of success in creating market demand for your products or technology.

Export statistics

It is customary in most countries that, when an export takes place, the exporter must report to some authority (such as customs and excise) the nature of the product under appropriate customs tariff headings, the volume of exports, and the value.

A study of home market export statistics will show:

● whether exports are taking place already
● where they are going
● volume and value of exports
● any seasonal pattern to exports in your product categories
● who is exporting.

Home market export statistics will normally be available from government sources (e.g. customs authorities) or through trade associations, chambers of commerce, libraries or government export promotion agencies.

If it is known that other countries are producing like products and are exporting them, then access to their export statistics will yield the same information on potential markets as I have noted above, and will additionally provide a basis for analysis of (from f.o.b. or c.i.f. value/volume comparisons):

- comparative export prices
- competitive export quantities
- magnitude of import trade to key markets.

Competitive country information will normally be available through the embassies of the foreign product source, your own government trade department or export promotion agencies, your own embassy in the foreign producer's country, or possibly interested trade associations at home that may like to monitor competition.

A thorough look at the export statistics available on comparable or similar products, substitute products or products where your own product would act as an input or ingredient in manufacturing or processing enables an evaluation to be made of the key countries at which you should look further — the target markets.

At this stage you should tabulate the information established and see what basic conclusions are apparent. It will frequently be found useful to tabulate initially in geographical regions (see Example 1).

Import data

Statistics   Now that you have a clear idea where the competitive sources of supply are and which are the key importing nations, the next step is to obtain detailed import statistics for the product category in the markets considered sizeable enough to be of interest to you. In export, as in most other business areas, concentration of effort in specific markets with specific products is often the most rewarding strategy.

Import figures can normally be obtained through the various government departments dealing with trade (e.g. the British Overseas Trade Board in the United Kingdom, or the United States Department of Commerce offices in the United States). If these figures are not available locally for any reason, an enquiry to the local commercial representative at the importing nation's embassy may either provide the information or assist in guiding you directly to sources in the countries being studied. Alternatively, contact with your own embassy's commercial attaché in the importing country may provide the information.

A study of the import statistics from these enquiries will start to put the flesh around the bones, greatly increasing your knowledge of the trading patterns with the data on:

- key sources of supply to the destination countries
- volumes by source of supply

Example 1

Tabulation of exports from major producers to identify potential import markets

Exporter / Importer	USA Volume Value	UK Volume Value	West Germany Volume Value	France Volume Value	Japan Volume Value
Latin America					
Argentina					
Brazil					
Chile					
Colombia					
Asia					
Indonesia					
Taiwan					
Thailand					
Philippines					
Middle East					
Saudi					
Kuwait					
Syria					
Jordan					
Egypt					
Africa					
Libya					
Algeria					
Kenya					
Zambia					
South Africa					
Europe					
France					
W. Germany					
Holland					
Italy					
Belgium					
Spain					
Greece					

- c.i.f. values by source of supply (enabling price comparisons to be made to assess competitiveness).

If there is any seasonal pattern to sales of your product, whether in supply, usage or consumer offtake, then a further breakdown of import (or export) statistics by month or quarter will probably be available through the same sources. This may have a commercial relevance, as with some seasonal products where it is necessary for customers to hold inventories for longer-than-normal periods to cover the short supply season. An exporter who can offer balanced shipments all year may be offering an indirect price advantage through reduced inventory financing. Moreover, supply availability when a competitor is in his off season may facilitate a first market entry.

Importers Normally, access to more detailed import records will show a breakdown by both value and volume, listing each importer by name, in the same way that export records will detail the exporters' names and shipping details (except where there is a provision for non-disclosure to protect companies that might be harmed by open access to their export details in customs records). This is an excellent way to identify who the dominant importers are, or to cross-check other sources that purport to list importers. In addition, it helps to check the veracity of importers who claim to be 'one of the biggest importers and oldest established firms' in the market. Exaggerated claims by potential importers and agents tend to be the norm rather than the exception among many entrepreneurial concerns in third world countries, and frequently it is difficult to obtain supporting data and substantiating cross-checks.

References from other exporters, reportedly represented exclusively by an importer, are an invaluable source of information on an importer's aggressiveness, performance and financial standing, and should be pursued as a matter of course. Normally, an exporter's opposite number at other companies will happily talk 'off the record' on his experiences in a market and give valuable commercial backgrounds on trading patterns and importers, regulations and customs known to him.

By this time you will have a far greater knowledge of potential markets and volumes and the prices at which recorded trade has taken place in the recent past. Since figures may often be up to three years old, you will probably be stretching your memory to recall accurately your own company's domestic or export prices at that time; in any event, it may not be too relevant a comparison if your own prices were not actually geared to quoting for exports at that time. However, your comparative analysis does give you an idea of ranking by price and volume of the competitive sources, and frequently these rankings will not have significantly changed over the short or medium term.

Identification of importers and distributors

The preceding research should have produced an initial list of some importers and distributors, but to complete the market survey a number of other sources can expand the list.

Government export agencies These agencies, such as the British Overseas Trade Board, will often have lists of potential or actual importers and distributors or be able to obtain such lists efficiently and rapidly from their staff in the commercial sections of their embassies located around the world. Frequently, however, these sources are incomplete or inaccurate. Lists may be incomplete if they rely upon foreign companies to make an approach to the embassy to request a listing as an importer or distributor, or if the list issued to the exporter includes only some contacts known to the embassy (it is a common practice for embassies not to provide a total list). Lists may be inaccurate if companies listing with the embassy have changed address or other contact details without advising the embassy; such changes are extremely frequent in developing nations, especially as a result of small traders going out of business and large traders needing to relocate to expand operations.

Chambers of commerce There may be a foreign chamber of commerce located in the country of interest (e.g. the British or American Chamber of Commerce located, say, in Mexico City). These organizations usually have a good base of local knowledge and contacts with commercial enterprises, and they are usually more commercially oriented than embassies and their staffs. It is nevertheless essential in drafting your enquiry to be very specific in your needs, in defining your target market sectors, and in describing your products and their uses and applications. The information you receive is a function of the quality of the enquiry you make.

Apart from foreign branches of domestic chambers of commerce, your local chamber of commerce is another useful source of data and information. They are likely both to keep a range of relevant trade directories and journals and to be able to direct you to sources with whom they have contact, such as the local chambers of commerce operating in some foreign countries. Where possible, always try to identify the name of a specific individual to whom you can personally direct any written enquiry, as this invariably produces a higher rate of response and, generally, better-quality information.

Banks All too often we think of the bank only in terms of paying and receiving funds. However, if your company has a relationship with a multinational bank, or if it banks directly with overseas associates or branches in the countries of interest to you, then an enquiry from your local manager to his foreign colleague or associate will generally prove to be an excellent source of information. Data may be available on:

- potential or actual importers banking with the foreign bank or branch
- financial status reports on potential importers
- general knowledge on trading problems with the foreign country, including currency and exchange matters, government priorities, rules and regulations.

Telephone directories If some of the more formal sources of information seem not to be producing adequate lists of contacts, why not try to find a 'Yellow Pages' directory for the major cities of the country of interest to you. These may be available through libraries, chambers of commerce, government export promotion agencies, or embassies and other foreign missions, and will invariably have sections relating to your product category. A very basic dictionary will overcome any language problems at this stage. If the potential contacts from this source seem scant, then try a telex or phone call to some of the listed contacts; explain your aims and objectives and ask advice on who you might contact. Most travelling exporters find that 'Yellow Pages' almost become their bible while sitting in hotel rooms trying to make 'cold contacts' in a country in which they are not experienced. After a brief explanation of who you are and what you represent, you will often be put on the right path to other leads that may be directly suited to your products.

Shipping lines Another source of information often neglected in the search for contacts is the shipping lines that move the goods to the markets of interest to you. A telephone call to a forwarding agent will enable you to identify which shipping lines go where, and a call to their sales service staff may give you access to potential importers through their own records or contact with their overseas branches or representatives. The bills of lading handled by the shipping lines give them excellent access to information on who is trading in what products. There may be ethical arguments against the release of information, but my own experience has always been that they are most cooperative.

Trade directories Most developed countries and many developing countries produce sophisticated trade directories of importers, distributors, exporters, manufacturers and service functions (e.g. *Thomas's Grocery Register* in the USA). These will often be available through chambers of commerce or government offices involved with international trade. Frequently, they not only list companies but provide additional information on size, volume, products, turnover and basic financial data.

Credit agencies   Publications by credit-checking and other commercial information services such as Dun & Bradstreet and Kompass contain a wealth of information enabling you to make some assessment of the strength of a company in the countries where such publications are available.

Trade associations   If there is a national trade association for your industry or for the industry to which you wish to sell in your home market, then it is very possible that they have contacts with their opposite numbers in foreign markets. Trade associations are most cooperative in helping potential exporters and may write introductory letters on your behalf to their foreign counterparts to help in contact identification.

Published market research   The *International Directory of Published Market Research* will contain much data on existing market research studies, some of which may be useful to the exporter and save costs of commissioning special research projects. It may be found in business and commercial libraries or through agencies such as the British Overseas Trade Board.

In addition to these standard and established sources of information on markets and importers, it is always useful to make a list of all organizations, associations, companies, etc., with whom you have contact in the home market, and then consider what assistance they may be able to provide in connection with your search for export markets. A few are mentioned below.

Market research agencies   These organizations frequently commission work for clients in foreign markets, and have a network of contacts and associates. They may well have access to market information likely to be of interest and relevance to a potential or established exporter, and a meeting to discuss your objectives and needs may prove beneficial.

Advertising agencies   The comments under the above section apply equally here, and an early approach to any home market advertising agency may prove most fruitful. They often will be especially helpful if they are a multinational agency with subsidiaries or affiliates in markets of interest to you, as clearly their hope is to handle any resultant advertising you may eventually plan in those foreign markets.

Auditors   If your domestic auditors are part of a multinational group, then they too will have access to contacts and market data through their foreign affiliates and will generally be most cooperative. Several of the major international auditing firms produce and publish extremely useful business guides on countries in which they have a practice, and these should be obtained.

While the information-gathering process seems straightforward and is a rather mechanical exercise, in practice it takes considerable time to elicit the information. Other people will not have your sense of priorities and urgency, and replies generally come in very slowly. You can only motivate the recipients of your initial communications by making the information requested seem interesting, available and relevant; make your contact really feel that he is making a significant contribution to a project that will progress.

At the conclusion of this stage of desk research, you should know:

● sources of exports of similar products
● import destinations, volumes and values
● potential importers, agents and distributors.

Further desk research

Additional desk research is needed into a number of areas before you can make the first export shipment.

Health and ingredient laws If you are dealing in foodstuffs, pharmaceuticals or a range of consumer products, information on health and ingredient regulations in the destination country is vital. Goods shipped that do not comply in all aspects with local laws are liable not to be allowed into the country. A mistake will be most costly if an importer finds goods not in compliance and refuses to pay a bill when due. Letters of credit may frequently specify that shipments must comply with all local rules and regulations applicable to the products being shipped.

Labelling and packaging The foreign country is likely to have its own rules and regulations on labelling and packaging, which may prove a hidden barrier to trade. Rules may cover language of the label, size of packages or units sold, size of lettering, position of labels, colours, product representations, production and expiry codes, product registration numbers, ingredient statements, names of distributors, and so on. This area of control often proves a major problem and trade barrier to producers of consumer goods, who may largely be selling to a domestic market and would find small special production runs an inconvenience. Thorough research at the outset will indicate if you can produce and be competitive while complying with all the laws.

Import licences and quotas   Many foreign countries have forms of import licences or quotas to control imports. These regulations enable the government agencies to:

● control the quantity and source of imports
● restrict imports of goods seen as 'non-essential'
● protect domestic industry
● control who is able to import
● control the allocation of foreign exchange reserves

Desk research once again will enable you to have a clear understanding of regulations relating to import control mechanisms. You need to establish:

● the absolute level of imports of your product permitted
● how often and by whom licences or quotas are allocated
● whether they are allocated on a 'first come, first served' basis or to historical importers
● whether the restrictions are imposed in monetary or volume terms
● whether licences or quotas are valid globally or for specific sources
● whether the quantities or values are fixed as part of a bilateral trade agreement or if they are variable at the whim of the government
● what is the customary period of validity of licences
● whether they are transferable from one party to another.

Establishing clear answers to these questions will aid you in assessing the degree of security with which you can start trading with the destination country; if you must make investments exclusively related to trade with that country, you can evaluate the risks against potential returns.

If licences are necessary and are issued on a historical basis, then that limits potential importers, unless a licence is transferable and your preferred importer has assured access to a transferred licence. You have much more flexibility where licences are issued on a 'first come, first served' basis. With a number of products seen as basic or essential, you may find the only importer is a government agency, which will handle all local sales and distribution. In this case, factors such as price, terms of trade and political considerations may override other commercial considerations such as quality, variety, delivery schedule, and your company's reputation. If you are dealing with a government agency, you will frequently need to spend enormous amounts of time establishing contacts in the decision-making process, which is often less clear-cut than in a private commercial enterprise.

Exchange restrictions   Availability of foreign exchange in your target country for your type of product is yet another factor in obtaining export orders. Should any restrictions exist, then your research should establish the guidelines for foreign exchange being made available. One common hidden barrier to trade is where one government agency is responsible for issuing licences, and another controls the availability of foreign exchange (and tells you this must be allocated prior to shipment of an order); your representative is left going back and forth trying to get the correct allocations with parallel validity from both agencies.

In some developing nations an importer must deposit a proportion of the value of any order before issue of licences or foreign exchange allocation. This acts as another deterrent to trade, because many importers are reliant on supplier credit to trade. Another delaying tactic inhibiting trade is where an importer pays his draft on time locally, but the central bank does not permit immediate remission of the funds overseas; instead, the bank releases remittances only according to some priority list, with the result that the supplier may wait months to receive his funds.

Internal market data

While analyses of export and import data show volumes and values of existing trade, they do not show the potential 'hidden' market, where the product (in existing or modified form) could be sold if access was obtained. Similar products may be locally produced and not imported either because of protective trade barriers or because they would just not be price competitive (as with soft drinks, which have a low ingredient cost and value).

The international marketeer should look beyond pure export opportunities to other ways of entering markets, and include in his field and desk research a programme to elicit data on countries where his products could be marketed other than by export, including licensing agreements or local manufacturing and distribution arrangements.

Most developed and many developing nations will have published data on production and consumption in a variety of product categories for local goods, and access to this will help seek out the additional market opportunities. Available market research, including omnibus studies, may highlight areas for consideration or further specialized research. Subsequent field visits will help identify the distribution channels and mechanisms available to organize local production if imports are not possible in competition with domestic goods.

Enquiry correspondence

The enquiry letter you first send to an overseas embassy, chamber of commerce or other contact is the key to eliciting germane information as part of your desk research programme. It is essential that the letter clearly and concisely communicate your objectives, who you are, and what you offer for sale. You are trying to motivate a busy recipient to seek out the data requested promptly and to respond diligently.

The foregoing sections of this chapter indicate that you may need data under any or all of the following information categories, depending on the nature of your products:

- recent import statistics
- lists of agents, importers and distributors
- size of local market for your products
- local economic data
- local labelling and packaging regulations
- requisite local product registrations or approvals
- health and ingredient rules and regulations
- import licence and quota regulations and administration
- foreign exchange controls
- tariffs (and any other non-tariff barriers not covered above).

The nature of your product may raise other questions to which you need answers prior to visiting the market, and it is well worth the time carefully to list any special circumstances before dispatching the enquiry letters.

The letter's recipient is unlikely to be sitting and waiting for your general enquiry letter, and will usually be more responsive if he sees that you have done some initial research. A professional, courteous and personally addressed letter will be more likely to produce the kind of reply you need. Whenever possible, before sending an enquiry letter, try to identify the specific name and title of the individual who can help you. A letter addressed only to the commercial counsellor or chamber director is much more likely to find its way into a wastepaper basket or pending file (see Example 2).

Frequently you may find that another government agency, such as the local office of the Department of Commerce or British Overseas Trade Board, wished to route all enquiries through its offices. From the exporter's perspective this is likely to reduce personal involvement and increase delays by the recipient. A direct letter to the specific individual overseas will often elicit a direct reply where that individual is aggressive and not too concerned over 'red tape', but you might consider sending a copy of correspondence to the local office of the appropriate government export agency.

Example 2
Introductory enquiry letter to an embassy

Mr John Smith
British Trade Commission
Bank of America Tower
12 Harcourt Road
Hong Kong

Dear Mr Smith

We are producers of speciality sugar and chocolate confectionery, mainly sold in gift boxes of from one to three pounds weight. While we do not yet export to Hong Kong, our initial research indicates an enormous market for imported confectionery in relation to the population, and I am given to understand that much of this is sold in connection with gift-giving seasons.

Our products and quality are well known, and I am enclosing a brochure to indicate our domestic product range. We can certainly consider modifications to this range if your local market requires that approach.

Specifically we would like your assistance in helping us enter your market by providing relevant information under the following categories:

- local import volume/value statistics
- local production and/or consumption statistics if available
- product registration and product approval regulations, if any
- health, ingredient and packaging and labelling regulations
- import tariffs, licensing or quota restrictions, foreign exchange regulations
- lists of potential agents, importers and distributors
- any additional information your experience indicates might be relevant

I would comment that an importer or distributor of foodstuffs would require cool storage facilities to handle and distribute our lines.

Your local knowledge will undoubtedly greatly assist our effort to commence exports to Hong Kong. Once we have your considered reply, I intend to visit the market in order to identify a specific representative, and at that time I shall look forward to meeting you personally.

Yours sincerely,

Summary

- In addition to researching your own country's export regulations, preliminary desk research should aim at identifying (using sources such as available export and import statistics) key potential markets, the volume and values of trade, competitive products sources, seasonal trade patterns, and competitive f.o.b. and c.i.f. prices to markets.

● Identify potential importers, agents and distributors, or users of your services by contact with government export promotion agencies, chambers of commerce, embassy contacts, trade directories, banks, shipping lines and forwarders, trade associations, credit agencies, and other groups or organizations that operate in the foreign market providing goods or services to companies likely to be of interest to you.

● At the pre-planning stage of desk research, using some of the contacts referred to above, identify all relevant rules, regulations and restrictions applicable to trade in your products with the foreign market, including ingredient, labelling, health and packaging regulations, and restrictions such as import quotas, licences or foreign exchange control.

Checklist

(A) EXPORT STATISTICS

● identify customs tariff headings for products
● obtain export statistics from customs & excise for relevant products
● analyse historical exports by:

> destination markets
> volume
> value
> seasonal trends

● identify competitive exporters, their products and prices
● obtain comparative export data for other source countries offering similar competitive products
● analyse such data as available or relevant by:

> destination
> volume
> value
> seasonal supply trends

(B) IMPORT STATISTICS

● supplement data in (A) by obtaining import statistics for markets considered significantly of interest (sources listed in text)
● analyse the data obtained above by:

> source
> volume
> value
> seasonal supply trends

(C) IMPORTERS

● obtain lists of potential agents/distributors/importers or end users (relevant for ingredients or industrial supplies)
 Potential sources include:

> BOTB/US Dept. of Commerce
> chambers of commerce
> banks and export finance bodies
> telephone directories
> shipping lines
> trade directories
> credit agencies
> trade associations
> advertising agencies
> market research agencies
> international auditors

(D) FURTHER DESK RESEARCH

● obtain data on following subjects from sources as in (C):

> health & ingredient laws
> labelling & packaging
> import licences & procedures
> import quotas
> export licences & quotas
> exchange control restrictions
> product registration/approval
> import duties/tariffs/taxes
> import/export documentation

(E) SUPPLEMENTARY CHECKLIST

● prepare a supplementary checklist of information requirements and sources relevant to your own particular products

3

Market Exploratory Visits

Introductory letters

After the completion of all the desk research that can satisfactorily be done without visiting markets comes the planning of initial market visits specifically to identify an importer. The desk research may have helped narrow the field, either because only a few companies have access to licences, or because the embassies or other trade associations contacted have presented comprehensive lists and advice on agents and their relative levels of likely interest and market activity.

At this stage, and prior to making a trip, it is useful to write an introductory letter to the identified contacts who might qualify as potential representatives. The letter should:

- introduce your company and products clearly and concisely
- request the recipient to advise you on his interest in representing such products (or if he has a conflicting agency); his experience of similar products; market structure for import and distribution; import regulations; all other relevant rules and regulations pertaining to trade in your product categories; competitive market pricing structures
- request the recipient to provide a full presentation of his company to enable you to evaluate his ability to represent you, including details on: size, turnover, employees, financial data, trade and bank references, facilities for handling, storage and distribution, and other product lines represented.

In order to motivate an early reply, it is important that you mention that you are proposing a market visit imminently. The depth and quality of replies will greatly assist you in assessing who is hungry for business and in deciding exactly with whom to schedule appointments on your initial market visit. Clearly the size of potential representatives will vary in every market, and generally you will be wise to schedule meetings with several importers, distributors or agents covering the spectrum of sizes, as it will not necessarily be to your company's advantage automatically to tie in with the largest. Frequently the larger sales representatives are less hungry and less geared to market development of an unknown product line.

Planning the trip

Generally you will plan to make a trip to encompass several different but geographically related markets to economize on both time and expense. The cost of travel on export trips is invariably far greater than for a home sales effort and frequently attracts the attention of senior management. Optimum routing can be worked out with your travel agent. Many professional exporters find the local holiday travel agent is not experienced in handling the complications and frustrations of planning a business trip, with the many last-minute changes, re-routings and visa requirements. It is well worth the time to seek out a professional business travel agent who can assist not only in optimum route planning and economy, but also in obtaining all requisite visas and other travel documents. There are many special air fares nowadays that can reduce your costs substantially below regular scheduled fares and many room rate variations with major international hotel groups; a reputable agency will fully realize that, by protecting your interests, they will have security in an ongoing relationship with you.

If you are visiting a country for the first time, it is usually useful to make your first appointment at the commercial section of your embassy, particularly if someone there has been especially productive in providing responses to your desk research enquiries. If they are advised well in advance of your visit and objectives, and any tentative itinerary and assistance you may need, including additional data, then much time can be saved. You can use this first appointment to obtain further advice on who you should meet and talk with. The embassy staff will often use their influence to ensure that you get an appointment with some elusive contacts at short notice: they invariably have a vast network of senior contacts both in government circles and in commercial concerns such as banks and trading companies.

Although you should pre-schedule a number of appointments, it is also very advantageous on your initial trip to any market to leave one or two days free, depending on the size and importance of the market, either for additional follow-up visits with contacts scheduled in the itinerary, or for the additional new contacts who will be identified as having something to contribute to your market studies.

It is absolutely essential to answer all your questions while in the market. Conclusions should be formed and an action plan prepared, to whatever extent is possible, with the cooperation and involvement of the importer you feel is most suitable as your representative. Good importers are plagued with an incessant flow of would-be exporters, and often lack the resources of the major multinational company to produce and implement sophisticated plans. You must demonstrate to your chosen representative that you can work with him, that he was justified in giving you his time, and that together you can prepare a marketing plan that is both simple and practical to implement, monitor and control without disrupting the established business of other principals.

If you are going to the Orient, then it is advisable to have business cards printed in acceptable local languages, such as Mandarin, Japanese and Korean; some airlines will offer facilities to produce these cards at reasonable notice.

Because of the need to 'achieve' while in the market, it is important that you do have with you everything you might expect to require to achieve your objectives. Make a checklist well in advance, and review it prior to leaving. Some of the essential items will include:

- product samples
- product specifications, brochures and all literature and price lists
- guideline freight rates and all other production costing data to prepare market costings on special products
- production and shipping schedules and lead times
- guidelines on the production plants' ability to modify products
- list of market contacts
- summary of relevant desk research data
- itinerary and appointment schedules.

And do not forget passport, visas, currency, travellers' cheques, air tickets, credit cards, pocket calculator, and so on. It is always useful when your secretary is preparing your itinerary to have her include programme details such as flights, check-in times, hotel reservation details, appointments, including addresses and phone numbers for easy access should you need to make changes. Professionalism and efficiency at the trip-planning stage will make your life easier when you encounter the frustrations that invariably arise on the journey. Since suitcases have a tendency to go astray in transit, many business travellers make it a point to carry all papers and travel documents (and sometimes a razor, etc.) with them on the plane in their document case.

Many foreign countries have rules on the importation of product samples, licences for commercial travellers, business visas, and other travel or visitor restrictions. It is essential that you are fully briefed by your travel agent or the appropriate government commercial agencies so that you do not arrive at the foreign airport and find that you or your samples cannot enter. Some countries may even have regulations relating to your personal tax status resulting from your visit. Venezuela, for example, has had regulations where, if you entered on a business visa, you were liable for tax on your home income for the period of your visit and could not leave without a tax-paid certificate. In general, you are better advised to travel as a tourist wherever possible. If entering a country or region where there is any risk to your personal safety, ensure that you give the programme of your visit to the local consulate offices of your home country.

Content and planning of meetings

Clearly, with the added cost of travel and accommodation to foreign markets, time devoted to meetings is at a premium. The person you are meeting will expect you to be prepared and know what you wish to talk about and accomplish. He will be impressed by professionalism, preparation, market and product knowledge, and a clear sense of strategy and direction.

It is generally a good idea to start the meeting with a brief but informative review of your company, its products and your objectives for the market, and not to waste time on unproductive conversation. At this stage of your first meeting with the new contact it is better to spend little time on your own company and products and devote more time to discussing the potential importer's company and ability to represent you. He will not be impressed by, and may react negatively to, a presentation that amounts to boasting. As language may be a barrier, visual aids are especially useful in communication.

At the commercial sections of embassies and chambers of commerce, banks and other institutions, you are likely to be seeking information to cover:

● potential agents, importers and distributors
● their strength in the market, including products represented, turnover, distribution capabilities, staffing, financial accounts, and credit status reports
● import history
● import regulations
● other relevant regulations including packaging, health, ingredients, local and imported competitive activity.

Banks and other agencies may greatly contribute to your knowledge under any or all of these headings.

Distribution channels

At an early stage in the evaluatory research processes the exporter needs to be considering what channels of distribution are open to him and at what cost, because each link in the distribution chain clearly adds a margin that increases the final price to the end user. The distribution chain may be very short, such as direct export to the end user, or long, as in the case of a consumer product requiring handling and storage and redistribution at several wholesale and retail levels before sale to an end user or consumer.

Some of the factors that should be considered when studying the product's distribution needs in relation to the market's available tiers and channels of distribution include:

- The need to achieve and maintain price competitiveness in the foreign market if the product is not sufficiently differentiated such that price is a lesser factor in the marketing mix.
- The physical distribution capabilities of those distributors able and willing to handle the products and the effective modes of distribution within the market infrastructure, e.g. road, rail, waterways, refrigerated storage and trucking, and other limitations on handling and storage.
- The number and geographical spread of effective and available distribution points, e.g. depots, industrial end users, wholesalers, retailers.
- Possible after-sales service needs.
- Traditional locally established distribution mechanisms and infrastructures, e.g. trading houses, importers, primary, secondary and tertiary wholesaling.
- Demographic characteristics of target market sectors.
- Available media for necessary or desired advertising and promotional support to target market sectors; i.e. certain media may be mainly effective in cities, whereas the product may have strictly rural demand.

Most exporters would consider that the primary factor to be considered is whether the product can be priced to reach the final user at a local market price that he can and will pay and at which the product represents perceived value for money. Each stage of the distribution chain has a directly measurable cost, as does each refinement in support and service, and the exporter has the task of evaluating the optimal balance to achieve his sales potential profitably. That may limit the length of distribution chain the exporter can effectively construct. The basic alternatives generally are:

- direct sales by the exporter through his personal representative calling on the end user
- sales on an indent basis through a locally appointed indent agent

- sales through a local importer/distributor who may carry stock or provide after-sales service and spare parts
- appointment of sub-distributors on a regional basis.

The choices facing the exporter may be limited or governed by such considerations as:

- who has access to or controls import permits or foreign exchange
- who has the necessary contacts with the end users and can handle local 'public relations'
- after-sales service requirements
- the need for local stocks to maintain ready availability to end users.

The market requirements or best approach will possibly vary. If the product has very few potential users, as may be the case with industrial plant or ingredients, the chain may consist only of exporter and end user. However, depending on the degree of service needed by the exporter, product or importer, even that chain may benefit by being lengthened. For example, it is unlikely that it would be cost-effective for an exporter of heavy plant and machinery to maintain inventory in a region where demand might be minimal, such as dairy plant in the Middle East; but the same exporter may well feel that a market such as North America warranted local branch operations and inventories of representative products.

In the case of branded consumer goods, the exporter is likely to find that he needs a lengthier distribution chain, probably similar to that in the home market. Main and sub-distributors may be necessary to hold stock or provide spare parts and service and to provide sales mechanisms to distribute to the wholesale and retail trade. Direct sales by the exporter to a number of competitive wholesalers frequently results in certain of the wholesalers trying to claim sole rights on the grounds that they represent the bulk of imports and sales. However, giving sole rights to a company seen locally as only another wholesaler (as opposed to main distributor) may result in other wholesalers ceasing their sales effort. A main distributor can be involved in managing marketing plans, including media, and offer goods on comparable terms to all local wholesalers, who will often be competing to the same retail outlets. Consumer demand, perhaps aided by advertising and promotional support, will often create pressure back from retailers to wholesalers to carry the product. However, a new branded consumer product frequently requires much effort and investment of time and resources to create the initial demand and distribution at consumer and retail levels in order to develop active wholesale support. A mass-market consumer item therefore needs a much greater margin between landed cost and retail price

Example 2

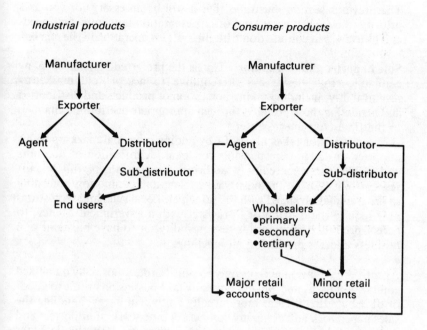

to support the frequently longer distribution chain, margins and promotional activity.

Early market investigations should ascertain the expected margin required by each tier in the distribution chain. Should the exporter not feel that his product can support the multi-tier margins and find an acceptable sales volume, it may be that the product will still find a limited market if aimed at a different segment from the home market. For example, a mass-market low-priced product in the home market may be aimed up-market in a foreign market, and sold at a higher price through few distribution points. As in the home market, a specialist consumer product with a narrow target market, such as designer clothes or cosmetics, may offer acceptable margins through a short and easily controllable distribution chain.

Typical tiers in the distribution chain could include any or all of the levels illustrated in the figure. The longer the chain, the more management effort may be required to control and manage market development.

The potential importer, agent or distributor

The previous section illustrates that it will be necessary for you as a priority to establish what kind of representation best suits your needs and objectives in conjunction with the systems operating in the market.

Sole importer and distributor   This is the preferred system for many companies that desire a representative to accept sole marketing responsibility, including taking possession of products and distributing and marketing those products through appropriate distribution channels to the final consumer or user.

The distributor takes his profit by adding a normal mark-up to his imported cost. He is responsible for local identification of accounts and local customer credit. In addition, he may accept full or part responsibility for any requisite advertising and promotion according to programmes arranged with the principal. Local rules and regulations may require the distributor to register with a government agency, to accept product liability as his responsibility, or to have his name and business address appear on all labelling.

Agent   A sales agent accepts only to solicit orders, normally on a fixed commission basis, and will not normally take possession or title to goods or distribute them. He is more usually an 'indent agent' handling the sales paperwork and company contact for a network of importers and distributors that may possibly cover either different geographical regions or trade sectors. He is responsible for motivating sales. An agent is usually chosen in a market situation where the principal feels no single importer or distributor can adequately represent his interests and ensure sales to all potential outlets. The agent will monitor stock levels and quality, solicit repeat orders, possibly help distributors make market sales to key accounts, and assist in managing local aspects of promotional and advertising programmes.

Importer with distributor   In some cases it may be found that an importer does not actually distribute to the market but resells to another distributor as soon as goods clear customs. Such a situation often arises where the importer exclusively holds certain import licences, or where other financial or quota situations dictate that the distributor needs the importer's services. Japan is a case in point, where a trading house will often provide middleman services by acting as importer but not distributor and be the banker for the transactions, while also being the sole liaison with the principal. The same trading house, while representing a principal to one or more distributors, may also represent the distributors without believing there is any actual or potential conflict of interest.

The main lesson the exporter learns by trading in many countries is to be flexible and adapt to the systems the market has already established. Trying to play 'big brother' and dictate your home market conditions and systems is very likely to alienate your contacts at an early stage of a relationship. Importers all round the world will tell you, 'Our market is unique', and you will gain no points by telling them that you know dozens of other markets that are effectively no different. Efforts to change a culture, whether business or social aspects, will invariably meet resistance and produce more negative attitudes than gently trying to modify some aspects, or trying to adapt a basically sound home product or concept to meet culturally acceptable standards.

Confirming houses   Confirming or export houses in the home country may often fill a middle role between seller and buyer. Such institutions basically undertake to pay the supplier for goods and to ship those goods to the foreign customer. They may extend credit to the consignee and make their margin of profit either by marking up the prices or by financing charges. They often are useful to manufacturers in the home market because they remove the payments risk from overseas transactions, frequently have a vast network of smaller customers who could not buy large initial quantities, and really can serve some companies as if they were the export division when special relationships develop. Some export or confirming houses choose to specialize in trade with certain limited regions, and may have access to bank or other lines of credit made available for those regions. An export manager can only benefit by developing contacts with these specialist institutions, which may often accept a limited customer protection without demanding market exclusivity.

Selection of the representative

Agent questionnaire   When interviewing a potential representative for the role of agent, distributor or importer, you will need to establish certain basic information to assist your evaluation; it may be helpful to prepare a written questionnaire, which can either be posted ahead of your visit or used at the first meeting as a guide to discussions (see Example 3 for sample chart format).
   Essential questions will include:

- correct legal title and company address
- details of all locations of offices, branches, subsidiaries, warehouses and any other relevant facilities
- ownership of the company and date of establishment
- paid-up capital and reserves

Example 3

Agent Questionnaire

Company name: Total employees:

Registered office: Employees:

Branch office locations: Employees:

Warehouse/other facility locations: Employees:

Paid-up capital: Owners or public company:

Asset value: Turnover last 3 years:

Bankers:

Date of company registration:

Details of exclusive companies and products represented and time
represented:

Comments on handling, storage & distribution facilities:

Comments on sales & marketing organization, including staffing levels:

Note: Please complete and return the above, along with relevant
supporting information such as accounts, to assist in evaluating
your company's potential as our agent.

- three years' accounts and financial data
- products represented and length of representation
- trade and bank references
- distribution capabilities, including warehousing and regional distribution facilities
- availability of any special facilities required for your products
- staffing levels and company organization charts
- sales and marketing organization
- sales performance history or current agency lines, and market share data.

You are seeking to establish whether the potential representative is well established and credible in the market; financially sound; capable of financing initial levels of imports and growing with the line. Is the agent able physically to distribute goods either nationally or regionally, or has he only limited geographical abilities. Does he grow by building on the base of existing agency lines or simply by taking on new lines to sell to a limited range of customers? Has he an effective management, sales and marketing organization, and management succession and training programmes? The export manager should personally visit all the relevant facilities of the potential importer to verify their existence and suitability. Every effort should be made to establish that staffing levels are as claimed, particularly if you are dealing with smaller, less established companies.

Customer contact At some point in the selection process it will be essential to visit potential customers and end users (for industrial products) to satisfy yourself that the potential agent has market acceptance and credibility, and to get a feel for how aggressive the potential agent may be in pushing your products. One useful approach is to visit some store buyers or end users alone and tell them you are seeking a sales representative and would welcome their advice. Generally you will be pleased with the helpful responses. If you also visit some potential customers with a salesman from your potential representative, you can then form initial views on his acceptance, trade relationships and professionalism in the market.

Should you be marketing consumer products, then there is no substitute for your own random store check to establish:

- strength of competitive products (distribution, display)
- which distributors are most effective in obtaining displayed distribution
- which distributors are known and respected by store managers
- local methods of merchandising and packaging products
- market pricing

- achievements of your potential agent with products already represented.

Contact reports

After completing all the in-market research and evaluation, it is essential to keep a formal record of your findings, conclusions and contact meetings. The same practice is also valuable for future market visits. Once you have established a relationship with a representative, it will be most helpful to him to receive a full copy or summary of your contact reports, because that will summarize market visit activities, record agreement on plans and programmes, and serve as a reminder of action to be taken by each party.

At the stage of initial market visits, your file contact report, which can be circulated as you feel appropriate within your own organization, should summarize:

- who you met (names and addresses, titles, etc.)
- purpose and content of discussions
- evaluations and conclusions
- market information obtained
- marketing programme to gain market entry
- action plan and points requiring further action and follow-up.

You will rapidly develop your own way of collating data and preparing contact reports. My own preferred system generally follows one of two basic styles in the information included, depending on whether it is a first market visit to identify data, trends and opportunities, or a repeat visit to an established representative as part of an ongoing market development programme.

Initial survey   The broad subheadings under which I would seek to develop data or evaluatory comments would include:

- objective of the trip
- import statistics and data
- import, health, ingredient, labelling, packaging, currency, and any other relevant regulations
- competitive activity
- store check notes
- notes on visits to buyers or end users
- notes on visits to all potential representatives contacted
- conclusions, agreements and action plans.

Any supporting statistical data or copies of regulations can be attached to the file copy of the report since most of your colleagues are unlikely to want or need copies of such information; their interest will mainly be in seeing a positive action plan. You will want to keep clear records so that you can refresh your memory prior to making the next market visit.

Repeat visit to agent   Once you have an established agent, importer or distributor, your contact report will normally record information under some of the following headings:

- any changes in regulations
- market sales, inventory and forward order position of importers
- pricing negotiations and agreements
- competitive activity
- sales, marketing, advertising and promotional programmes (generally prepared in outline for, say, twelve months and updated each interim visit)
- financial, payment and credit matters
- distribution checks
- staff training in product and sales-related matters.

Even with the most sophisticated distributors and agents, you will only be one of a multiplicity of principals and product lines demanding time and attention. The plans and programmes that are easiest to implement and monitor will receive greatest attention and effort by the importer, and therefore have the greatest chance of achieving your objectives. Professionalism from you, the principal, will influence the importer's attitude towards you, your company and its products, and generate commitment and involvement in making a success of your marketing programme. When an agent starts telling you stories about another company's export manager who only wanted to sit by the pool during the day and tour the entertainment spots at night, read into that the message that a busy agent does not respect or need visits from any but those who want to contribute to mutual benefit.

Follow-up

The obvious is often neglected. The best time to prepare notes and contact reports is in the many hours you will spend sitting around hotels and airports, or in flight between markets. It is very wise to prepare all your notes and 'thank you' letters and whatever other correspondence the trip generates before arriving back at your home office. Once you arrive home, there will be a desk piled high with other matters needing you urgent attention; if you can just hand over your taped notes or hand-written drafts to a secretary to prepare while you attack the in-coming mail, nothing will be neglected as a result of your market visits.

The contact report can usefully identify in the margin who is responsible for implementation or specific action, but do not assume it will happen without your direct follow-up with the person whose initials you have placed in the margin. As a courtesy, if you are requesting action by a colleague to assist you in implementing your full programme, such as preparing special costings or product samples or modifications, then let your colleague read a copy of your contact report so that he feels involved and committed to the success of the overall project.

To maintain goodwill and continuity of contact, you should write immediately upon your return home to all the contacts who have assisted you. Commercial contacts in embassies will be interested in knowing how you have progressed towards finding an agent. Other institutions may just warrant a polite note thanking them for any information they were able to provide on your visit. Potential agents, importers or distributors need to be told where they stand in respect of plans to appoint one of them to represent you, and they should be thanked for the interest they have shown in representing you. Above all, the selected agent must be communicated with to confirm his appointment and to arrange any agency agreement matters in a formal manner. In the early days of a new business relationship, occasional follow-up on matters by telephone will aid the building of relationships and keep your company's plans higher on the agent's priority list. All too often plans and programmes made during a market visit fall by the wayside and are not implemented on schedule because the exporter fails to communicate with his agent professionally and continuously.

Summary

- Advance preparation for market visits should include introductory letters to all potential agents, importers and distributors you may wish to visit, along with other contacts such as embassy commercial officers and banks.
- Agency questionnaires can usefully be prepared and dispatched to potential companies prior to market visits to assist in shortlisting who to visit, and can be accompanied by summary details on your company and its products.
- Your 'market visit kit' should include adequate supplies of product samples, brochures, specifications, price lists, product costing data, guideline shipping and distribution costs, and summaries of desk research, in addition to your appointment schedules and travel documents.

- Initial meetings with potential representatives should be concise, incorporating a brief company and product introduction using visual aids, and aim at eliciting the maximum information relevant to your decision-making process, particularly that relating to financial standing and ability to handle, distribute and market your products.
- Marketing and sales programmes need to be formulated in outline with the participation of the new representative, and contact reports can usefully serve as an ongoing means of communicating agreed decisions, plans and programmes, along with notes on action points to which each party is committed.

Checklist

PRE VISIT

- introductory letter to potential importers and/or representatives

include:	company brochure/product catalogue
request:	expression of interest
	company description including size, turnover, facilities, financial data, products represented
	trade and bank references
	information on competitive environment

- introductory letter to the commercial officer at your embassy

advising:	proposed visit dates
	information requirements
	assistance required in making contacts

MARKET VISITS

- optimum route planning in association with travel agents

> book flights
> hotels
> visas
> currency

- confirm all appointments by letter or telex
- prepare market visit kit

include:	samples
	brochures/company accounts
	product specifications
	product costings
	freight rates
	production/shipping lead times
	summary of collected market data

itinerary/appointment schedule
contact lists

● prepare agency questionnaire (see text) to give a structure to interviews (and possibly post ahead)
● conduct in-market surveys on:

outlet types
competitive distribution/pricing
credibility/acceptance of potential representatives

● prepare contact reports on

relevant discussions and meetings
conclusions
action plans
other relevant data or aspects

POST VISIT

● follow-up as required in contact report

4

Identifying and Creating Product Opportunities

The flexible thought process

With the multiplicity of consumer and industrial goods and services available, clearly it would be an impractical task in this chapter to try and identify new or additional opportunities for specific items for specific markets. What I shall do, however, is consider the need for a flexible thought process, look at some anecdotal examples, and formalize an investigative list of factors to consider in new versus old products.

There is the age-old story every exporter has heard about the shoe salesmen sent to Africa early this century. One cabled home: 'Returning home immediately; they don't wear shoes here.' The other more optimistically cabled: 'Send more samples urgently; they haven't got any shoes here.' The salesman who can see or create an opportunity is often a very different animal from the one who can manage only an existing business base. Entrepreneurial skills are always at a premium.

A confectionery salesman going to the Middle East twenty years ago might simply have concluded that the excessively hot climate was not conducive to building a market for confectionery sales. Storage, handling and distribution would possibly have seemed an enormous task to ensure that the product arrived with the consumer in good condition. But the perceptive confectionery salesmen who did go there realized that the Arab peoples had sweet teeth for delicacies, mainly in the form of cakes, and that the addition of confectionery to the diet was complementary to existing cultural habits. The net result was that during the late 1960s and 1970s the Middle East grew to be the major international market for British confectionery exporters. In Africa, it was a different matter trying to sell confectionery, partly because of the hot, humid climate and the more restrictive import regulations in these less rich and developed countries; however, from a marketing point of view the bigger drawback was the basic lack of sweet items in the typical African diet. When something new was being added to the culture that required a cash transaction amongst cash-poor inhabitants, market development was going to be a much longer-term project.

If you are a manufacturer of parking meters, should you go to a market and say 'they don't use meters there', or should you include as part of your market development programme a visually-aided training and introduction programme to show the local government authorities in each market the benefits both in terms of extra revenue and in terms of traffic control derived from the introduction of parking meters in key city centre neighbourhoods? Such a product needs an importer who can persuade the politicians and civilian authorities that the cost of maintaining and policing a meter system is far less than the financial revenues and environmental benefits.

If you have consumer products that really require advertising and promotion but the media are state controlled, then perhaps you can start a lobby programme along with other interested parties to demonstrate to the controlling authorities that there are significant financial benefits to the authorities in treating even state-controlled media as a business centre that should be designed to pay its own way and not be a drain on the taxpayer.

If your expertise is in making biscuits and sweets or other baked goods, then you have the alternative of: exporting domestic market products; producing products for export nearer to the acceptable taste preference of consumers in the foreign market; setting up a plant, possibly as a joint venture, in the foreign market to produce and distribute acceptable products locally; supplying baking technology in exchange for a royalty under some form of technology transfer agreement.

If your expertise is in canning for the home market, then foreign markets present an opportunity to use your canning expertise to open a plant in those markets either to supply needs locally for locally preferred products or to pack a locally available item such as, say, tuna, shrimp or mushrooms, for export back to your home market, where your distribution system can handle sales and marketing.

If your business is dairy products, can you develop and produce a cheese that will suit the taste of consumers in a foreign market more than those you currently offer on your domestic market? Or, if the foreign market has no strong local dairy industry, is there an opportunity for you to use your technology and ingredients to set up a small-scale plant in the foreign market and seek government protection from imports?

Can a manufacturer of electric toasters and coffee percolators adapt his plant to produce an electric rice cooker and develop a market to the Orient, where more and more married couples are also finding it necessary for the wife to work and therefore have to seek the use of convenience foods and cooking aids? Could you produce an electric wok?

A toiletries manufacturer may find additional markets if certain local popular fragrances are incorporated in perfumes and cosmetics.

Do not automatically assume that you cannot compete with less expensive labour in foreign markets. Frequently the foreign market is also importing raw materials and may be facing rising labour costs as the country develops. The point will be reached where you can sell competitively at marginal cost against a foreign plant having to cost production fully. Rising labour and production costs in Japan have resulted in many Japanese companies moving production to less costly countries, such as Taiwan, in order to remain competitive in some of their foreign markets. You should also consider the possibility of producing your products within a region where you can have trade preference and tariff protection in order to develop markets. For example, if your product can be produced with reasonable investment in, say, Singapore, then you have preferential access to the Asian markets of Southeast Asia; the longer-term benefits of such a foreign plant to your company may outweigh the utilization of spare home production capacity, which, in any event, may reduce as the home market grows.

If you are a shoe manufacturer seeking exports to hot countries where you find only sandals are in demand, your opportunities may be either to create an up-market designer type range of quality sandals to compete with locally produced mass market generic products, or, alternatively, to use your technology to produce a synthetic material in sandal form that offers consumer benefits in terms of either price or durability.

If you are a manufacturer of school or laboratory equipment mainly aimed at the educational markets, you may find that to develop your long-term markets you need to provide the authorities in the foreign market with such extra services as a programme offering assistance in designing the laboratory layout or classroom format. The close relationship you develop with the individuals responsible, say, for the education programme should hopefully result in preferential treatment of your supply bids.

If your company provides heavy industrial equipment for material processing and handling, then seek out those markets that are rich in raw materials but currently export them in crude form. You have an opportunity to persuade private or government interests that their economic development is aided by adding value through processing a raw material at least to the next stage of preparation for industrial usage before it is shipped, creating additional local employment and the acquisition of more sophisticated industrial skills. As part of such a sales programme, you may need to supply total consultative services to aid in designing and constructing a plant, but this can usually be arranged in consort with other suitably qualified companies with which you have established associations in the home market. Do not be shy to form joint arrangements with other parties in your effort to exploit export and international opportunities; there is no benefit in operating in isolation if you do not obtain business. Indeed, consortiums are becoming the norm rather than the exception in major industrial projects. It is absolutely essential, however, that each party to a joint project group is clearly and legally bound to performance standards for his section of a project within specific parameters. If there are penalty clauses that may be invoked against the consortium for non-performance or quality aspects of a contract, then the agreement between the parties forming the consortium must identify each individual participant's liability and obligations as part of the collective responsibility. It may be that the consortium agreement requires each party to provide a performance bond in respect of its contribution to the project, whether it be provision of designs, or actual construction or engineering services.

The key word in creating or developing markets is thus FLEXIBILITY − flexibility of thought in seeking opportunities, and flexibility of product in taking advantage of an opportunity once you have identified or created a potential need for your goods or services.

The exporter should not just think of taking ideas from the home market to the foreign market. In your travels you will frequently see interesting ideas and products that may have some home market potential. For example, while in India you may see a food item that could be added to your company's food product range back in England for supply to the large minority Indian population, and your company could possibly import and distribute items in addition to exporting. A supplier of bakery ingredients from the USA to the Philippines may find opportunities to import and distribute handmade and creatively designed bread baskets for the dinner table. Your export travels may provide an opportunity to contribute to cost recovery by providing a buying and importing service to smaller importers and distributors in your home market, provided the time element involved is marginal. Your own company may be using imported ingredients obtained through middlemen, such as imported frozen fruit, and you could possibly provide a cost saving by locating direct export sources. Look for foreign products that are synergistic with those your company produces or markets to the home or export markets, or that you could import and distribute profitably. New product opportunities result from a flexible mind becoming a questioning mind.

International product development

If we now consider how to put some formalization into the process of decision making as it applies to standardized versus modified products, there are some basic questions the exporter needs to put to himself:

- Can existing domestic products be sold in some or all markets without modification in design, function or packaging, and in compliance with local rules and regulations?
- Can modifications in design, function or packaging be made that enable the domestic product concept to find acceptance in the foreign markets?
- What local tastes, preferences, cultural and social habits exist in the foreign market that relate to the exporter's industry or potential product markets?
- Can new products for specific use in foreign markets be developed and produced that use the company's existing expertise, technology and production facilities?
- Are there other ways the same inputs or ingredients could be utilized to find markets and acceptance overseas?

Once the exporter has taken the decision, based upon market research, whether he can effectively market existing products or develop and produce modified or new products, then the next questions relate to product promotion:

- Can existing home market advertising and promotional material be relevantly used in the foreign markets, i.e. is it culturally transferable?
- Can the home market material be modified, i.e. with new voice-overs or scripts?
- Does new material need to be developed and/or produced in the foreign market to reflect local tastes, preferences, social and cultural environments or foreign regulations relating to advertising content or production and use?

The process of product modification and new product development for foreign markets will involve a combination of market, process and product development research, none of which is cheap. Many manufacturers are therefore rightly reluctant to develop new products for developing nations where they have little market security and where initial development costs might not be recoverable in the short run. It is more common to prefer to market existing or modified products, even though this may be known not to maximize potential sales.

Product modification is often essential to comply with rules and regulations or conditions of use in foreign markets. In addition, many basic items of equipment may receive much rougher handling and less maintenance than in the home market, and users may be less concerned with style and appearance than with functional performance.

In considering the case for marketing standard or new/modified products, there are no really hard and fast rules, but we can develop a checklist of factors that may weigh more heavily in favour of one or other approach, and the export marketer could consider the costs and benefits of some or all of these factors in his evaluatory process.

	Product standardization	Product modification
Consumer tastes*		+
Cultural environment		+
Packaging		+
Advertising		+
Rules and regulations		+
Physical environment		+
Production scale economies	+	
R & D costs	+	
Product/packaging inventories	+	
Target market – locals		+
– travellers	+	
Industrial goods	+	
High-technology good	+	
Education/technical skills		+
Local service facilities		+
Consumer disposable incomes		+

*This depends greatly on market sector; e.g. food tastes differ more around the world perhaps than, say, fashion (where a Paris, Rome or London label assists world sales) or high-technology consumer goods such as cameras and hi-fi.

If trade conditions dictate local manufacture under licence or local production or joint ventures as the only practical route to market entry (because of high import duties, quotas, licences, taxes, foreign exchange control, or local government policies) then the manufacturer has an opportunity to design the foreign production plant or process specifically to produce products that suit local tastes and requirements.

Summary

- The key to finding new markets for existing products, or new products for existing markets, or new products for new markets, is a questioning mind and flexible thought process and approach to the use of plant and materials and technology.
- Consider the practicalities of using existing spare plant capacity

to produce products currently in demand in a foreign market but not now made by you.

- Consider how to use your advanced technology to create products that satisfy local cultural needs or practices and that offer consumer or user benefits in terms of cost, convenience or economy of operation.
- Are there products or concepts in the foreign market that you could adapt for use in the home market and produce on your facilities, or that offer a synergistic fit such that you could import and profitably distribute them to supplement your current product range?

5

Agency and Distributor Agreements

Every potential agent customarily requests total market exclusivity and will indicate that he only puts his full efforts and abilities behind those products that he alone can represent. And that may be a reasonable starting point for both parties. Intensive export marketing effort can often only be planned and achieved where there is a responsible and controlled agent or importer involved who will competently manage promotional activities and provide full reports on marketing matters to the principal. Nowadays, most companies considered medium or large tend to develop a structured export department to handle marketing, sales, shipping, production and financial planning, and they have a network of overseas distributors managed from the home base or overseas branch offices.

The main alternatives facing the exporter are:

● An exclusive sales agreement with an importer or distributor in the foreign market.
● Representation in the market by an independent agent in the foreign market, who will normally not accept the *del credere* risk for customers but will solicit orders on behalf of the principal in exchange for an agreed agency commission, usually fixed on the basis of f.o.b. or c.i.f. prices.
● Encouraging potential overseas customers to place their orders through a confirming house or independent export company.
● A network of branch offices to manage his own sales operations in each country, which may include working with other distributors.
● A subsidiary company in the foreign market to handle total distribution operations.

The easiest initial solution for the smaller exporter just getting started is simply to have a 'gentleman's agreement' that you will permit an agent or importer to have trial exclusivity for a period of, say, six or twelve months while he demonstrates his ability to develop sales without the interference of other parties also offering your products to the same customers. The importer, if he agrees to this approach, which can avoid you legal costs and possibly limit your legal commitment and obligations to the importer, will expect you to honour your arrangement and produce a formal agreement at the appropriate time if the importer has performed satisfactorily.

Sometimes it may be necessary to divide market representation either geographically or by market sector − for example, if no one distributor can successfully cover the whole country, or where a distributor does not adequately cover certain market sectors such as governmental, military or institutional sales.

Exclusive sales agreements

The agreement will normally require that the seller grant the overseas trader a territorial sales exclusivity in respect of specific goods or services in return for an agreement from the buyer to use the seller exclusively as the sole source of supply of those same goods and services. The contract may go beyond just being a contract to represent the principal, and may have very specific performance clauses concerning minimum quantities of goods to be purchased and delivered over a specified time period.

Care must be taken that restrictive practice laws in the foreign market are not infringed by any terms and conditions in an exclusive agreement.

In an exclusive distribution agreement the seller is not concerned with the credit risk for a multiplicity of small customers in the foreign market, but in an exclusive agency agreement the exporter may still have this credit risk for customers indenting through the agent where the agent does not accept the credit risk.

Export distribution agreement

Some smaller manufacturers may consider the best approach to their export ambitions is to appoint a domestic company specializing in export sales to be their exclusive exporter. They may have an agreement that does not specify minimum sales requirements and, in fact, find it administratively easier to pass any export enquiries received directly on to their export agent. The export agent will normally only pass on orders to match his firm sales, and does not carry stock. However, he will accept the credit risk for his own shipments and prepare all necessary export documentation. In that respect the export agent is almost acting like a division of the manufacturer, and he may either make his profit by receiving a commission on sales or by buying the goods on agreeably advantageous terms and adding his profit margin before billing the foreign customer at the marked-up price.

An export agent is unlikely to have any long-term expectation of security in his arrangement to represent any manufacturer, because the manufacturer will normally want to set up his own export department to administer exports once the volume justifies that expansion in resources.

Clauses in exclusive agreements

Before entering into any exclusive agency or representation agreement, check the local laws that may be applicable to such agreements in the foreign market. The final agreement will identify duties and responsibilities of the two parties — seller and agent or distributor — and also have clauses dealing with such matters as disputes and termination of the contract.

Some countries have agency laws that will give protection to agents, after termination of a contract, in respect of future commissions on business from customers introduced by them. They may also protect an importer who has been required by a sole distribution agreement to make special investments in order to comply with aspects of the handling and distribution of the exporter's product.

The agreement will essentially cover:

- territorial exclusivity
- product exclusivity and product range or extensions
- special storage, handling and packaging
- promotional responsibilities and materials
- reporting/marketing information reports
- performance clauses
- payment terms or commission arrangements
- dispute handling
- duties of agent and principal
- duration of agreement
- pricing and costing guidelines
- applicable country for legal enforcement and interpretation
- training of agent or distributor's personnel
- assignability
- trademark/patent protection
- termination.

A little thought to the special commercial requirements of your own products will help you prepare a list of key points to incorporate in an agreement, and these can then provide the basis for discussion with a lawyer. The more thorough your own preparation, the lower you can expect accompanying legal charges to be. Since there can be such a range of clauses, both parties must have the intention of producing an agreement that is fair and equitable to each other in order to progress, and the agreement must be adapted to the trade practices and conditions in the foreign market.

Define the territory The geographical definition of the territory may consist of a region of the country (e.g. Northeast United States), one entire country (e.g. Japan), or a collection of political units (e.g. the European Economic Community).

Future territorial extensions may be covered or referred to.

Any export rights from the defined territory can be addressed, as the buyer may wish to know if he can re-export to other markets or customers where he feels he has an advantageous relationship.

The seller's obligation not to by-pass the distributor and sell directly to any customers should be covered. The seller may wish to retain sales rights to certain accounts or institutions (e.g. government agencies or military establishments), but may even agree to pay a nominal commission on such 'house accounts'.

Any exclusions should be clearly identified and understood (e.g. NATO bases).

The goods The contract should define the goods or specific range of products or brands that the buyer will have exclusive sales rights to represent in the territory. Sometimes this is included in an appendix to the agreement rather than in the body.

The contract should give the manufacturer or exporter a 'get out' clause for any products he ceases to produce or offer in export markets so that the seller cannot be obligated to the buyer to produce small and unprofitable production runs.

Any special packaging requirements can be mentioned in the body of the agreement or a reference made to either appendices or subsequent exchanges of correspondence that will cover such matters. A general clause may often contain a phrase such as 'suitably packaged for export and to comply with all local laws and regulations dealing with the packaging and presentation of such products'. If the products require any special storage or handling then it is essential that this is identified to the distributor and that he is contractually committed to comply with the product requirements.

New product lines should be able to be added to the sales and distribution agreement under a 'range extension' clause.

Exclusivity It may be wise clearly to identify that the importer acts as buyer and not agent of the manufacturer so that the buyer clearly understands that he has no power to bind the manufacturer in any matters of local contracts or prices and cannot create any obligation or liability for the exporter or manufacturer.

In return for exclusivity the buyer may be required to accept certain performance clauses to distribute and actively promote the products, or to take certain minimum quantities in each quarter or year. This clause is designed to stop an importer or agent just collecting agencies that they then fail to develop and promote.

A mutual exclusivity of buyer and seller binds the two parties to work together actively to build a mutually profitable business in the assigned market.

Promotions and market information   The seller wants to see the market grow and frequently clauses can bind buyer and seller individually or jointly to finance advertising and promotional activity, particularly if the product is an internationally known consumer product, but also in the case of some industrial products.

It may be that both parties contribute equally to an advertising fund, or that only either the seller or the buyer contributes. I have personally always favoured a joint approach to optimize the commitment to success of promotional activities. Possibly the buyer will agree to spend a certain fixed level of funds in one year or to provide an agreed percentage, say 4 per cent of sales revenues; or perhaps the arrangement will simply be that the buyer will pay for an agreed number of advertisements in the local newspaper. Whatever your own preferred formula, the contract can set the tone for cooperation in this area.

The distributor is often requested within a contract to provide certain reports such as monthly or quarterly information covering:

- sales by product or account
- competitive prices and products
- competitive promotional activity
- new products
- stock levels and forward order positions
- measurable promotional activity results.

State clearly where responsibility for planning and controlling the marketing programme lies and possibly include a reference to the supply of any promotional aids from the principal.

The seller will want to protect his patents and trademarks, and will want a clause binding the buyer not to seek pre-emptive registrations in his own name, and to advise of any threats to trademark protection that he may become aware of in the form of competitive registration applications or apparent infringements in the market place. The buyer may be obligated to assist in any legal activity necessary to protect patents and trademarks adequately or defend them locally.

Other clauses   The time period of exclusivity should be agreed upon and defined, and conditions to be fulfilled prior to enactment of the contract stated.

Methods of handling disputes and terminations need to be specified, including notice periods, transfer of residual stocks, and arbitration procedures.

Any rights by either party to assign the agreement to another party not included in the original contract should be covered. For example, a principal will normally reserve the right to terminate the agreement if the distributor sells his company or it effectively changes ownership, because it has been known that a distributor may come under control of competing interests.

General sales conditions are commonly referred to in an agreement, such as commission or payment terms. Sometimes a general clause will simply say something to the effect: 'The payment for goods shipped will be by irrevocable letter of credit confirmed by a US or British bank except where subsequently agreed', and 'Prices will be as agreed from time to time by the issue of an export price list by the seller to the distributor'.

Any laws governing agency or distributor agreements or restrictive practices in the foreign market must be considered; information on this may be available from your embassy or BOTB in the United Kingdom. For example, some countries will not accept a clause stating that judicial jurisdiction in disputes can be in the seller's country.

If the principal wishes to have the right or access to train the sales or other personnel of the agent or distributor, then this should be identified and accepted by inclusion of a suitable clause within the initial agreement.

The principal may wish to include a *force majeure* clause to cover him against an inability to ship for reasons outside his control.

Agency versus distribution agreements   The distributor buys the goods on his own account and is solely responsible for his customers' creditworthiness, although he has marketing responsibilities to the seller or principal.

The agent may have other rights and responsibilities and duties. He may be able to bind the seller to contracts, prices, delivery schedules and performance clauses. He may also be able to agree on payment or credit terms with customers, while not personally having any credit risk. Sometimes his contract may require him to, or he may voluntarily, take over title to goods where a buyer fails to clear these through customs or pay for them. The contract can spell out the limits that the seller agrees to put on the agent's authority.

A potential agent who is going to have any authority to bind the seller in any way must be very carefully researched to establish reputation, creditworthiness, financial standing and worth, and trade and bank references should be thoroughly checked. The contract may exclude the agent from having any power to bind the seller to specific terms and conditions, but purely make the agent a negotiator between seller and buyer, leaving the buyer with all rights to conclude terms. It is always unwise to appoint any agent or sole distributor without prior personal knowledge of the organization obtained by direct market visits.

The agent or importer should satisfy you on the following criteria:

● They have high standing and reputation in the business community and are seen as experts in the products they represent.
● They have no conflicting interests in respect of similar agency lines or management or financial involvement with any customer where that could limit your opportunity to sell to other parties, cause direct conflict where the agent recommends beneficial terms to his associate, or provide false credit data because of associations.
● They have the organization to perform to your requirements.
● They have the financial standing to pay for goods if they may be required to take up distressed consignments, and they have proven records and data to support their credit recommendations for buyers.

An agent may or may not disclose his interest with a manufacturer when dealing with a customer. If he does not disclose his principal, the agent may be held liable or face suits as if he were the principal himself. Equally, a customer or confirming house may have rights to sue a manufacturer directly if goods do not conform to specifications and standards agreed upon at the time the manufacturer accepted the order. Usually it is better to ensure that the agent is obligated to tell his customers of his interest in representing the manufacturer and that he is agent for the principal.

Duties of principal and agent

The agent
The agent must disclose all relevant facts both to his principal and to his customers relating to each and every transaction.

He must exercise diligence in carrying out duties, and he has no authority to give any warranty other than that provided by the manufacturer. Agents have a habit in some countries of stretching a point to make a sale with such comments as 'you know Alpha Beta Company will stand behind you and their products', which implies a general commitment that is outside the control of the supplier, and the buyer may use a product in an unapproved manner.

He cannot act as both commission sales agent for the seller and commission or otherwise paid agent for the buyer. Personal interest in every contract should be disclosed. Japan is an interesting case in point, where, in fact, a trading house may effectively be involved with both buyer and seller to financial benefit. Principals frequently find this frustrating yet are obligated to work within the established systems.

The agent should not give or accept bribes or make any other secret profits out of a transaction or his representation of the principal. Within this guideline, one must recognize that in certain third world countries the whole purpose of having a 'connected' agent is that he can spread his largess around to the direct benefit of his principal, and legal restriction on this covert activity imposed by a manufacturer's home authorities only leaves open additional market opportunities to competitors.

The agent must keep confidential that information provided to him by the principal in the pursuit of mutual business, where the principal specifies such information is not for disclosure (e.g. formulas, recipes, drawings, designs, costings, etc.).

The agent should keep accurate records and accounts of all transactions on behalf of the principal.

The principal

The principal must pay commissions on sales according to agreed terms. Commission will not normally be due for payment until the buyer has remitted funds to the principal, and will not be due on bad debts. Occasionally, possibly for a higher level of commission, the agent will accept the *del credere* risk for buyers, but most agents seek to avoid such obligations.

The contract should clearly state who is responsible for the agent's costs and expenses incurred in connection with obtaining orders. Generally, the agent is responsible for all his own normal operating expenses, but it may be agreed that the principal will reimburse costs connected with clearing samples through customs.

The contract should specify the principal's responsibility to pay commissions on business emanating from the agent's territory but not directly procured by him. There can frequently be disputes on this matter, because the agent will expect commission on every dispatch into his territory, and possibly on dispatches into other territories where he has a claim to motivating the purchase, for example if a foreign branch of a company located in his territory subsequently orders. Any exclusions for house or multinational accounts should be discussed and agreed upon early on. In the case of a multinational account, with a head office in one territory and branch in another, a split commission arrangement may be acceptable to the respective agents in the two territories, since both may contribute to motivating purchases.

The agent will expect commission on all repeat orders, even if sent directly to the principal, at least for the duration of his agency agreement. It is necessary to check local agency laws to establish liability for any ongoing commissions in the event of termination of the contract. Some countries provide protection to agents for all accounts that are initially introduced by them to a principal.

The principal has duties to support the agent with data, samples and such other sales aids as will enable the agent to represent the products effectively to potential customers. The agent is entitled to expect efficiency and promptness in the principal's handling of communications, and vice versa.

The principal should reserve the right to accept or reject each individual order, and the agent must understand that commission will only be due on an order accepted, shipped and paid for in full. Disputes sometimes arise where an agent claims that he obtained orders and it is not his fault if the manufacturer cannot or will not ship the goods.

Supplementary agency matters

Del credere risk   As has been mentioned previously, the principal may require the agent to accept the *del credere* risk and indemnify the principal for any loss resulting from failure of a consignee to clear and pay for a consignment shipped against an order obtained by the agent.

Stocks   Some agents may be required to hold stocks of a product, possibly on consignment (i.e. not paid for by the agent until or unless they are sold to a customer), to meet certain market demands, such as unusual seasonal fluctuations, delays in vessels arriving with regular orders, replacements for goods damaged or lost in transit, or possibly spare parts for machinery or equipment. In such cases it would normally be agreed that the agent could release such contingency stocks to established customers without referring back to the principal in advance, provided the customer was in good credit standing, but advise the principal of the transaction for invoicing purposes. The contract should consider the matter of responsibility in disposing of such contingency stocks, and the agent or distributor should be required to report on inventories at agreed intervals. The export representative of the principal should verify stock levels on regular visits. It may also be that the agent would be given local responsibility for collection of payment for stocks released under his control, rather than the principal issuing invoices to the customer from the home office. As your relationship develops with your agent, there will be many practices that will become the norm yet may not be contractually covered. In general, if your agent does not have your respect and trust, then you have the wrong agent or distributor.

Confirming houses If a principal is dealing with a confirming house or export company, then that institution will normally have made itself obligated to the supplier to take all goods it has ordered and to pay for such goods according to agreed terms. If the final foreign customer cancels the order or fails to pay, that does not release the confirming house or export company from its obligations to the supplier. Again, in practice, if the final overseas customer cancels an order before it is produced to special order or dispatched, the supplier may cooperate with the exporter in not insisting that the transaction be completed, but the exporter should understand that favour is not a forgoing of general rights to enforce contracts. A manufacturer who has made goods to special specifications or packaging requirements is likely to want to hold the confirming house or export company to its contract, or to collect any losses resulting from distressed sale of goods that possibly may not be suited to the home market.

The confirming house or export company, while responsible for all matters of payment and shipment to the customer, does not normally have responsibility for ensuring that goods comply with specifications from the customer, or for matters relating to quality or quantity of the goods. The exporter will pass on the customer's specifications exactly as received by him, and principals dealing with confirming houses should carefully read the purchase contract applicable to each separate order to establish exactly what responsibilities the confirming house or exporter is transferring to the principal.

Agent of necessity On occasion, a situation may arise when an 'agent of necessity' is needed. You may have appointed an agent with limited authority who, to safeguard your interests, must take urgent action without reference to you in particular circumstances. For example, if you are shipping a highly perishable product such as fruit or frozen goods and the customer fails to clear goods through customs promptly, or the frozen container is left on the dock not plugged into electricity for an excessive period, the agent may, in your interest, have to sell these goods off the dock for best obtainable prices. Your agent may have some protection in law for overstepping your authority if he can demonstrate that he acted in your interest in unusual circumstances. Be careful to ascertain that the buyer of distressed goods at bargain prices was not the original consignee or his nominee, as that tactic has been used many times in places where you cannot control events. If that happens, you may have a claim either against your agent or the original consignee for losses below contract terms.

When you know your agent well, a trust relationship will develop, and you will form a comfort level in how much leeway to give. My own experience has always been that a good, reliable agent, even in the most difficult operational conditions, will seek genuinely to serve your best interests.

Country of jurisdiction　Several times I have referred to the developing practice of countries' giving various degrees of protection to sole agents or distributors that may entitle them to fees or commissions or other obligatory or goodwill compensations after the termination of an agreement. You should not assume that even by including a clause, accepted by your distributor, 'that this contract shall be governed by and interpreted in all respects according to the applicable laws of the State of New York, USA, whose courts shall have sole jurisdiction in the event of a dispute' you are protected. The acceptability and validity of such a clause needs to be researched for each country in which you have contractual arrangements.

European Economic Community law　If your sole representation agreement involves countries within the EEC, then at the contract drafting stage you should seek legal advice to ensure that the terms of the agreement do not breach articles 85 and 86 of the EEC Treaty, which are designed to prevent compartmentalization and fragmentation within the Community. EEC law disapproves of any clause that restricts where a person can buy or sell within the EEC, and market price fixing arrangements.

Style of agreement　The simpler the agreement can be, both in style and language, the easier it is for all parties to understand and comply with its terms and conditions. If the language of the country to which the agreement applies is not English, then you should consider a professional translation into the appropriate language to ensure that your agent is clear on all aspects of your agreed relationship. Lawyers perhaps have a tendency to use legalistic jargon or stylized prose that the layman has trouble comprehending. Try to avoid such a presentation in contracts submitted to foreigners.

The appendix to this chapter gives an example of the first draft of an agreement to sell and represent a confectionery product range as such a draft might look when first prepared by the export manager for discussion with his potential representative and his company lawyers. This draft would then be worked into the final document and legal terminology.

Summary

● A representation agreement will normally appoint the representative as exclusive sales agent, exclusive importer or sole distributor for a defined geographical market or market trade sector.

● Local laws in the foreign market applicable to agency and distribution agreements should be checked for restrictions, including protection afforded to appointed representatives.

● An agreement should clearly identify and define all the terms and conditions of representation, along with the rights, duties and responsibilities of each party.

● Clauses generally will cover such matters as: territorial exclusivity, product range and exclusivity, storage and handling requirements, marketing and promotional responsibilities and planning procedures, funding of advertising and promotions, reporting requirements, performance clauses, handling of unsaleable and returned products, payment terms, dispute handling, trademark and patent protection, legal jurisdiction, obligations and arrangements in the event of contract termination.

Appendix: Sample of a draft agreement prepared by an export manager for review by the company lawyer

Agreement between Sugar Candy Company and Worldwide Import Company for Product Distribution in the Philippines

(1) The following definitions shall apply to the following terms used in this agreement:

  (a) *territory*: this is the national boundaries for the country known as the Philippines.

  (b) *the products*: these should include all products produced by Sugar Candy Company, Inc. and listed in an appendix to this agreement or subsequently offered to Worldwide Import Company in any exchange of correspondence.

(2) This agreement is between the Sugar Candy Company, Ltd (hereafter referred to as Sugar Candy) of 1 Main Street, Hightown, England and the Worldwide Import Company (hereafter referred to as Worldwide) of Suite 200, World Trade Center, Manila, Philippines.

(3) Sugar Candy appoints Worldwide as its exclusive importer and distributor for the Philippines and the geographical limits on the exclusive territory shall be the national boundaries of all territories forming part of the Philippine sovereign nation. Worldwide shall import and distribute the range of confectionery products from time to time offered to it by Sugar Candy and initially defined in the list referred to as Appendix I attached to this agreement. Additions to or deletions from this initial list shall be communicated to Worldwide as such changes occur by letter or by the issue of new product data or price lists. Worldwide shall have no rights to offer any of the Sugar

Candy products for re-export from the assigned territory or knowingly to permit re-export through any of the customers purchasing the products from Worldwide within the territory.

(4)   Worldwide agrees it will not import or represent any other confectionery product ranges without the prior written permission of Sugar Candy.

(5)   Worldwide agrees it will actively import, distribute and promote the range of products offered by Sugar Candy to all potential wholesale and retail outlets deemed to be creditworthy and that offer or display similar confectionery items for sale in the territory.

(6)   Worldwide agrees it will place regular orders with Sugar Candy, subject to any licensing, quota or exchange control regulations currently in force or subsequently introduced, and that it will on average maintain minimum inventories of each item equal to approximately two months' average sales. In general, Worldwide will seek to place orders on a regular monthly basis to optimize product rotation and freshness. Minium import and sales targets will be agreed each year prior to the calendar year to which they apply and Worldwide accepts that such targets will constitute the minimum acceptable import performance standards for the year under this agreement and will be committed to such imports subject to any limitations which might be enforced by regulatory bodies as under the preceeding section of this clause.

(7)   In the event that Worldwide fails to meet minimum import targets for any reason and Sugar Candy has other importers willing to purchase and import the products then Sugar Candy reserves the right to accept and fill such orders but agrees to reserve 5% commission on the c.i.f. value for the account of Worldwide on all such despatches made into the territory during the currency of this agreement.

(8)   Sugar Candy reserves the right to sell directly to and without consulting Worldwide nor reserving any commission all house accounts which shall include all foreign military establishments within the territory and such other foreign based multinational companies or organisations with a place of business in the territory but who place orders through offshore offices or companies.

(9)   Worldwide will give no warranties expressed or implied to any party in respect of the products except those warranties communicated to Worldwide by Sugar Candy.

(10) Sugar Candy will supply all merchandise to Worldwide on a c.i.f. destination port basis and Worldwide will be responsible for all handling, storage, clearing and other charges after that point. Prices will be quoted in the currency of the destination country and adjusted from time to time with the objective of remaining competitive at the retail level consistent with clause 9 below and to take account of fluctuations in cost factors or exchange conversion rates.

(11) Worldwide agrees to pay for all goods ordered and shipped by irrevocable letters of credit confirmed by a British bank except where

other payment terms are subsequently agreed between Sugar Candy and Worldwide.

(12) It is expected that Worldwide will resell product at a price that gives a gross contribution of between fifteen and twenty per cent over the landed duty paid cost of the goods. Worldwide agrees to provide Sugar Candy with copies of all relevant costings relating to the products and to resell goods only at prices and margins agreed with Sugar Candy prior to implementation. It is the objective of both parties to maintain a competitive pricing structure with other similar imported confectionery items offered for sale in the territory. Worldwide agrees to maintain accurate and current accounts and customer records in respect of sales and stocks of the products and to permit any authorised representative of Sugar Candy to examine all such records at the offices of Worldwide during normal working hours.

(13) Sugar Candy is responsible for ensuring that all merchandise sold and shipped to Worldwide is in good merchantable and saleable order at the time and point of shipment and that all products and packaging will be as agreed in specifications and orders and suitable for sale in the territory by compliance with all relevant rules and regulations pertaining to the sale of foodstuffs and confectionery products.

(14) Worldwide is responsible for payment of all invoices for goods ordered and shipped, all subsequent costs of clearing merchandise through customs including duties and any taxes; and all costs of handling, storage, distribution and product replaced or returned by customers within the market. Worldwide is solely responsible for any credit it extends to its customers including resultant bad debts.

(15) Worldwide is responsible for ensuring that all laws, rules and regulations relating to the importation and sale of confectionery in the territory, including those on ingredients, packaging and labelling, are communicated by letter to Sugar Candy with copies of relevant regulations and authorized translations.

(16) Worldwide agrees to store all products imported from Sugar Candy in air-conditioned storage facilities at temperatures in the range of 7°C to 16°C and free from all infestation, contamination and other factors that can contribute to the deterioration of product quality. Worldwide also agrees to distribute product in air-conditioned or chilled trucks.

(17) Worldwide agrees to uplift and exchange all product from wholesale or retail establishments identified by customers or the representatives of Worldwide or Sugar Candy as not suitable for sale or consumption for any reason including age, deterioration in quality or damage to packaging.

(18) Sugar Candy and Worldwide will work together to prepare an annual marketing and promotion plan with the objective of promoting and increasing sales and distribution. Worldwide will then be responsible for implementing agreed plans and reporting monthly on the achievements, progress and sales against the plan. Sugar Candy will

contribute up to five per cent of the f.o.b. invoiced value of goods dispatched to Worldwide in any one year as a contribution to agreed advertising and promotional activities forming part of the marketing plan, provided Worldwide contributes an euual and matching contribution. Sugar Candy reserves the right to appoint and approve all agencies used in connection with advertising, promotional activity and market research projects in the territory.

Worldwide agrees to the ongoing and regular training of all its staff involved in the distribution and selling of the products by the management of Sugar Candy in the territory and to follow the techniques and procedures relating to selling, marketing and distribution recommended by the management of Sugar Candy. Should it be considered mutually beneficial for any personnel of Worldwide to visit Sugar Candy in Britain for training, then the two parties agree to share the costs of transport and subsistence.

(19)   Worldwide agrees to provide Sugar Candy with a monthly report including detailed distributor sales information by product, brand, pack size and outlet type, or other report formats as subsequently agreed. A report should also be submitted monthly to encompass competitive promotional activity and pricing policies, market imports and sales, and any other data considered relevant from time to time to the effective planning and implementation of programmes to promote Sugar Candy's products in the territory.

(20)   Sugar Candy will be responsible for the registration and protection of all trademarks and patents in the territory and Worldwide agrees not to attempt pre-emptive registration of any patents or trademarks it has reason to know or believe Sugar Candy to have an interest in, or that are registered by Sugar Candy or an associate company in their home market. Worldwide agrees to assist in any practical matters relating to the registration of patents and trademarks in the name of Sugar Candy, and to advise Sugar Candy of any infringements it learns of in the territory and to assist Sugar Candy in the defence of any trademarks or patents against infringement. All costs of initial or ongoing trademark or patent registrations and their defence will be borne by Sugar Candy unless subsequently agreed differently.

(21)   Worldwide agrees to keep secrets confidential and secure all information and data that refers to the marketing plans and programmes agreed with Sugar Candy, and all pricing and costing schedules, product specification and data sheets and any manuals provided by Sugar Candy relating to sales or other systems or operating procedures, and such other exchanges of information whether in written or verbal form and communicated to Worldwide in the normal course of business and designed to assist Worldwide in developing the sales and markets for the products. Worldwide will communicate information to its employees only to the extent that such information is necessary to enable them to perform their job functions efficiently and after making them aware of their responsibilities under this clause and agreement. The directors of

Worldwide indemnify Sugar Candy in respect of resultant losses caused through any breach of this secrecy agreement by present or future employees or other persons who gain unauthorised access to confidential information. In the event of termination of this agreement all manuals, specifications, and other product related data will be returned to Sugar Candy along with any copies in any form that are known to exist.

(22) Sugar Candy reserves the right to grant licences for the production and marketing of the products within the territory and using the trademarks and other brand names of the products to any company at any time and without prior consultation with worldwide. In the event of any such licence being granted this agreement would terminate upon the commencement of production by a licensee and Sugar Candy will have no liability to Worldwide for any reason or in any form.

(23) This agreement shall remain in force for one year from the date the first order is shipped by Sugar Candy to Worldwide, which shall be within one month from the date of signing of this agreement by the parties, and prior to the first shipment Worldwide shall satisfy Sugar Candy of its ability to comply with all the other clauses in this agreement that relate to sales, marketing, handling, storage and distribution of the products. The agreement shall be void in the event Worldwide is not in compliance with the foregoing.

(24) In the event of termination of this agreement for any reason, Worldwide agrees not to disrupt the marketing of Sugar Candy's products in the territory and to sell back to Sugar Candy or other nominated party all remaining stocks of products at the landed duty paid cost plus any verifiable clearing charges. Until the date of final termination under the terms of notice, all other clauses, conditions, responsibilities and duties covered in this agreement or any subsequent mutually agreed exchange of correspondence will be honoured in full by both parties.

(25) Sugar Candy may terminate this agreement by giving three months written notice to Worldwide for failure to perform contractual obligations incorporated in any of the clauses in this agreement, or on such other grounds where, in the opinion of Sugar Candy, Worldwide is not acting in the best interests of Sugar Candy in promoting and representing their products in the market, provided that Sugar Candy has given Worldwide thirty days to rectify the matter in question by communicating details of the unacceptable problem or practice in writing.

(26) In the event of termination of this agreement by either party, Worldwide agrees that Sugar Candy will have no obligations, either financially or legally or in any other respect, in connection with assets owned, leased or employed by Worldwide and utilized in the promotion and distribution of the products, or for any outstanding customer debts to Worldwide, or profits or commissions that may relate to the trade of Worldwide in distributing the products of Sugar Candy in the territory, and Worldwide will have no further claim,

financial or otherwise, against Sugar Candy arising out of this distribution agreement.

(27) This agreement will terminate automatically without notice if the ownership of Worldwide changes unless Sugar Candy has been notified of any pending change in ownership and agreed that the distribution agreement may continue in all respects unchanged and binding on the new owners. It will also terminate automatically if Worldwide defaults on any payments to Sugar Candy or enters into any proceedings leading to bankruptcy or insolvency or if the owners or officers of Worldwide are charged or convicted of offences under the criminal codes of the territory.

(28) This agreement may be assigned in whole or part by Sugar Candy to any parent, associate or subsidiary company at any time and Worldwide would be notified of such assignment. Worldwide may not assign this agreement to any party except with the prior written approval of Sugar Candy.

(29) Worldwide shall not represent itself as agent of Sugar Candy in any way and shall have no powers to commit or bind Sugar Candy in any contract or create any liability against Sugar Candy, and Worldwide shall conduct itself and represent itself only as distributor of the products of Sugar Candy according to the terms of this agreement with no form of partnership between the parties existing.

(30) This agreement shall be interpreted in all respects according to the laws of the United Kingdom, whose courts shall have sole jurisdiction in any dispute not resolved by arbitration. Should Sugar Candy not enforce any of its rights under this agreement or modify its requirements for any particular reason at any particular point in time such failure to enforce its rights shall not constitute a waiver of those rights.

(31) In the event of any dispute this shall first be referred for arbitration to an arbiter or committee of arbiters appointed by the London International Chamber of Commerce, and arbitration will take place in England. The decision of the arbiters shall be binding and enforceable on both parties. Should Sugar Candy agree on any future occasion to permit arbitration in the Philippines, then that arbitration shall take place only under the auspices of the International Chamber of Commerce under its standard rules and conditions, and such agreement in any instance shall not constitute a waiver of any rights Sugar Candy has in this clause or clause 24 preceding for arbitration or recourse to legal action in the United Kingdom unless the outcome of such arbitration in the Philippines is accepted by both parties.

Signed for Sugar Candy Company, Ltd.:

Signed for Worldwide Import Company:

Date:

Note: Comment on sample agreement   This agreement is offered only as a sample of some of the issues and types of clauses that can address such issues involved in arranging an agency or sole distribution agreement. You are the best person to know the commercial aspects you wish to cover in an agreement, and can beneficially devote time to the first rough draft before involving your company lawyers. Generally, an export representative should carry blank draft standard agency, importer or distributor agreements with him on market visits so that the content can be discussed in the market place with any companies that may seriously be considered to represent the exporter.

The more simple the style and content of the agreement, the less arguments and discussions will generally result on the finer points. Nevertheless, the objective of any agreement must be to clearly establish and recognize the ground rules both parties must work by; to consider duties, obligations, rights, responsibilities, disputes and terminations in return for the commissions or profits on sales.

In principle, if you end up in disputes that lead to legal action or arbitration, then it is likely that your relationship is in such jeopardy that you may be better off mutually to agree to terminate the formal arrangement and appoint a new representative.

Checklist of clauses and scope of agency agreements

- definition of terms used
- territorial exclusivity
- limitations on exports outside the geographical territory
- market sector limitations
- product range

> define the goods
> sole source
> new products
> packaging
> compliance with laws
> product deletions
> other exclusions

- competitive product lines
- minimum sales performance clauses
- order frequency
- inventory levels
- consignment stocks
- spare parts/servicing/maintenance
- markets returns
- handling and storage

- physical distribution
- market pricing policies
- marketing programmes and plans
- advertising and promotional costs
- commissions
- standard payment terms
- marketing and sales reports
- training of agent's personnel
- duties and responsibilities of parties
- disputes/arbitration (rules/venues)
- duration of agreement
- renewal/extension clauses
- agreement enactment date (often subject to certain conditions being met)
- termination clauses

> causes
> notice
> stock disposal
> compensation

- assignability of agreement
- *force majeure* clause
- laws applicable to enforcement
- secrecy clause
- rights to license production

PART TWO

PRICING, PACKAGING AND PROMOTIONAL CONSIDERATIONS

6

Export Costing and Pricing

Although you may have already decided in principle or in practice that you wish to develop export markets, the policy question you must now answer at senior management levels within your company is whether you really want exports to become a significant outlet for the unutilized or marginal capacity in your production facilities. All too often the approach taken in traditional industries and companies that have grown rapidly to strength in the home market is that fulfilling export orders is nothing but an inconvenience that distracts management from other priorities and productive activities and disrupts existing systems and production programmes.

As a result of this kind of management attitude, a typical pricing formula takes the home market price as a base and adds on amounts to cover extra staff time, labour, packaging, inventories, financing, administration, and so on. This we may call the 'domestic plus' pricing system, and it basically entails a price overload to the foreign market because deductions have not normally been made for domestic marketing, sales and distribution costs, or domestic trade credit. An export order sold against letters of credit will often produce funds more rapidly than a domestic order for which payment is not received perhaps for thirty or sixty days.

There are costs specific to exporting over and above the actual cost of producing goods. These include special packaging and quality control, ingredient and formula modifications, export administration and documentation, financing for goods in store or transit prior to payment being received, and allowances for the costs of the export sales department. However, costs specific to home market sales and distribution should be eliminated from the export transaction if you are to be competitive and achieve sales.

At this point it is worth considering a few issues where the pricing of exports may prove very significant to the manner in which you conduct business and the resultant sales achievements.

Parallel exports and imports

Where exports are made from the home market to an export market by companies other than the manufacturer (i.e. where the manufacturer's products are being offered by other parties such as export traders), then you have a situation generally referred to as 'parallel exports'. Sharp exporters frequently find that they can buy a manufacturer's home product cheaper through discount wholesale outlets in the home market, especially when sales promotions are in effect, and offer these same goods to importers other than the manufacturer's exclusive representative in the foreign market. The independent exporter probably has lower overheads than the manufacturer and generally sells against letters of credit, thereby avoiding the export financing costs the manufacturer may have. In addition, while the home market goods may bear an element of home market sales, promotional and distribution costs, this may be minimal during the discount promotion. The goods offered for export by the independent exporter may also, and frequently are, in different packaging or sizes than those directly exported by the manufacturer, as the goods were clearly not produced specifically for export. They may also not comply fully with the labelling and ingredient laws of the foreign country to which they are subsequently shipped.

The net effect of parallel exports is to add a disrupting factor to the export strategy and markets the manufacturer is trying to develop, and the manufacturer may find his credibility reduced both with his foreign importer and with the customers in that market. The official importer may find himself held responsible for an incorrectly packaged and unapproved product that he has not imported, and may have some difficulty in identifying the true parallel importer because customers will frequently not disclose product sources if they are knowingly trading in parallel imports.

The manufacturer and his official sole importer may find that they have no legal recourse to prevent parallel trade, although some countries now will seek to provide a degree of protection in recognition of exclusive distribution agreements. Local chambers of commerce and other trade associations often seek such protection on behalf of their members, who tend to be the more ethical companies in the market.

The parallel importer will also be benefiting from any advertising and promotional activity organized by the principal and official importer, yet the unofficial imports are unlikely to include any costing allowance contributing to the promotional funds. The official importer is certainly not going to pay a contribution, if one was due on his official imports, on that element of imports not shipped through his company, even if such parallel imports could accurately be quantified.

A barrier to parallel trade exists where the importing country does have specific laws relating to packaging and labelling, unit sizes, ingredient declarations and inclusion on labels of product registration details or names and addresses of importers. However, these only create a barrier when the sales outlet, such as a retail store, in addition to the importer, is held liable for products sold in non-compliance with all regulations. In that case no reputable retail establishment will risk offering for sale goods clearly not complying with local standards and regulations. Hence, there are benefits in such regulations that may initially appear a nuisance, in that they may assist orderly market development. The official importer who finds incorrectly packaged parallel imports in any outlet can both advise the authorities and the outlet, thereby ensuring that he is not subsequently held liable for any resultant complaint involving such products.

Where the export product is marginally costed (and I shall review this shortly) and only relevant additions relating to the specific costs of export operations are added back into the costing formula, then it is likely that the home market priced product, even on promotion, will not prove an attractive proposition to the parallel traders. Both the manufacturer and official importer should try to avoid the consumer confusion that results when a product is found in a variety of labels and sizes, as this can seriously harm market sales, particularly in a market where consumers fear 'fake' products.

Cross-border smuggling

Occasionally you will encounter a situation where a low-duty country is next to a higher-duty country, and where traders or systems operate to facilitate illegal cross-border transactions into the higher-duty country. If this is happening with your products, while you may not directly believe you are losing, your sole importer in the higher-duty country will be losing profit contributions and motivation to push sales. In addition, the smuggled product may result in an imbalance where the advertising funds incorporated in product costings are earned and allocated. If all advertising funds are included by the manufacturer at source, he can reallocate some from the budget of the lower-duty country to the higher-duty country. However, if there is provision for the importer in the lower-duty country to contribute, it is highly unlikely that he will recognize any obligation to donate part of his contribution to the neighbouring market, or any benefit from so doing. The manufacturer is more likely to optimize sales in both markets by finding a balancing formula to relate the level of promotion in both markets not to the level of shipments to the respective importers, but in direct relation to the consumption levels of the two markets, if this can reasonably be assessed.

In reality, the official importer in the higher-duty country will tend to be over-conservative in ordering, constantly fearing that the actual or potential smuggling of goods will restrict his sales. The smugglers, meantime, also have an insecure outlet and tend not to satisfy all potential demand. The net result is below-optimum product sales in the higher-duty market.

One solution the manufacturer should carefully study and consider is to increase his basic export price to the lower-duty country to the point where smugglers would no longer see benefit in illegal cross-border trade for the small returns left to them. This may give more security to the importer in the higher-duty market, who may then increase his orders and conduct an orderly growth programme. How much more he can sell will depend on whether the smuggled goods were reaching the consumers at lower prices, or whether the price benefit was being absorbed by the wholesale and retail trade in the form of better profit margins. In the lower-duty market, prices should not be increased to the extent that local sales decline by more than the potential net increase in the two markets added together after the change in pricing structure. Bear in mind that, since most importers work on a percentage margin on cost or sales, any price increase you pass on to them will be magnified when they use their mark-up formula of, say, 20 per cent of cost.

You will need to consider very carefully all of the above factors and any others particular to your situation or products before implementing such changes to reduce disruptive smuggling. In the early 1970s, such price adjustments were used very successfully to reduce smuggling of confectionery products out of the lower-duty Kuwait market into the higher-duty Saudi Arabian market, with a net overall increase in business resulting from the appointed Saudi importer's ability and willingness to import in much greater volume without fear of cheaper smuggled goods. In that particular instance, the growth in Saudi Arabia was several hundred times the percentage loss in business for the Kuwaiti market.

If a situation exists where a particular country has trade barriers that:

- limit legal import by quotas,
- limit imports by other licensing or currency restrictions,
- do not permit any legal imports of your product,

then it may be that smuggling of your product into that country both gives you the benefits of an overall higher sales volume and keeps your product name in front of end users or consumers in the restricted market. Many manufacturers have successfully developed contacts and tactics to supply worthwhile or potential future markets via 'the back door'.

Marginal costings

Marginal costing normally follows the basic principle that the extra cost of additional production units will be less than for previously produced units, down to the point where a fully marginally costed unit requires inclusion only of the variable cost of inputs such as materials, packaging, additional labour or utilities, and specific handling, storage and distribution costs.

If we consider this further, the typical company produces an annual sales production plan and budget, which will aim to recover all basic costs of production and overheads over the volume of output and sales in the plan. The plan has made specific assumptions on costs of raw materials, utilities, office overheads, labour and production, distribution, marketing, and so on. That plan may have included or excluded some export sales volume. Any additional sales volume may have the effect of both spreading the budgeted costs over larger output and possibly enabling actual expenditure per unit to drop, for example by buying larger volumes of ingredients or packaging material. Therefore, any additional margin over and above identifiable variable costs of additional goods produced for export is an extra profit contribution for the company.

You will find that an exact analysis of your true marginal cost is a frustrating study of an elusive figure, because there will be so many variables, the effect of which may not accurately be assessed in advance, even by the most sophisticated cost and management accountant. Accountants tend by nature to be more conservative than the sales personnel. If you have a serious prospective export enquiry or order, your responsibility to the compny is to negotiate the highest possible price at which you can secure the order; at the same time you should be liaising with the cost accountant to establish at what price he will say the order is unacceptably unprofitable. You may be amazed at how he will change his position daily, but this may not be because he is being obstructive, rather that he genuinely knows there are so many variables in marginal costing that a price unacceptable one week, say when the plants are running at full capacity, may be very acceptable in a week when production capacity is not fully utilized.

In preparing your export costings, it will be helpful if you start at the initial planning stage by persuading your company cost accountant to identify all the fixed and variable costs separately when budgets are being prepared. Generally, the accountant will be using a 'standard costing' system for inputs and, as previously mentioned, it may be found that additional sales volumes result in lower unit costs of some inputs through increased volume usage or buying power.

Your basic aim is to reach a clear decision on whether or not to accept sales at a certain price level. The two principal steps, in summary, are:

- identification of the marginal cost of producing those extra units you wish to contract to sell in export markets
- arranging the product costing in a format that enables you to make an estimate (possibly only based on standard costing data at this stage) of the profit contribution from this contract.

Bear in mind that you have a sound position for considering goods already in store or in production as marginally costed if you have the production capacity to replace them at the time they are needed for delivery elsewhere, and if they are already in exportable form (i.e. no special modifications are needed except those for which you can charge the customer in your quote). If modifications are needed, then that element may be marginally costed unless it really is impossible to make the modifications beyond a certain point in the production process.

Your profit estimate, or gross contribution, may be calculated simply by preparing a tabulation showing the gross sales revenue less all the marginal costs of production and specific additional costs in completing the order for export (see Example 4). With ongoing shipments of consumer goods, it is often not seen as a worthwhile exercise to attempt a profit estimate on each transaction, but it is beneficial in the case of commodity transactions or industrial product contracts such as supplying components or capital equipment.

Another point to consider in marginal costing, when seeking to exclude those costs you consider fixed, is that in some businesses the fixed costs per unit will vary month by month if they are treated as occurring at a point in time yet production volumes are not the same in each month. Frequently there are significant seasonal variations in production, and you may work with your cost accountant to assess seasonal cost factors to consider in the marginal costing process.

Marginal costs may similarly vary month by month – for example, if you are using as ingredients one or more commodities that fluctuate in price frequently, and where either you do not have longer-term contracts or your costs of replacing the commodities for regular production would be different. This is particularly likely to be the case if you have a significant proportion of an agriculturally based commodity (such as sugar, milk or grain products) or certain metals (such as gold, silver, etc.). The standard cost used by your cost accountant may differ up or down from the replacement cost if you have booked only commodity cover to meet the initial production plan. When you have a situation where one or more basic commodities traded freely on world markets are a major input and cost factor, then you must be extremely sharp in assessing when you may be competitive and book contracts for export deliveries. There may be seasonal swings, typical with many agricultural products, when customers look for the

Example 4
Profit contribution estimate

Gross sales revenue (f.o.b. port)   £100,000

Less marginal cost of goods sold:

Raw materials	£45,000
Direct labour	20,000
Indirect labour	5,000
Factory supplies	1,500
Utilities	1,000
Packaging supplies	3,500
Storage	500
Insurance in store	100
Additional quality control	200
Spoilage	500
Financing (from production to payment receipt)	1,500
Transport & distribution to exit port	2,000
Export documentation, etc.	100
	£80,900

Gross profit contribution   £19,100

Note: In this assessment of gross profit contribution, I have not made a deduction for the overheads of the export department or any other department, on the assumption that these were fixed costs.

best deals either from the northern or southern hemisphere, and take advantage of the lower seasonal production costs.

When standard products are being produced on mass production lines, there is usually little if any variation in production or ingredient costs from month to month; hence, the marginal cost may vary little, particularly if ingredient supplies are well covered under medium- or longer-term contracts that reduce the effect of seasonal price variations.

In your role as exporter building a business in a tough and competitive environment you will not just be facing competition from two or three domestic manufacturers who, in the home market, coincidentally seem to have very similar prices. You have to compete head-on with the major suppliers from many other nations, all seeking to enter new export markets with marginally costed products, and many of them having very different cost structures from yours.

However, in summarizing this section, the exporter should seriously consider taking a contract if:

● the price covers the marginal cost of production and distribution and any costs specifically and identifiably related to the export order
● if there is an identifiable gross margin between price and marginal costs.

Example 5 illustrates some typical elements of costings that may be considered as fixed or marginal costs. The export manager usually has to be much more familiar with the construction and elements of product costings in his company than the home market sales manager.

Example 5
Typical variable and fixed cost factors

Typical variable cost factors
Indirect labour*
Direct labour*
Factory supplies
Overtime premiums
Extra shifts
Repairs and maintenance*
Utilities*
Insurance on goods in store
Stock financing
Packaging materials
Raw materials
Spoilage
Export distribution costs
Export documentation costs

Typical fixed cost factors
Central office and administration costs
Production & quality control supervision
Rent
Property taxes
Basic insurances
Research and development
Certain utilities*
Repairs and maintenance*

---

* Certain cost elements may justifiably be treated by your accountant in either category, depending on particular company practices.

Pricing considerations

Pricing is an independent exercise from costing. Fundamentally, your price is governed by what the customer will accept to pay and confirm the order. Producing elaborate price lists and never getting orders is a wasteful exercise. There are basically two main elements that assist you in arriving at a market price:

- assessing the value potential customers will put on your product and be prepared to pay, and
- assessing your true cost of producing for sale the particular units you are offering for sale.

If the potential price is higher than the measurable costs, then it is worth quoting and seeking business.

Some points to consider in arriving at a potential price are:

- Establish all relevant market data on competitive prices for similar products; this will include weight/value or volume/value comparisons. You can usefully tabulate this data. Your comparison should include both retail and wholesale prices.
- Identify and compare competitive wholesale and retail trade margins of profit so that you can ensure you offer competitive margins, but not necessarily excessive margins (traders rarely send you a 'thank you' note for such generosity). If you find your costing would enable you to offer bigger margins and still be price-competitive, then consider the alternative of using the difference for sales promotional activity and treating it as an advertising and promotion reserve rather than offering excessive trade margins.
- Attempt neutrally to assess the consumer-perceived quality or other attributes and benefits in your product versus competitors' in order to establish where in the price rankings to target your product and meet your sales expectations. For example, if you are selling designer-named French perfume, perceived as the top quality source, you would probably not do yourself justice by pricing to compete at the bottom end of the market. You might achieve higher volume but no more gross profit contribution.
- Your price must include adequate margin over your actual production and distribution costs to cover advertising and promotional expenses, market returns and spoilage allowances, and your distributor's costs of handling, storage and distribution in addition to the expected levels of profit contribution for the distributor, wholesalers and retailers. There may also be local sales taxes to incorporate in the price if these are not separately charged at the point of sale.

Example 6
Elements in a pricing calculation for a product shipped from the United Kingdom to the USA

Optimum assessed market retail sales price			$200
Less Standard retailer's margin (20% on sales)[1]	$40.0		
Wholesale margin (5% on wholesaler's price)[2]	$ 8.0		
Importer's margin (15% on importer's price)[3]	$22.8		
Local advertising reserve (5% of importer's price)[3]	$ 7.6		
Spoilage allowance (1% of importer's price)[3]	$ 1.5		
Importer's cost of customs clearance[4]	$ 2.1		
Customs duties (10% of c.i.f. value)[5]	$10.7		
	$92.7		
C.i.f. price at foreign port in foreign currency			$107.3
C.i.f. price at foreign port in exporter's home currency[6]			£71.5
Less Ocean freight & insurance		£6.5	
Exporter's f.o.b. vessel price			£65.0
Less Export documentation costs		£1.0	
Distribution costs from plant to vessel		£2.0	
MAXIMUM PRICE EXPORTER CAN CHARGE EX-PLANT			£62.0
Less Production costs of export merchandise		£48.0	
GROSS PROFIT CONTRIBUTION			£14.0

Notes:
  [1] 20% of retail price of $200.
  [2] 5% of wholesale price, which is $160 (retail price less retail margin).
  [3] Percentage based on importer's sales price, which is retail price less retail margin and less wholesale margin (i.e. $152 per unit).
  [4] These costs are generally estimated by an importer either as an absolute cost per unit measure or as a small percentage of landed duty paid cost.
  [5] If duty taxes are, say, 10% of c.i.f. cost, then the c.i.f. can be calculated by dividing the landed duty paid price by 1.10, the difference being the duty.
  [6] Exchange rate taken as $1.50 = £1.00.

We can tabulate this reverse calculation from market sales price to the price you can charge ex-plant as in Example 6. Clearly, what your distributor can achieve as a local sales price in his market, less all cost factors and trade margins and less all costs of distribution to ship goods to the foreign market, governs the price you can hope to achieve as your quoted ex-plant price. And this figure, less all your costs of producing and packaging the goods for export, will give a gross margin contribution to your own company. If you are going to compete in export markets and be profitable, then obviously you must arrive at a positive contribution in this reverse calculation. If you show a negative contribution, then you would be exporting at a loss to compete with foreign market sales prices.

In setting your prices, you will be getting into such marketing discussion points as market positioning, on the one hand, and pressures on you to get volume business to keep plants running at capacity, on the other. You must work to achieve a balance between what may sometimes appear as conflicting objectives. Is your objective related to a marketing strategy aimed at achieving longer-term sales volumes consistent with a market position or to get short-term, marginally costed, high-volume sales to fill a production line? Where are you trying to position your product in the foreign market? Is it a luxury consumer product that demands and responds best to a high-price image, or is it a mass-market, disposable item with a less brand-conscious target market? Is it an internationally famous brand, perhaps, with a youthful cult image? Or is it an industrial product used as a component in other manufactured goods? Does it have clearly perceived technological advantages? Is it just a regular commodity obtainable on world markets from a variety of sources with little identifiable quality or functional differences?

The more unique your product or the more exclusive features or uses it has, the greater flexibility you have as the exporter in pricing the product to sell and to yield a positive profit contribution. The closer it is to a commodity-type product, the more the 'market' dictates at any point in time what you may charge. Another factor is availability. Are there many producers of similar products or just a few? What spare production capacity do your competitors have to compete with you for exports? If you have few competitors with limited spare capacity, they may be less aggressive in exporting, enabling you to obtain better prices.

With all the variables to be considered in export pricing, you are justified in concluding that there can be no hard and fast rule or formula for arriving at an export price. Export managers seeking business opportunities will sharpen their business disciplines and training by exposure to the procedures and processes of product costing. When you have to make most of your critical decisions relevant to any export deal, you will probably be far away from the home office in a foreign market, unable to walk into a colleague's office to discuss merits of the transaction under review. Hence, to make binding decisions competently, you need an unusually thorough knowledge of your company, its products and all the variable factors that affect costing and pricing, and your best friend back at the home office is likely to be your cost accountant.

The pricing exercise is ongoing. Changes in relative exchange rates between the home and export market will necessitate regular review. If your home currency strengthens relative to the importer's currency, yet foreign market prices are not rising, you may have to consider dropping your export price in home currency terms to remain competitive. However, if your currency becomes relatively weaker, you may be able to increase prices. The importer often takes the position that he, not you, should reap the benefit of windfall gains if your currency weakens, but he rarely considers that he should take the loss in contribution if your currency strengthens, and then sees the only alternative as a local price increase. Many larger manufacturers avoid this potential source of conflict with their distributors and importers by quoting their ex-plant or f.o.b. sales prices in the foreign currency and taking the currency risks themselves. In practice, the finance division will normally reduce that risk by selling the foreign currency forward as soon as a contract is exchanged and there is some certainty about when the foreign funds will be received.

Your importer should be requested to provide you with monthly reports on competitive pricing and promotional activities, including analysis of the customs reports showing volumes and values of imports of similar products from the alternative sources supplying the market. This assists the exporter in studying competitive imports, which generally bear a direct relation to market sales, and movements in c.i.f. values, which, in turn, may indicate likely market price adjustments.

Exporting is not just packing a suitcase and travelling to exotic islands. Successful exporting involves considerable time devoted to ongoing desk work in preparing and analysing data, and planning and monitoring marketing activities. You may never develop as much expertise in your foreign markets as your local distributors, but you certainly should aim to have a thorough and up-to-date understanding of the mechanisms and magnitudes of trade in the market in order to present a professional image and contribute to and manage the market development. If you find yourself preparing market analyses based upon data supplied by your distributor or other sources, then, in general, it is a useful courtesy to send a copy of your studies to your distributor, or to take them with you for discussion on your next visit. Successful exporter–importer relationships only develop by total mutual commitment in developing the right products for the market and the right market for the products.

Export price lists

Once you have decided on the price at which you wish to offer your products to your foreign customers, the next stage is to produce a formal price list. This should contain the following basic data:

- product names and/or descriptions and reference codes
- pack sizes (i.e. number of units per carton)
- package weights and dimensions
- price quote per unit to point of exchange of ownership (e.g. ex-plant, f.a.s., f.o.b. vessel, f.o.b. port of exit, c & f destination, c.i.f. destination)
- terms of sale, payment terms and conditions, insurance coverage
- warranties or exclusions
- period of validity of quote.

You may need to include additional information particular to your company or products. When you have prepared your draft price list, it is well worth passing it to a colleague in another department for his comments on the understandability of the document. If he finds it too confusing, then the chances are that your non-English-speaking customers will find it equally or more difficult to interpret.

If your products do not lend themselves to formal price lists, possibly because of their commodity nature or because they are being exclusively produced for a customer, you may have to do individual costing and pricing exercises for each separate transaction or quote. In some markets it is the custom and practice to haggle over prices and the exporter may expect to offer discounts or reductions to close a sale.

Price-controlled imports

Many developing countries have strict regulations governing the permissible retail prices for basic commodities and foodstuffs, such as bread, rice, flour and other staples. You need to establish if your product will land and sell within the price control limits if it is a controlled item, and still give the customary trade margins. It may be that all controlled items can be purchased and imported only by a specific government agency, such as the Mexican government agency and corporation, Conasupo, which has sole permission to bring in controlled raw material food imports.

Points of ownership transfer

It is customary in the export trade to quote a price that relates to the geographical location where legal title to the merchandise changes from the seller to the buyer. The manufacturer of, say, consumer goods, may have a standard practice of quoting f.o.b. ('free on board') vessel to all his customers, because they find this an easy location to associate with transfer of title. In order to understand exactly what obligations and costs fall on both you, the seller, and the buyer you should obtain and study the *International Rules for the Interpretation of Trade Terms* (commonly referred to as *'Incoterms'*) published as document No. 350 by the International Chamber of Commerce. It is then frequently advisable or suitable in a quote to refer to a price in a manner such as 'Incoterms c.i.f.' or 'Incoterms c.i.f. plus war risk insurance'.

A brief comment on normal transfer of title locations may assist you in relation to preparing quotes, particularly if your products are more commodity related.

Ex-works: merchandise delivered only to the edge of the exporter's factory dock, with no other cost inclusions for loading or handling. The buyer is responsible for collection of goods and loading onto truck, railcar or container.

F.o.b. factory: merchandise delivered 'free on board' the collecting vehicle at the plant, and the exporter will have costed his loading charges. After taking title when goods are placed on his pick-up vehicle, the buyer is solely responsible for all subsequent charges, including product insurance.

F.o.b. other intermediate point: a contract may specify goods delivered to any other intermediate point, such as a container collection terminal or railway connection. Also, the terms of sale may transfer title either when goods are loaded onto the ongoing transport, or simply when the seller's truck offloads them at the transfer point. There needs to be an understanding in the sales note about who is responsible for on-loading charges, with a comment such as 'free delivered to railway'. The seller is responsible for freight to the point of title transfer at this inland handover point.

F.a.s.: 'free alongside ship' may sometimes have a marginally different meaning from 'free on board port', because f.a.s. puts the responsibility for the costs of getting goods right onto the dockside with the seller.

F.o.b. port is often confused with f.a.s., but, in f.o.b. port, title transfers before goods pass the dock gates, and charges associated with the dock and port fall to the buyer.

F.o.b. vessel: in most countries the simple term, f.o.b., means 'free on board vessel', but it is customary in the USA to clarify that. In the USA, title transfers when goods hit the vessel deck, and the seller is responsible for all charges and risks to that point.

C & f ('cost and freight') customer's destination: the customer may name a foreign port where title transfers, and the seller owns the goods and pays all charges related to freight to the foreign port. From the foreign dock, the buyer takes over and accepts the duties, clearing and handling charges associated with entering the goods into the country. Insurance is the buyer's responsibility.

C.i.f. ('cost, insurance and freight') customer's destination: here the shipper is obliged to insure the goods in transit to the destination designated by the customer, in addition to paying all associated costs and freight charges to the agreed destination.

Ex-quay customer's destination: the seller will pay all costs and, if agreed, duties associated with entering the goods into the foreign market as far as the dock gates, where the buyer collects them. Sometimes the term 'landed duty paid' is taken to have similar meaning, but it is advisable that the contract terms on an 'ex-quay' contract do specifically mention what local charges are to be included to the seller's account.

F.o.b. inland point: if the customer's facilities are well inland, he may request the seller to be responsible for delivery to the inland named city and to organize the onward transport from the port to, say, an inland rail or container point. The sales contract should clearly identify where responsibility for goods and related costs transfers, including duties and local taxes.

Free domicile: the seller delivers the goods to the customer's final named destination, possibly a factory or warehouse, and is responsible for all duties and taxes, handling, storage and transport charges legally arising before that point. Many sellers prefer not to be involved in retaining responsibility to such a stage because it is difficult for the seller to know accurately many of the charges he may incur and need to include in a costing. For example, in some countries a sales tax may be due on imports as they clear customs; in others it may not be due until goods are resold in the market.

At the stage of negotiating the contract of sale, the seller should be very clear with the buyer on how each party understands the conditions of sale in relation to where responsibility for merchandise, transport, title, insurance and so on transfers. (The exporter should refer to the International Chamber of Commerce's *Incoterms* for more precise legal definitions of the standard terms of trade.)

Summary

- Export costing should take account of any additional special functions or modifications to products, including: costs of distribution; special packaging; ingredient, formula or specification modifications; quality control; and export administration and marketing.
- Marginal costing of a product for export will enable the exporter

to judge his competitiveness on world markets and take advantage of opportunities to achieve extra volume. It recognizes the need to exclude fixed costs from costing quotes and to identify and include all variable costs such as those related to raw materials, packaging, production and other inputs, and related services.

- As long as the gross sales revenue exceeds the established marginal cost of goods for export, then the export sale will make a positive contribution to gross margins, and sales can beneficially be pursued.
- Market pricing may be an independent exercise from costing, and include such considerations as the maximum price the consumer will pay (possibly governed by competitive activity), desired market positioning, perceived product benefits and differentiation from competitive or substitute products.
- An ex-plant price can be derived by a reverse calculation from the maximum foreign market price attainable, less all costs associated with distribution, handling, storage, marketing and promotion, trade and importer margins, duties and taxes. If the attainable ex-plant price exceeds the marginal production cost, then exporting is a viable project.
- The exporter's price structure can be varied between markets to maximize sales potential and counter or encourage such unofficial sales avenues as smuggling and parallel exports.
- The export price list must minimally include full product names and identifying descriptions, pack sizes, weights and dimensions, quoted prices to point of transfer of ownership, and a statement of all terms and conditions of sale or warranty.

7

Packaging for Export

Export packaging has a number of functions and objectives. It must ensure that the product arrives in the market and with the final end user or consumer in as good condition as it leaves the exporter's factory, and in perfect working order, free from heat, humidity and other climatic damage and without physical damage of any form. It must comply with all laws, rules, regulations or trade conventions that apply to the packaging of goods for sale in that market, and to the international carriage of such goods (e.g. goods considered dangerous). It must identify the product clearly to the end user in the export market and relate to local culture so as not to be considered offensive or unacceptable in any aspect of presentation or design. It must comply in each and every respect with the specifications and requirements of the importer and agreed upon at the time of concluding the supply contract.

Physical suitability

The transportation of an export order from the supplier to the final customer is likely to involve several modes of transport, and it may involve many rigours not encountered in a home market sale. Truck, sea and rail are all likely to be used at some point in the journey, and goods may be containerized while on the ocean but shipped loose on the final inland stretch in the destination country. There will be a variety of climatic variations to take account of, and probably much rougher handling and storage conditions than your product faces at home. Packaging design and structure need to reflect the factors of transport mode, manual or mechanical handling, perishability, effects of climate, and nature of the goods (would they be classed as 'dangerous').

Physical protection You should therefore start by assuming that your export packaging needs to be much stronger and more durable than packaging used domestically. First examine the outer case or carton in which the products are shipped domestically. Many packaging scientists like to conduct transit tests by sending a single carton over the roughest expected conditions to the foreign importer, and then having this returned carefully by air for study. It may be that either the weight of carton board used, or the packing configuration of individual units can be varied in order to reduce the risk of damage. Carton dividers or various polystyrene fillers may help provide extra strength and protection from physical damage. Sealing the carton with tape in addition to normal gluing may also reduce risks of physical or climatic damage.

The individual unit of the product in turn may need its own extra protection. For example, if there is a risk that the product could rust in transit, it may need protection in the form of a moisture barrier such as an impervious sealed polythene film wrapper round the unit container. It may benefit from polystyrene corner protectors to prevent physical damage. Consumer durables are likely to need more protection than industrial components.

Heat and humidity protection   Perishable foodstuffs and many canned goods require careful attention to adequate protective packaging to prevent heat and moisture damage that could result in mould or rusting. In addition, the product may be subject to insect infestation in transit or before sale in the foreign market. Past experience has shown me that weevils often acquire a taste for imported delicacy food items even before the local population, and enormous cockroaches are not intimidated by the flimsy boxes frequently used in the home market to protect breakfast cereals. Good sealing on the outer carton is the first stage of protection. A polythene heat-sealed overwrap may be considered necessary for some products. Inner cartons can likewise be protected by a shrink-wrapped polythene cover. Impregnation of cartons may assist in reducing infestation by insects if the chemicals used are food-safe. The final product within the display box, such as a cereal, may need to be foil-wrapped to protect against heat, humidity and insects.

Many of the markets to which you ship will not yet have all the sophisticated and hygienic facilities of the home market, including adequate refrigeration and pest control equipment. Indeed, many stores in hot countries even turn off air conditioning overnight to cut the prohibitive cooling costs involved. If you, as the supplier, do not recognize and protect against known risks, your product sales will suffer in the market. In this brief commentary I cannot offer you all the solutions; I can only really alert you to the potential problems. You will have available to you the specific advice of professional packaging scientists, either at your home office or through the service of your packaging supplier.

As an illustration of a situation where packaging affected market sales drastically, there was an instance of a confectionery product being marketed in Hong Kong, where the climate varies from unbearably hot and humid to pleasantly temperate. After launch, this product had phenomenal sales, especially at Christmas and Chinese New Year. In the normal air-conditioned supermarkets the product was well stored and displayed, and sales were consistent all year. In the more open street-side traditional stores, sales were initially voluminous in the first gift-giving season after product launch, and barely slowed down into the hot and humid summer. However, the second gift season resulted in a dramatic decline of sales through the non-supermarket outlets, despite trade and consumer acceptance for the product. And sales in non-air-conditioned stores, which were the greatest market sector, continued to decline. Extensive store checking and product sampling revealed that, although the product was displayed everywhere and highly accepted, product offtake had dropped because the particular confectionery item had a light, malted milk type centre, which collapsed under humid conditions to a chewy ball − not what the consumer expected and had initially accepted. The alternatives here were:

- improve the packaging to be suitably heat and humidity proof
- limit distribution to air-conditioned stores only
- introduce a new and better produce freshness and uplift policy for the damaged product.

In fact, the practical solution was a combination. It proved impossible adequately to package the confectionery product to give total heat and humidity protection at any reasonable cost where chocolate was involved. The outer carton could be wrapped with a polythene overwrap to reduce humidity damage while goods were still kept in the thirty-six count outer box. In addition, the distributor had to persuade the small stores to treat the product as a gift-giving seasonal item only, so that consumers could be guaranteed the quality in the cooler weather, and introduce a product return policy. The price was increased to build in a reserve fund that could be used to pay for the greatly increased level of expected end-of-season returns, or to run end-of-season store promotions to clear the pipeline stocks. In the height of the hot and humid summer season, sales were restricted to air-conditioned stores, which, although it caused a short-term drop in sales into outlets, resulted in consumers knowing that the fresh product was available through non-air-conditioned outlets only in the cooler season. Special gift packs were developed where a multiple of individual packs were placed in a decorated tin container, giving added protection. The end result was that, in the following gift-giving season, sales volume again escalated to new peaks because of increased and renewed consumer satisfaction.

Basically, when designing packaging, the packaging must plan to protect your product from sensitivity to:

- excessive heat and temperature variations in the market
- humidity and its seasonal variations
- transit handling and storage risks
- damage through inherent vice and infestation.

Rules and regulations

Label information You should consider what the authorities in the foreign market may wish to have known about the product when it is offered to the public. Rules and regulations frequently act as a non-tariff barrier to trade and, in practice, are more often applied to consumer goods than to products for industrial processing.

The regulatory authorities do not usually get too involved in regulating outer packaging such as cartons, beyond simple specifications perhaps on print size, language and basic data you should incorporate (such as name and address of manufacturer, name of contents and number of units contained therein). The manufacturer usually has more data he considers necessary for inclusion, such as expiry dates of perishables, indications about the correct side to face up, and so on. On the individual product unit offered for sale, it is normal to find additional and specific regulations relating to ingredient specifications, manufacturer, expiry dates, manner of usage, product representations, product registration details, importer's name and address, language of labelling, permissible ingredients. They will also generally regulate the location and size of print for all compulsory information. For example, you will often see references to the main panel incorporating much of this information, and that can be taken to mean the side of the box displayed towards the consumer at the point of sale.

Language If two or more languages are used, then the usual rule is that the local language must be in print at least as large, and appear on the same panel location, as the foreign language.

The practice of requiring the use of the local language on product labelling and on any other information or instruction sheets has grown rapidly in recent years as more countries have felt the surge of nationalism, and as consumer protection has come to the fore. Most marketers will see this as both beneficial and reasonable, although imposing more demands upon the production and planning departments. Some companies respond to this matter by seeking to design one multilingual label for their major markets (e.g. incorporating Spanish, French, English and German). There is the risk that a cluttered label leaves a confused image with the consumer, and two languages are considered by many exporters as the limit on a label. The more pack sizes and labels you are obliged to have, the more strains placed upon your production, planning and inventory control departments if you are producing consumer-packaged goods. If, however, you are selling bulk products or industrial products, it may be that you simply store the standard product in unlabelled form until you know to which market it will finally be shipped and then label it accordingly. No company wants any more inventory of different pack sizes, designs, labels or finished goods than necessary, as this causes both unwieldy control problems and more working capital.

Label approvals The technical terms permissible in obligatory ingredient or component declarations may vary from country to country. It is essential that you obtain copies of the respective regulations for each market in which you offer products for sale and ensure compliance. Translations may be available via your embassy or agent, and it is always wise to confirm the acceptability of labels by sending samples to your agent or distributor and requesting that he prepare his own comments and seek any appropriate local approvals before you incorporate the proposals in printed materials. Agencies frequently involved in labelling approvals may include any or all of the following: health departments, consumer affairs bureaus, weights and measures departments, any price control agencies, import control agencies, government analytical laboratories, customs and excise authorities.

Apart from assistance from your agent in labelling matters, you may feel more comfortable by establishing a relationship with a suitably qualified lawyer in the export market; once again, your embassy is best placed to make recommendations.

Dangerous goods Customs authorities or other regulatory bodies specify the nature of packing, shipment, handling and storage that apply to goods considered 'dangerous'. The carrier can usually give specific advice and guidelines applicable to his routes and mode of transport, or in the UK information will be available through the Department of Trade and Industry. Substances including explosives, poisons, chemicals, gases, inflammable liquids and solids, corrosives, radioactive materials, and other products considered a hazard whilst in transit or store are subject to regulations.

If the product or container is susceptible to expansion or contraction as temperatures change, or to become a fire or explosive risk, packaging may have to allow for potential volume changes or risks. If the product is combustible or explosive under conditions of movement, vibration or temperature, the goods may need to be shipped at controlled temperatures and in a movement-free environment. If the goods can contaminate others, they may need separate storage or container facilities.

Packaging should be both resistant to its contents and to the environment encountered in store or transit. Various guidelines, regulations and codes exist, such as those of the International Air Transport Association and International Maritime Dangerous Goods Codes.

Clearly, each stage of packing should bear suitable and clear labelling instructions on handling, storage and action to be taken in the event of possible emergencies. Some products may simply be unsuitable for shipment by a particular mode of transport.

Product identification and positioning

Quite apart from the official rules and regulations governing your product labelling, your first concern as a marketing manager is to ensure instant product recognition by the consumer at the point of sale, and to design the packaging to convey your quality image, in addition to it serving its functional purpose of product protection.

Local culture   There are cultural aspects of packaging that must be considered along with the objectives of international brand recognition. Generally you will find it easier to add something to a culture than to change something within that culture. During the early efforts of the fast-food chains to establish themselves in Southeast Asia, the hamburger and pizza organizations seemed to find it easier to gain acceptance initially than the fried chicken operations. The consistent response to travellers who asked friends and associates why this might be the case was that the Chinese had been cooking chicken in their own traditional way for many generations and preferred its taste to the fried form.

Colour may have an important role to play in packaging. Local attitudes and superstitions may need to be considered, and you should investigate these through your distributor and foreign advertising agency at an early point in the planning process. Chinese communities historically favour red and gold as warmer colours suitable for packaging gift-type items, and white is seen as associated with death and unhappy events. So it may be quite inappropriate to have an expensive gift perfume boxed in white. Even the shade of a colour can significantly affect attitudes and sales. On one occasion, when designing a gift box for confectionery scheduled to be launched one Chinese New Year in Hong Kong, a principal and his agent, along with their advertising agency, were all in favour of a particular shade of red. However, as a quick check, since they knew how important it was to get the right shade, they took twenty-five of the male and female clerical staff in the distributor's office and walked them past the alternative shades being considered one by one, seeking an instant comment on preference. It may not have been a very scientific test by research standards, but the response was twenty-five against their choice and in favour of another alternative.

Forgeries Where possible, if you can use a distinct name or description of the product in the local language, it will be beneficial, particularly for a product being launched into a country where the written language bears no relationship to your own, such as Thai, Arabic, Chinese and Japanese. The branded goods' exporter is frequently plagued by rough copies of his product in developing markets, and often the copy tries to use a crude variation on the foreign brand name, which, in any event, most of the local customers can neither pronounce nor read correctly. Even a registered trademark may be hard to police in many countries. Every traveller has seen the poor copies of Cartier watches and Gucci accessories that come out of the Orient. Local manufacturers will always seek a quick profit if they find they can produce a cheap copy without much capital investment. So anything you can do to make the copying process both difficult and risky (by enforcing trademarks, brands, patents and copyrights) should be done; this will assist the brand development of the original item, because sales are likely to be significantly reduced if consumers come to fear that their purchase could be of a forgery. Copying may be a form of flattery, but if your distributor of fashion accessories is an exclusive retailer, he will justifiably be upset if the street vendors are offering close copies at vastly reduced prices.

Purchase motivations Market habits and purchase motivations can be important considerations at the stage of packaging design. For example, gift giving in Japan is a major feature and event at certain times of the year, and retailers give over much of their display space to suitable gift items. Since the gift should clearly not put an obvious value upon a person's friendship, it is less acceptable to give a standard retail item, such as a regular-size bottle of Scotch whisky, than to give a specially packaged and sized item where the inherent value is disguised, say the same Scotch but sold in a fancy glass decanter. Cosmetic and toiletry items could be in fancy multiple-product gift boxes rather than sold in the normal single-item form.

   The exporter must consider most carefully for each separate market who will buy his product, what will be the likely purchase and use occasions, when it will be purchased; his knowledge and judgement on these matters should be incorporated in any relevant manner in the design of the packaging. Above all, be flexible, because what may be a mass-market line in one country may be best sold as an up-market luxury in another. If you are not limited by a prescribed international brand image of a consumer item, then pay heed to the local advice from distributors and advertising agencies on aspects of packaging and presenting your product, including acceptable unit sizes, shapes, design, logos and labelling.

Product use information   The descriptive phrases used in labelling or advertising the product need to inform the consumer clearly how to consume or use the product if that is not immediately obvious from the nature of the product. In many foreign and developing countries, consumers are constantly being bombarded with new products and product concepts that may initially be outside their experience. Apart from packaging to ensure recognition of a particular brand and to establish a market position for that brand, it is important to ensure that you are telling the consumer what to do with that product or how to use it correctly and safely. With a breakfast cereal, you may benefit by illustrating the eating occasion along with the schematic showing of the need to add milk. Other convenience foods may need more elaborate illustrations showing how the product is prepared in the oven or on the stove top. Household cleaning items may need fuller descriptions on applications if they are new products to a market. Consumer durables are likely to benefit from comprehensive and extra instructions on use, care and maintenance, and safety, as in the case of electric drills or other tools aimed at new home handyman markets.

Consider all the additional potential problems you may face in selling your product to the new market at the stage of designing packaging and literature, and a thorough and professional approach at this stage will reduce the risk of lost sales because of consumer ignorance of the product.

Customer's specifications

Order requirements   Should your customer have specified certain packaging requirements at the time of placing the order, and should you not have agreed to any changes or amendments with the customer, then you are bound and obligated to comply with the requested specifications. It may be that the customer's order purely repeated your packaging specifications contained in your price list or quotation, but do not assume that; check your customer's order thoroughly. If you are selling against a letter of credit, then even such a small point as an incorrect item of packaging could warrant non-payment under the terms of the letter of credit. A difference between the standard packaging and that specified by your customer might only be a typing error at his office, but that should not be assumed.

Customers may specify a change from your standard label, possibly with the addition of their name and address, or a change in ingredient declarations, unit size, multiple of units in a carton, and so on. Some requests you may be able to comply with; others you should not comply with. It is well known in developing countries that an importer may request changes in labelling or product descriptions to enable an otherwise restricted product to enter the country, or to enable the importer to pay a lower import duty by it being reclassified. If your product contains a non-approved ingredient or colour and you cannot change your ingredient to an approved item, then do not risk a false or incorrect label declaration at the request of an importer, as your company may have more to lose by falling foul of the foreign authorities than your importer in the long term.

Customer packaging expectations When you ship merchandise to your foreign customer, he is entitled to expect and receive:

● packaging in line with the custom of the trade
● packaging that is adequate to ensure the product arrives safely at its destination and that has protected the product from transit risks
● packaging that complies with rules and regulations in the receiving country for the particular product.

This chapter has dealt with the second and third of these points, but the first point is something not to be overlooked. If your industry and product have an acceptable standard form of packaging, for example a certain type of bag for an agricultural product, then your shipment should be at least as well packed. If your shipment of, say, milk powder in bulk 25 kg bags only uses 2-ply bags when the normally accepted bag is a 4-ply unit, then your customer may have grounds for complaint or claim. Similarly, consider at this point the mode of shipment. If you are offering to deliver goods that normally require refrigeration and the product arrives unrefrigerated, then your customer may have a basis for claiming that any c.i.f. quote you sold against was fairly assumed to be commensurate with the product requirement of refrigerated stowage in transit, and claims may ensue or your bills may not be paid.

The rule for the exporter is to check with the customer on all points concerning each order, and issue an order acceptance and confirmation that not only details the packaging but also the volume, value and method of shipment, and other specifics relevant to a particular product.

F.o.b. and c.i.f. price quotes customarily include suitable export packing unless otherwise specified. Phrases used might be such as: 'goods packed for export in heavy duty cases, with supporting dividers, and individual product units are polythene overwrapped', or 'goods are supplied in standard domestic market cartons and packaging, but may be protectively packed at an additional charge of £20 per fifty units in specially constructed wooden crates'. Your price list should always contain a summary of your standard terms and conditions of sale, along with notes on packaging for export, to reduce the risk of complaints by customers that they were insufficiently informed of your practices and procedures.

Packaging and freight The mode of packing for export – for example, whether the goods are palletized or containerized or simply shipped loose stowage – may make a difference in freight and handling charges. Also, the weight and dimensions of cartons may affect whether you pay freight by volume or weight measure. The general principle, both to reduce the risk of damage in transit and to minimize freight costs, is to make the packaging a precise fit at each stage of packing; i.e. product into initial inner container; inner container into multi-unit (or single-unit, as appropriate) outer container. Efficient choice of the most effective form of protective packaging to minimize size, weight and general bulk may even result in a faster form of shipment such as air freight becoming a cost effective mode of transport. Of course, the mode of shipment will also depend to a degree on the value of the merchandise being shipped, because the smaller the ratio of freight costs to market value the more attractive it will be to exporters and importers to consider faster, if more expensive, modes of shipment.

If the exporter is to receive a clean bill of lading at shipment, then the packaging used must have at least been adequate to ensure no visible defects or damage when goods were loaded onto the vessel. Goods shipped in sealed containers may result in the issue of a bill of lading bearing a note such as 'a container said to contain five hundred cartons of canned soup', without reference to the goods being received in good order as they cannot easily be checked.

In summary, check the initial order, the shipping documents and the payment documents to ensure that at each stage you are fully in compliance with instructions concerning the type, quantity, quality and packaging of goods ordered by your export customer.

Summary

- Export packaging should provide complete physical protection from all transit and market risks to ensure that the product arrives with the final user in perfect usable condition.
- It should comply in all respects with the importing country's rules and regulations, including those relating to labelling, design and product representation, ingredient declarations, language, print size and positioning.
- It should clearly identify the product to users, and include on packs or in separate literature full instructions, in the local language, covering operation, use and maintenance.

- Packaging design and format should be acceptable to local cultural standards, for example in respect of colour or illustrations of products or persons.
- All packaging should comply with any specifications agreed with the foreign customer.

8

Advertising and Promotion

The need to advertise and promote will depend greatly on the type of product you produce and offer for sale, and the degree of security your products have in respect of import controls such as import licences and quotas. If there are finite import limits in respect of volume or value, then the level of expenditure should probably be no higher than is necessary to move the volume of imports through the distribution pipeline either within the limits of shelf life, if a perishable product, or before the next quota issue.

An industrial product may need a very different approach from a consumer product, and a consumer durable product will need a different programme from non-durable items. One chapter cannot cover this vast subject, but it may serve to provide an outline of facets to consider.

Industrial products

Journals and buyers' guides Industrial products generally benefit most from advertising and editorials in local or international *trade* and *technical journals*. They need to be promoted to a particular market, such as the buyers of processing companies or the manufacturers of machinery or industrial plant and equipment. Listings and advertising insertions in buyers' guides aimed at a particular trade sector, such as the construction industry, are extremely beneficial in eliciting response providing the insertion is very clear in describing what you are offering, in summarizing the product's use, and in stating who to contact at the manufacturer's office to obtain specification details and price quotes. If you promote through a regional guide or journal, then you should list the local importers who carry stock or handle market sales efforts.

There are so many new trade and regional directories coming on the market that you need to research who is producing the directory and its circulation. I have known publishers to solicit directory entries for a fee in some markets, and then take several years to get the first edition into print. Establish the reputation of a directory by asking a few buyers of your products in the home market which directories they would refer to in seeking such products, and then call the publishers of those specific directories to obtain international circulation data by market. Major trade directories, such as *Thomas's Grocery Register* published from the USA, are very well worth listing a product or service in if you offer foodstuffs or related services. The *Food Engineering Master Guide* is invaluable if you are selling food-processing equipment or ingredients. A phone call to trade or professional associations or chambers of commerce will usually help you establish which directories they value and to which they subscribe.

Trade shows Exposure at trade shows can be very beneficial because these shows tend to attract the specialist buyer or technical personnel such as researchers or production personnel. In recent years, however, a multiplicity of minor trade shows have been promoted, and one must question the benefit of many of these shows to any except the professional show organizers. Do carefully evaluate which of the major shows around the world are considered by your target audience as worth attending. A considerable number of buyers and technical persons travel to the major international and regional trade shows, but local shows are often poorly attended, in part because some of the motivation in making a trip to a major show, say in the USA or Europe, is to meet old contacts and have a nice overseas trip on company expenses.

Usually the least expensive trade promotional efforts occur when your embassy in the foreign market puts on a mini-trade show and hosts local buyers and company representatives. Before you involve yourself in this and possibly send representatives and samples, ask for a specific list of who will be invited and expected to attend.

The costs of participating in some export trade shows may attract subsidies from a government or trade agency concerned with export promotion, but these are normally only partial subsidies for the total cost of booths, travel and samples. The costs of attending a small regional show are likely to be more per attendee than participation in a major show, such as the Anuga or Sial food shows in Europe. Once you have made the decision to display at any trade show, then it is wise to advise all your existing agents, importers and buying contacts of your planned presence and booth number so that any contacts planning attendance at the show may schedule a visit with you. Your booth needs to be staffed with personnel fully competent to answer questions of a technical nature, and to give firm price quotations to potential customers. Plenty of trade literature and relevant samples need to be available, and you should have a system for recording who has visited your booth so that you or your importers can follow up in each market to develop business.

Advertising Advertising for industrial-type products will generally convey a different message from that for consumer goods. Often your advertising copy needs to elaborate on quite technical specification and applications data so that a potential buyer can quickly identify a use or need or potential opportunity. In addition, the buyer must be encouraged and motivated to contact the manufacturer or his agent for further specific data relating to use in his plant or industry. It is therefore common to include some form of customer enquiry form.

A few guidelines to consider in preparing your industrial product advertisement:

- show the product clearly with a good product photograph
- be cautious if your advertising agency suggests too abstract a copy theme, because a busy buyer normally only skims through journals and has little time to give to the mental gymnastics of understanding and interpreting the purpose of vague advertising
- keep the copy as brief and simple as possible
- inform the reader of the product's uses and applications, basic specifications and performance details
- outline the benefits to the buyer and user of incorporating your product in his processes or finished products. This may include price, performance, economy of energy, safety
- tell the buyer who makes the product and where he can both get more information and see local demonstrations (in some instances, if you are advertising in a multinational journal and have a network of distributors, it may be adequate to say 'Consult your local Yellow Pages for the name of your local distributor').

Consumer goods

Durable consumer goods These can generally be promoted and advertised in a similar fashion to the home market programme. However, for developing markets where you are trying to establish a need and create demand, you may need to give emphasis to product use and applications. You can possibly take advantage of your international reputation to make the consumer feel secure with the expected quality and performance. If the item may need any spare parts or servicing, it is essential that the potential buyer knows what local support services you or your distributor can offer and where these will be made available.

Lifestyle advertising is much used to promote a developed-market product in the less developed countries – copy or illustrations show potential users how 'the other half' lives. Consumers all round the world desire to improve their standard of living and are heavily influenced by exposure to western films and journals.

Consumer durables also benefit from promotional activities that emphasize convenience and labour-saving aspects. Even in so-called 'developing' nations, more and more family units are finding the need for both the husband and wife to seek employment, either to supplement the family budget or because modern living leaves the wife with less demand on her time from domestic chores and more of a feeling of self-worth and desire to contribute to society by pursuing a career.

Because many of the durable products being promoted internationally may be aimed at markets and consumers who are less familiar with usage than the home market consumer, it is essential that instruction leaflets are translated into the local language of the foreign market. The consumer must not be exposed to any risk of incorrect use or assembly through inadequate instruction, and the authorities in the foreign market may have regulations concerning prior approval of any packaging or instruction literature. If the item is electrical, then it should be already adapted for use at the correct local voltage and current strength. If the item is for regular use in hot and humid climates, then it is essential you have thoroughly tested its ability to perform under such climatic conditions, and that it will neither rust nor malfunction because some part corrodes or expands. Your company's reputation will take longer to repair than the product if early shipments do not perform in line with your advertising claims or consumer expectations.

Frequently used promotional techniques for consumer durables include:

- television and radio advertising
- poster campaigns
- advertisements in newspapers and periodicals aimed at the target market
- in-store promotions and demonstrations
- displays and exhibitions at consumer and trade shows
- consumer competitions using the promoted items as prizes
- piggyback promotions, e.g. 'buy a refrigerator and get a free coffee percolator'.

If you decide with your distributor to run any in-store or consumer promotion, then it is essential to keep the programme as simple as practical administratively so that your distributor can successfully handle it with his limited resources.

Branded non-durable consumer products Items such as toiletries and foodstuffs can frequently take a number of years to develop to maturity in a market, partly because in many cases the importer is initially facing limited sales opportunities to the more affluent element of the local population. However, displayed distribution will create interest and desire among a much wider population, because in many of the developing countries the younger people tend to spend many hours simply window-shopping and admiring the products they would like to have.

Some of the promotional techniques used successfully with non-durable goods include:

- media advertising (radio/television/cinema)
- posters (particularly in less affluent markets where few own televisions)
- magazines, particularly those with 'lifestyle' image
- in-store demonstrations and promotions
- couponing
- consumer competitions involving purchase requirement (where legal)
- retailer competitions related to sales volume or feature displays.

Advertising   It is essential that you seriously assess your sales potential for the product and the degree of security with which you can import before committing yourself to an advertising budget. Consideration must be given to the level of effective distribution and product display achievable and to consumer spending power to ensure that you do not overspend at too early a stage. Advertising agents will generally propagate the pulling power of advertising through media, perhaps with some merit, but at an early stage of market penetration with consumer non-durables many exporters find the first priority to be obtaining displayed distribution of the product.

Media advertising should be in the local language to reach the target market effectively. Some countries actually require this and even that films intended for use in their market should be locally produced. That adds greatly to the cost of a programme, and the exporter initially is better advised, where practical, to devote more of the limited budget to actual advertising and less to producing costly and fancy films. A thorough review of your domestic advertising films may well reveal some that are suitable for use in foreign markets initially, even if they are considered old, for a very low expenditure on local language voice-overs. In fact, once you establish a track record for achieving export sales, it is worth making the case to the domestic marketing department that consideration be given when new films are being produced either to producing an export version at the same time for nominal additional cost, or to making a modified version with minimal need for lip synchronization with foreign language voice-overs.

When you finally start a media programme in any foreign country, it is beneficial to appoint and work with a local agency or affiliate of your domestic agency. There is no substitute for local experience and knowledge, in addition to local monitoring and controlling of advertising schedules to ensure that programmes booked actually are enacted by the television or radio station. The local agency may offer comment on culturally unacceptable aspects of your home market films, possibly for racial reasons or acceptable public standards. For example, in most Moslem countries it will not be acceptable for advertisements to incorporate bathing beauties. If your film features persons clearly of several different races in one film, local viewers could take offence if their race is interpreted as subordinate to another by being featured either later or in a less important role. One exporter experienced a situation where government agencies rejected a film because their impression of the film was that a doorman at a hotel was of their race, and was holding open an automobile door for a person of another race; they could not accept this apparent impression of inferiority. Many such complaints are, in fact, justified, because the creative staff at the home market advertising agency have not necessarily acquired the requisite level of foreign market experience.

Consumer promotions Apart from media advertising, consumer promotions can greatly contribute to product trial and awareness in many developing markets. However, all too frequently the cost of the promotion outweighs the benefit to the manufacturer. To the professional marketer, the purpose of a promotion is not just to demonstrate use of a budget, but to use that budget as a scarce resource and maximize DISPLAY, DISTRIBUTION and CONSUMER TRIAL. It is essential for forward planning purposes to make the most accurate possible post-promotion estimates of the results achieved under each of these categories. We have all seen the many instances of bright consumer marketing men who organize a sophisticated promotion such as a redemption offer, yet the retailers and distributors make no special effort to promote it with extra display features. Hence, in the early stages of market development in new markets consideration must be given to the order of priorities – get the distribution, then the display, then motivate the offtake. The three are not mutually independent, of course, but the most effective promotion is likely to be one that tackles all three response areas.

If we get back to the basics, the first stage is to assess your potential distribution outlets. Surveys may already exist for the local market showing, say, the locations of each food outlet or toiletries retailer. If such information is not readily available, then there may be relatively inexpensive ways to build your own list. Your distributor and you may feel the priority is to tackle the major cities. In that case you could hire college students at low cost in vacation periods to make a comprehensive street-by-street survey of all outlets currently selling similar or competitive products. Some basic follow-up checking on the students' report sheets will enable you to assess their accuracy. Field follow-checks by export marketers using such an approach to identifying outlets indicated that the students have been 80–90 per cent thorough, and that is surely far better than having no decent outlet base. Frequently the distributor can identify many new outlets and potential customers for other products he represents from your survey and it is therefore worth trying to gain commitment by conducting the survey on a cost-sharing basis.

Once a basic survey of target outlets exists, a distribution objective for a specific promotion can be set and then monitored by subsequent retail checks. Plan and provide simple point-of-sale material that will not offend a retailer or obstruct his customers, yet will gain attention at the display point. For example, in markets where many retail outlets are open stall-type streetside shops, stickers and hanging display cards often have more permanence than larger posters, which either get torn down or obstruct the retailer's limited sales area. Since the salesmen in many markets are on commission, and may be reluctant to give time to installing display material, it may be beneficial to have a salesman's bonus for each outlet accepting display material, or a competition for the best displays on each sales territory. Either can be monitored on follow-up checks by the sales supervisors.

Similarly, a key objective is the retention of feature displays for the duration of a promotion. Ideally some form of special display box could be located at the key sales point. A dealer display competition is one way to motivate this. There are various approaches to this, and you can experiment and find for each market and distributor which is effective. Some examples include:

- a dealer competition for best displays, where the sales supervisor can give instant prizes (such as a discount voucher for next purchase) to retailers featuring the key point display during random store checks
- a salesman photographs displays and submits the photographs for judging. The winning retailers receive a worthwhile prize for display originality or prominence, and if they still have the display in place when the supervisor calls to award the prize.

Display retention can be assisted by clearly communicating to retailers the media advertising programme supporting the promotion.

The consumer must be able to find leaflets for competitions or premium offers clearly displayed in the retail outlets during a promotion. These leaflets should be in the local language and explain the rules and procedures for entry simply.

In many developing markets the exporter is not dealing with the degree of retailer and consumer sophistication found in the home market. Define and quantify realistic and achievable marketing objectives, and make a specific plan with your distributor to achieve growth under each criterion. Ensure that your plan considers each variable that can influence the outcome of the promotion. Your initial draft notes on the promotion may look something like this:

(1)	*Distribution objective*:	increase in distribution from 20% to 45% of all outlets
	Method:	– salesmen's new account incentive bonus
		– new retailer bonus of 2 for price of 1
(2)	*Display objective*:	50% of stockists with feature display (22½% all outlets)
	Method:	– point-of-sale display aids and product feature boxes
		– media support on television and in press
		– dealer display bonus or competition
		– salesmen's display competition
(3)	*Consumer trial*:	20% new consumer trial
	Method:	– consumer premium offer (label redemption programme)
		– advertising support on television and in press
		– point-of-sale material and leaflets
		– feature displays in retail outlets
		– in-store demonstrations and sampling in 50 main outlets.

The objectives and the methods to motivate results obviously interrelate, and from this outline plan the full promotion can be planned in detail to ensure timely production of all display material and sales aids, and the booking of media spots. If the promotion has worthwhile objectives, then it is worth thorough planning. If it is worth the budgeted expenditure, it is worth the management time and effort training the sales personnel to ensure effective implementation. If achievement of the objectives is important to sales development, then the results are worth monitoring and quantifying. Visit the market during the promotion period and conduct extensive random store checks on display distribution and to assess effective accessibility of point-of-sale feature displays and the quality and condition of displayed product.

In-store demonstrations These have been mentioned in passing as an aid to consumer trial. Attention needs to be given to the cost-effectiveness of such promotional techniques. Frequently it is found that the demonstrators are not very effective and have little product knowledge. The costs of the wages and sampling programme are often greater than the additional gross sales revenue achieved. Therefore, if you feel that your product merits experimentation with sampling and demonstration programmes in order to increase consumer trial – often it is the only way to motivate a major store to give you a feature display space – then do take the extra time needed personally to select and train your demonstrators.

The marketing of consumer and industrial products has been the subject of many more specialized texts than this. The message that this short commentary on basic export marketing should leave you with is the following:

● To be successful in a remote market where you have little direct control over a distributor, limited market strength with retailers and little consumer awareness, keep promotions simple and set fundamental objectives that are accepted by all parties as both achievable and measurable.

● Plan each aspect of a promotion in detail with your distributor to give a measurable sales benefit for each pound spent. Discussion of 'intangible' benefits at a post-promotion review is often purely an excuse for designing a poor promotion or failing to seek tangible, quantifiable results.

● Measure the quantifiable benefits to your distributor and advertising agencies so that successful aspects can be incorporated in future promotions, and ineffective elements can be discarded.

Financing advertising and promotions

Advertising reserves If your products need promotional activity to create or maintain demand, then you need to incorporate a budget for such activity in your costing programme. The simplest system is to build in a percentage of the ex-plant or f.o.b. price, which need not be the same percentage for each market if expenditure will be at different levels in each market. Some markets may actually develop through a lower price and less promotional activity, particularly if consumer spending power is low. Others may need heavy media support to aid efforts to gain display and distribution.

A fundamental concept in marketing is to push your strengths. That may be liberally interpreted in export markets as placing emphasis on the markets and products with the most potential, where potential may be measured in such terms as consumer incomes and spending power, population size and growth, assessments of market sophistication in matters of distribution or acceptance of westernized culture, and freedom from import or exchange controls. Where there are clear risks to your market development programme, such as unstable governments and arbitrary changes in regulations, or where you can clearly see that developing a consumer franchise is a major long-term project, then, although you perhaps should not abandon the market, relegate it in the priority list and allocate very limited promotional funds in the initial stages. In fact, in such situations there is frequently merit in seeking more local contributions from your importer, within the limits of acceptable market prices, to use on limited-scale local promotional activity.

As the timing of promotional expenditures may not be directly related to when the funds are earned from product sales, a system should be agreed upon with the company accountants whereby accruals for advertising and promotion are noted separately in the accounts as a reserve and should not be allocated back to profit if not dispersed in the same period as the accrual is earned. Generally, at the end of each financial year the accountants will ask you to detail what bills and commitments are outstanding and will consider that any excess should then be allocated to the profit account, since accruals will rarely be allowed to continue unused beyond one year in most corporations.

Distributor's contributions In addition to the margin the exporter includes in his price as an advertising reserve, it is often possible and beneficial to request the distributor to incorporate a local reserve for advertising and promotion. Such a local reserve has the practical benefit that it commits the distributor more fully to promotional programmes and their measurable success if he sees expenditure go through his books, and, in addition, it may mean less total import duty is paid on that element of the f.o.b. price that would form the manufacturer's reserve. The higher the local rate of import duty, the greater the benefit in incorporating the advertising reserve at the distributor's end of the transaction.

As a practical matter, the exporter normally finds more control problems occur with the element of advertising and promotional funds reserved by the distributor. Some distributors become reluctant to commit themselves to promotional programmes because they may be reluctant to spend local advertising reserves; they may hope to incorporate unused reserves into profits at the end of the year, especially if they will not agree to reserves being carried forward into another financial year. Occasionally an importer wants to draw against the advertising reserve to cover adverse currency fluctuations, while not wanting to reciprocate by contributing extra to the reserve when his currency strengthens. That factor may be removed by the exporter taking the currency risk and pricing only in the foreign currency.

Careful budget planning is essential if you are neither to overinvest in promotional activity nor to fall out with your distributor over sources and uses of funds. The chapter on agency agreements has indicated that at an early stage some clear contractual basis could be given to the mutual obligations of the parties in respect of advertising and promotion, including the respective contributions and the mechanics of management control over planning and disbursements against accrued reserves. In the final analysis, only mutual confidence and mutual business benefit will produce cooperation without conflict.

The advertising and promotion plan

The preparation of an annual advertising and promotion programme is an essential process in planned market development. It may be an internal control and requirement from the export manager's superiors, and it should not be prepared in isolation from the distributor, who will have significant experience and local market knowledge to contribute to the document. In any event, as with most marketing programmes, subsequent developments and events often cause change from the outline; such change need not signify a bad plan, just the need to adapt flexibly to any short-term or unforeseen circumstances.

The final version of the annual promotion programme should include relevant comment on such topics as:

● timing of promotion for each product, taking account of seasonal factors such as gift-giving periods and vacations
● promotion objectives
● promotional media support or general media support (bear in mind that if there is a clear seasonal sales trend, a pound spent in the peak sales period generally creates a greater impact on sales than a pound spent in the low period)
● promotional aids and material, including preparation lead times
● special packaging requirements and production lead times
● shipping and distribution lead times for special promotional goods.

The planning stage must ensure adequate lead times for all preparation and production of each special aspect of the promotion, including artwork, scheduling advertising, packaging and production of merchandise, even though there may be an element of flexibility in the final promotion dates. Your distributor and advertising agency should be kept fully appraised of all aspects of planning, and be clearly briefed on their respective responsibilities, although the exporter's job will include monitoring the performance of their respective contributions within the plan time-span. Preparation of the plan in a simple schematic, such as Example 7, may assist control of the various stages in implementing the marketing programme.

Each separate promotion programme should have a fully detailed written plan, in addition to the outline annual plan referred to above, incorporating such information as:

Example 7

Outline promotion programme: Ireland   Product range: Personal Care   Budget year: 1984

	Jan	Feb	Mar	Apr	May	June	July	Aug	Sept	Oct	Nov	Dec
Male toiletries range *'Macho'*												
TV advertising				↕						↕		
Dealer 'loader'				↕						↕		
Dealer display competition					↕						↑	
Salesmen's incentive					↕						↕	
Consumer premium pack					↕						↕	
Salesmen's display competition					↕						↕	
Magazine advertising					↕						↕	
Holiday 'travel kit' (free toiletries bag)					↕							
Retailer's display incentive					↕				↕			
Summer skin-care range												
Dealer 'loader'					↕							
Salesmen's incentive					↕	↕						
In-store display programme (counter display units)						↕						
Consumer premium (sunglasses with 2 bottle tops + £2)							↕	↕				
Magazine advertising							↕					

- budgeted expenditure in total and by item of expense
- lead times for preparation of each aspect of copy and artwork connected with design of packaging, display material and media advertisements
- production quantities of each item of advertising and display material, packaging and product
- rules of consumer, retailer and salesmen's competitions
- criteria and programme to evaluate success
- reference to the legality of any aspect of that specific promotion that may be questionable or require approvals, such as lotteries.

In the plan in Example 7, export promotions for a toiletry range sold into Ireland give the base for the matrix, and there are two main promotions within the budget for the year. First, there is a summer 'travel kit' promotion, which could be a four-item assortment with a free toiletries bag for the consumer. This is supported by magazine advertising in 'lifestyle' image journals. To get the product in displayed distribution, the display period is preceded by a dealer 'loader' (say, one box free with twelve) to fill the pipeline with stock, and a salesmen's bonus competition. Secondly, there is a Christmas promotion as the main event of the year, based on the marketing experience of the exporter that toiletries are popular gift items. This is supported by TV advertising, magazine advertising, feature displays, dealer 'loaders', salesmen's incentives, and competitions for best displays. The summer promotion would concentrate on summer skin-care items, such as suntan oils and lotions, and after-sun treatments. The winter programme would concentrate on colognes, perfumes, after-shaves and similar items, and complementary 'luxury' products.

Our example, of course, is not all-encompassing. Every product has promotional techniques to which it best responds, and every company has product attributes and benefits that its own expertise and marketing team best know how to exploit. Liaison between the export marketer and the domestic marketing team will promote a cross-flow of ideas and experience to the benefit of the export marketing programme.

Your professionalism as the main company representative with whom your distributor has relationships in preparing and presenting promotional plans, and your ability successfully to implement and manage a programme for positive results, will infectiously motivate your distributor to enthusiastic cooperation in the future.

Summary

- Industrial products are frequently successfully promoted through trade journals and editorial commentaries, trade shows and exhibitions, directing of goods and services aimed at buyers.

- In developing advertising copy for industrial products, simplicity in the theme can be supported by information on use, performance, specifications, applications and benefits to the buyer or end user. The buyer needs to be assured that supplies and support services will continue to be available.

- Durable consumer goods may benefit from 'lifestyle' advertising themes, media campaigns in periodicals and on television and radio, poster campaigns, in-store promotions and demonstrations, consumer exhibitions and competitions.

- Branded non-durable consumer products benefit from media advertising, couponing, in-store demonstrations, premium and price-off promotions, consumer and retailer competitions.

- Because of the importance of display and distribution to the successful launch of a new product, particularly in less sophisticated markets, emphasis can include salesmen's and retailer competitions and incentives geared to increasing and maintaining displayed distribution.

- Promotion plans should be formally prepared annually in conjunction with the distributor or importer and modified as circumstances dictate subsequently. They should ideally be simple to implement, manage, monitor and control, and they should be clear in their objectives.

Advertising and promotion checklist

ANNUAL ADVERTISING AND PROMOTION PLAN

- Develop an annual *advertising and promotion plan* including:

  budget details
  advertising and promotion objectives
  media support
  timing and lead times for preparation and implementation
  special packaging requirements
  promotional aids and materials requirements
  legal approvals of promotion regulatory compliance

INDUSTRIAL PRODUCTS

- Media frequently preferred include:

  trade and technical journals
  international buyers' guides

- Advertisements should include:

  brief technical description and specifications
  product illustrations
  product attributes

> product benefits
> sources of product
> after sales servicing facilities and availability
> source of further information

● Promotion of industrial products is common through:

> specialist trade shows
> national and international exhibitions

CONSUMER PRODUCTS

● Advertising can increase demand and distribution by:

> illustrating product use and applications
> emphasising after sales service
> demonstrating product attributes and benefits
> creating brand name awareness
> creating or emphasising market positioning

● Advertising media commonly used can include:

> television
> cinema
> radio
> press
> life-style journals and magazines
> posters
> special interest magazines
> exhibitions
> point of sale material

● Promotional means include:

> in-store demonstrations
> product sampling
> couponing
> consumer and trade competitions
> flash-pack (price-off) offers
> self liquidating premium promotional offers
> in-store price reduction feature displays
> special offers at exhibitions
> free gifts of another product (probably from same
>   manufacturer) with purchase
> sponsorships of local worthwhile causes (relating to
>   return of labels etc.)

PART THREE

PROCEDURAL ASPECTS OF ADMINISTRATION AND DISTRIBUTION

9

Export Department Administration

Essential to the success of any export sales manager are the support services provided by his export shipping and administration department. The controls, procedures and report systems developed and operated within the administration section need to be thorough, accurate, detailed and timely in presentation. The primary function of a shipping department is to be responsible for all aspects of physically fulfilling the customer's order requirements,. moving the goods from the production plant to the consignee's nominated destination, and raising all documents necessary to facilitate both shipment to the destination and remission of payment back to the exporter. If mistakes occur in the mechanics of shipment or supporting documentation, these could be very costly, possibly even losing you control or possession of goods, or causing payment problems. In this chapter I shall consider and examine some basic procedural systems of control. Other publications available to the exporter very competently provide pro forma export shipping documents and examples of all standard forms in use (such as *Systematic Export Documentation*, published by the Simplification of International Trade Procedures Board).

On the assumption that your export department is initially too small to be computerized, at this stage a manual system of controls will be considered. When subsequently you can computerize some or all of your workload, you will then have a more thorough knowledge of what your own specific data and records need to include and will be able in particular to computerize customer shipment records and total all transactions by market and product to provide the summary sales data needed to monitor progress and provide a basis for future budget preparations.

The following sections discuss and review some of the major areas in which the exporter generally needs to institute control systems.

Shipping log book

In essence, the shipping log book is a department diary, an instrument to discipline you and your shipping manager to document transactions and record the content of telephone calls pertinent to the conduct of department business. The content would generally cover, for example, telephone conversations with shipping forwarders, truckers and any other carrier, the production plant personnel and possibly any contact necessary with suppliers of materials needed to facilitate production, in addition to bank contacts or matters relating to documentation. Notes should specifically record the purpose of the contact, points discussed and agreements reached, with a note of any follow-up action by either party, but particularly the shipping manager, to ensure that time schedules are met. A vessel will not wait for a late arrival at the dock, whether caused by delays in preparation of documents or by any other apparently valid reason.

Typical comments that the shipping log might beneficially note could include:

- 'Asked ABC company for freight rate to Dubai on January 2nd. Follow up January 4th.'
- 'Ellie at XYZ company quoted verbally £90 per metric tonne to Nigeria, from Liverpool. Confirmation requested.'
- 'Bill Jones at Glasgow plant gave January 31st inventory of export cans at 100 units. Reorder.'

Keeping a shorthand record is just good housekeeping and reduces the risk of problems resulting from someone forgetting to follow up on their promise to perform a specific task relating to your export transactions. In general, more detailed memoranda would be prepared and appropriately circulated on any issue of real significance.

Quote book

Telexes, letters and telephone calls requesting quotes will rapidly accumulate, and the need for a control system to monitor your own handling of the enquiries will soon become apparent. The control system should also be followed by any of your colleagues who progress a quote while you are away. Using one single instrument, the quote book, for the whole department to record the progress of requests for price quotes again acts as a discipline reducing the risks of forgetting to act on a request.

If you have a standard export price list covering very standard types of products, your problems may be less. Perhaps all you need do is send a standard response to each enquiry, including a copy of the price list. However, if your products are commodities whose prices can vary hourly or daily or any form of customized product, you will probably have to treat each quote request quite separately, and spend some time preparing calculations prior to a response; it is these quote requests that it is particularly beneficial to log to ensure that you actually do reply within a reasonable time.

Example 8

Quote book layout

Quote request	Product availability	Ex-plant cost	Profit contribution	Distribution costs: documentation, insurance, freight	Quote given	Customer acceptance	Notes
Dairy Importers Barbados 100 metric tonnes mild cheddar Mar. 15th '84	Now	$1,650	$100	$180	$1,930	Mar 25th '84 Subject to L/C	New contact. Request for price in dollars
Star Markets Dubai 5 tonnes fresh turkeys 3rd week Dec.	23rd Dec. Air shipment	£0.50 per lb.	£0.13 per lb.	£0.12 per lb.	£0.75	Payment in advance required. Await customer response.	Usually replies late.

A standard account record book from any stationers can provide a suitable quote book. Use it to write in, however briefly, a summary of requests for quotes, and to check on the various stages leading to issue of a reply (see Example 8). Some products may lend themselves better to a separate quote sheet for each request if a significant quantity of data is involved; in that case a loose-leaf binder may suit the needs of keeping all documentation related to a quote together. Remember that common courtesy demands a reply to every enquiry.

All the rough calculations, exchanges of communications, telexes and relevant documentation to support the enquiry and resultant quote should be stapled together, and, if an order materializes, would normally go into the shipping file relating to that order. If no order materializes within the period of validity of the quote, then I suggest not keeping the full file indefinitely, but perhaps for six months; thereafter dispose of the dead file and transfer the name and address of the enquirer to a potential customer file in case of future enquiries.

If you are quoting by telex or letter, your response must clearly answer all the points relevant to effect confirmation, and include:

- f.o.b., c.i.f. or other price quote exactly as specified
- period of validity of quote, and conditions applying to validity
- terms of payment acceptable (give your bankers for letter of credit)
- pro forma invoice if requested
- potential shipping date relating to product availability
- packaging to be used, units per carton, etc.
- quantity quoted against (price quote may be on a per tonne basis)
- method of shipping, e.g. refrigerated container
- technical specifications guaranteed for goods to be shipped, if relevant to the product, e.g. a raw material.

Order progress record

An export order requires great attention to detail as it progresses through the many stages in the process from order acceptance to final shipment and receipt of payment. Errors may be much more difficult to rectify than with a home market transaction, partly because of the many and varied documents, and partly because goods or ownership may have passed outside the exporter's control. Therefore, a simple record can beneficially be kept of each and every stage. Again, it is simple to use a ledger sheet with up to twenty columns for entry of the appropriate information.

Experience will generally show that the stages or points in time that it is critical to monitor on the order progress record are:

- customer name
- pro forma invoice number and issue date
- order receipt date
- customer order number
- exporter order confirmation/acceptance
- product availability date and location (plant or warehouse)
- vessel name
- vessel sailing date
- product movement order to plant or warehouse
- shipping documents prepared
- invoice number and date
- invoice value (f.o.b. or c.i.f.)
- freight cost
- consignment weight
- estimated time of arrival of vessel at destination
- payment terms
- payment due
- payment received.

The reason for recording against most of these column headings (and obviously the shipping manager would develop his own shorthand notations is self-evident in the process of controlling the progress of the order. However, each company's circumstances or special product requirements, such as packaging, may give rise to other critical points to monitor. Control requires only the most basic entry of key numbers and dates for each critical point from the time you receive the request for a pro-forma invoice until you actually receive payment, which frequently is at a later date than the 'payment due' date.

This kind of control document reduces the risk of overlooking any key point or date relating to a consignment only if its use becomes a fundamental part of the daily operating routine, with strict adherence to the entering of relevant data immediately it is established. You will probably find that because many dates, such as vessel sailing dates, are initially tentative it is better to make entries in pencil.

A practical operational point: once you allocate a pro forma invoice number to a transaction, it will be easier to collate and follow up all subsequent internal documents if you use only that same reference number (for example on product movement orders and final invoices), rather than using a different reference number on each internal document.

Other standard control documents or checklists could and should be developed to suit the specific needs of your products and operational management.

Export sales analysis

Analyses of shipments   If you wish to institute a manual system of collating information to monitor your export performance, then first identify the performance criteria that can beneficially be measured. More usually you will want to establish progress and measurement against some or all of the following:

● The individual performance of your company against national total exports of the relevant product categories, as identified in customs export statistics. Figures can compare volumes, values and percentage share of each itemized customs category.
● Your company's share of exports in the relevant category to specific markets, by volume, value and percentage share of exports to each market.
● Your company's performance by product or product type recorded each month, and compared with, say, the same month last year in volume and value. This generally should be done both for total exports to all markets and on an individual market-by-market basis.
● Cumulative performance in total, and market by market, for the current year to date (updated monthly) versus last year to date, both by volume and value.

If you have a relevant budget figure, this should appear at each point of measurement on each of these analysis sheets, and you can show achievement by individual market month by month, total exports month by month, and percentage achievement and cumulative achievements against the budget or plan. This draws your attention to potential problems where plans are not being met, may assist in identifying seasonal patterns not previously taken into consideration (if, say, you simply allocated the same plan volume to each month), and enables future plan preparation to be more accurate and sophisticated as you build up a historical data base.

Your initial sales, market and dispatch analyses may not need to be very sophisticated or detailed if you start from a small base of operations. As exports grow, however, you will be pressured to produce more data to facilitate control and planning, and measure achievements in more detail. Problems will then develop in measuring only against recorded customs export figures, as these are likely to be less finely tuned into specifically relevant product categories than you would like. But constantly bear in mind that there is no benefit in producing data just for the exercise in statistics. Production of statistical data is worthwhile only if:

● it measures performance against comparable relevant criteria
● it aids the planning process.

To start the information recording process, an account ledger book may again prove a useful instrument, or you could design a simple shipping record card — as in Example 9, in which the exports of alcoholic beverages to a single market are monitored for a California wine exporter. For each separate month, say February, you can then extract the total by product and the grand total for each individual market, and place these figures on a market shipment summary that details all active export markets and shows monthly, year to date (Y.T.D.) and a comparison with the last year to date (L.Y.T.D.). Additionally, you can make a percentage comparison of this year versus last year (T.Y./L.Y.). Example 10 illustrates a suitable record sheet for this purpose. Using the same format, you can transfer the month-by-month totals from the bottom of the market shipment summaries for each separate month and build these to give month-by-month comparisons (see Example 11).

In essence, at this point of recording and analysis, you have available data on:

- month-by-month and product-by-product shipments to each active market (Example 9)
- a summary of your worldwide 'all markets' month-by-month activity (Example 10)
- a cumulative 'all markets' product-by-product performance record (Example 11).

Clearly, there are many alternative combinations of comparisons that can be prepared if you have the time and staff, but before asking a colleague to prepare data the following questions should be asked: Who will see the data? Who will use them? How will they contribute to monitoring performance, improving performance and planning processes?

Of course, figures and statistics are of use only if some interesting or meaningful interpretations can be attached to them. Example 9 on the Canary Isles indicates that February 1983 was a larger month for shipments than January. This may reflect either a post-Christmas downturn in demand, as consumers were satiated with Christmas liquor, or perhaps that stores were still carrying heavy inventory to the extent that the distributor needed less stock. The higher dispatches in February could simply indicate a return to normal as inventories were balanced, or even a boost in sales through some special event such as the much-celebrated Mardi Gras. Your own knowledge of the market and comparisons with previous years aid a correct interpretation. Example 10 indicates immediately that dollar sales are increasing at a faster percentage rate than volume, but this purely reflects inflation, in that there was an end-of-year price increase from $24 to $25 per case. Year-

Example 9

Market dispatch analysis: Canary Isles
Year: 1983
California Wine Exporters Inc.

Product

Order number	Date	ROSÉ Value $	Volume (cases)	WHITE Value $	Volume (cases)	RED Value $	Volume (cases)	TOTAL Value $	Volume (cases)
1234	12 Jan	1,400	56	2,000	80	2,000	80	5,400	216
1230	29 Jan	1,200	48	2,500	100	2,000	80	5,700	228
	JAN	2,600	104	4,500	180	4,000	160	11,100	444
	YTD	2,600	104	4,500	180	4,000	160	11,100	444
1249	12 Feb	1,200	48	4,500	180	4,000	160	9,700	388
1263	26 Feb	1,750	70	1,250	50	1,250	50	4,250	170
	FEB	2,950	118	5,750	230	5,250	210	13,950	558
	YTD	5,550	222	10,250	410	9,250	370	25,050	1,002

Units: Cases and f.o.b. values.
YTD = year to date.

Example 10

Market shipment summary: all markets
Month: February   Year 1984
California Wine Exporters Inc.
Product

Country	ROSÉ Value $	Volume (cases)	WHITE Value $	Volume (cases)	RED Value $	Volume (cases)	Value $	Volume (cases)	TOTAL Value $	Volume (cases)
Canary Isles										
Month	2,950	118	5,750	230	5,250	210			13,950	558
YTD	5,550	222	10,250	410	9,250	370			25,050	1002
LYTD	3,600	150	9,120	380	8,400	350			21,120	880
%TY/LY	154%	111%	112%	108%	110%	106%			119%	114%
Nigeria										
Month	15,000	600	12,500	500	11,250	450			38,750	1,550
YTD	27,500	1,100	22,500	900	22,500	900			72,500	2,900
LYTD	24,000	1,000	19,200	800	19,200	800			62,400	2,600
%TY/LY	115%	110%	117%	113%	117%	113%			116%	112%
Singapore										
Month	12,500	500	10,000	400	7,500	300			30,000	1,200
YTD	22,500	900	20,000	800	17,500	700			60,000	2,400
LYTD	19,200	800	19,200	800	14,400	600			52,800	2,200
%TY/LY	117%	113%	104%	100%	122%	117%			114%	109%
All markets										
Month	30,450	1,218	28,250	1,130	24,000	960			82,700	3,308
YTD	55,550	2,222	52,750	2,110	49,250	1,970			157,550	6,302
LYTD	46,800	1,950	47,520	1,980	42,000	1,750			136,320	5,680
%TY/LY	119%	114%	111%	107%	117%	113%			116%	111%

Units: Cases and f.o.b. values.

YTD = year to date.
LYTD = last year to date.
%TY/LY = percentage comparison of this year to date versus last year to date.

Example 11

Market shipment summary, cumulative data: all markets
Year: 1984
California Wine Exporters Inc.

Country		ROSÉ Value $	Volume (cases)	WHITE Value $	Volume (cases)	RED Value $	Volume (cases)	Value $	Volume (cases)	TOTAL Value $	Volume (cases)
January	Month	25,100	1,004	24,500	980	25,250	1,010			74,850	2,994
	YTD	25,100	1,004	24,500	980	25,250	1,010			74,850	2,994
	LYTD	22,080	920	22,560	940	22,080	920			66,720	2,780
	%TY/LY	114%	107%	109%	104%	114%	110%			112%	108%
February	Month	30,450	1,218	28,250	1,130	24,000	960			82,700	3,308
	YTD	55,550	2,222	52,750	2,110	49,250	1,970			157,550	6,302
	LYTD	46,800	1,950	47,520	1,980	42,000	1,750			136,320	5,680
	%TY/LY	119%	114%	111%	107%	117%	113%			116%	111%
March	Month										
	YTD										
	LYTD										
	%TY/LY										
April	Month										
	YTD										
	LYTD										
	%TY/LY										

Units: Cases & f.o.b. values.

YTD = year to date.
LYTD = last year to date.

to-date versus last-year-to-date comparisons are generally more meaningful in export analyses because there are so many distortions to affect any single month, such as delays in vessels. Example 10 indicates a healthy growth trend for all the individual and total markets, and Example 11 shows that the growth is continuing month by month.

Market share   Once you have built up your analyses of dispatches to each market and in total in whatever fashion you find most relevant and convenient, the next likely information needed to give a performance measure is your market share on a country-by-country basis.

In practice, for many markets you will simply not obtain any locally meaningful or timely data on the size of that market for many types of products. Local manufacturers may not be required to report production data at all, or reports may be highly suspect. Even import statistics, useful if a large share of the product sales is imported, may be very late becoming available.

Therefore, the first estimate of performance that in any way relates to a share of a market is generally to monitor your share of total exports from your home country to the foreign market, which gives you a simple comparison of your performance against other domestic exporters to each market. This comparison is probably not worth preparing any more frequently, say, than every quarter or half year, because the leads and lags each exporter experiences will make any more frequent comparison of limited meaningfulness. In this analysis, value is generally a more accurate measure than volume, unless volume is specified as kilograms, tonnes or other weight or volume measures, such as litres, that eliminate errors in comparison or resultant assumptions if, say, similar items of vastly different quality and prices are being shipped by the various exporters.

A layout is illustrated in Example 12, and you may like to experiment with others that more conveniently suit your information needs. For simplicity, in this example I have assumed that the customs export data do not distinguish between different varieties of wine, and that we can get comparisons only with total wine exports to each destination from the home country.

From the illustration in Example 12, a comparison is drawn between the company's and the country's exports of wines to the markets to which the company ships. In this simple example the value figures for both company and national exports have risen faster than volume exports, reflecting price increases in export product between this year and last year. The figures also show that the company's share of value and volume has risen for the named markets this year versus last year. However, there is a slight decline in the company's 'all countries' share of value of exports, although the volume share is maintained.

Example 12

Share of exports
Wines
Period: Jan – June 1984
Value: $'000s   Volume: '000 litres

Destination country		Company		National		Company's exports as % of national exports	
		Value	Volume	Value	Volume	Value	Volume
Canary Isles	TY	38	9.1	66	18.8	58%	48%
	LY	34	8.5	60	18.0	57%	47%
	%TY/LY	112%	107%	110%	105%		
Nigeria	TY	60	14.4	211	47.0	28%	31%
	LY	55	13.7	204	47.0	27%	29%
	%TY/LY	109%	105%	103%	100%		
Oman	TY	12	2.9	14	3.1	86%	94%
	LY	10	2.5	15	3.5	66%	71%
	%TY/LY	120%	116%	93%	89%		
Peru	TY	84	20.1	194	43.1	43%	47%
	LY	79	19.7	189	43.6	42%	45%
	%TY/LY	106%	102%	103%	99%		
Singapore	TY	20	4.8	60	13.3	33%	36%
	LY	19	4.7	59	13.6	32%	36%
	%TY/LY	105%	102%	102%	98%		
All countries	TY	1,516	363.8	3,420	760.0	44%	48%
	LY	1,420	355.0	3,190	736.2	46%	48%
	%TY/LY	107%	102%	107%	103%		

TY = this year.
LY = last year.

Note: Percentages rounded to nearest whole number.

Distribution statistics

Market share Apart from the company's share of home country exports to the various markets to which you are now shipping, your share of the market achieved by each of your distributors will be key to assessing your progress and the effectiveness of marketing programmes. If the foreign country is also a producer of goods similar to your own, then theoretically you can deduce market share by adding imports to local production and deducting exports, and dividing your own imports by this figure. However, this takes no account of changes in inventories year on year, and that figure may be particularly hard to ascertain. The correct and approximate equations look like this (volume or value):

Correct:

$$\frac{\text{company total imports} + \text{company opening inventory} - \text{company closing inventory}}{\text{local production} + \text{opening inventory} - \text{closing inventory} + \text{imports} - \text{exports}}$$

Approximate:

$$\frac{\text{company total imports}}{\text{local production} + \text{imports} - \text{exports}}$$

The approximate market share calculation assumes no net change in importer or local manufacturer market inventories.

It may be especially difficult to get the degree of category analysis you want to assess your share accurately, because the local or import figures may not finely identify sub-categories of main product groupings. Developing countries often have limited local reporting of production, and any reporting may be of dubious accuracy.

If the market either has no local production of the products you ship, or if local production is not reported, then you may reasonably use the difference between locally reported import figures and export figures as your market share base:

$$\text{market share} = \frac{\text{company total imports}}{\text{imports} - \text{exports}}$$

Once again, this calculation has limited accuracy because it assumes that no estimate can fairly be made of inventories at either end of the period being measured.

In more sophisticated markets, it is likely that various government agencies will closely monitor all local production, imports and exports, and accurate figures would then be available to assess a market share. Quite possibly manufacturers and distributors might have to report on sales either to a government agency or on a voluntary basis to a trade association.

You need to work with your distributor to identify what local data are available, and where they can be accessed for the purpose of preparing your most important measure of marketing progress – the market share. Once you know what data are available, then it is a simple task to design a standard form on which to enter figures and present your share analysis for circulation to interested parties.

Sales performance   In order to monitor market sales activity by the
distributor, it is customary to seek monthly statistical reports on stocks
and sales. A minimum report should cover:

- opening stocks (for each product/pack size)
- shipments received into stock during current month
- market sales
- closing stocks

In addition, you may want a forward sales forecast that includes provision for forward orders to cover anticipated sales. Ideally, depending
on shipping lead times, your distributor will need to plan to hold
between one and two months' stocks, based upon forecast sales for
each item.

Your distributor will probably be quite experienced in controlling
stock levels, but in smaller markets is unlikely to have computerized
systems. You may therefore find it useful at this point to review a few
basic formats of simple forms that the distributor might use to control
his business in your products.

Example 13 illustrates a simplified form of an *annual sales
budget*. On the same table, monthly totals for actual sales against
budget and for percentage achievement, as well as comparisons with
the same time last year, can all be monitored. In this instance,
the example considers a manufacturer of various sundry electric items
shipping to Singapore. The only figures entered are for the men's
electric razor, which we see is highly seasonal in sales. The 1983
budget presumably was closely based on the previous year's actual
sales, with an overall growth factor of just over 10 per cent, mainly
geared to planned increased Christmas season sales. You may wish
to fill in some figures for the other products if you feel practice
in budgeting would be of benefit.

Example 14 is a very basic *stock, order and sales control* form, which
can be used by a distributor to assist in forward planning of orders.
In general, firm orders are likely to be committed for about two or
three months ahead, because of long shipping lead times. I usually
advise putting tentative or budgeted figures in pencil initially, erasing
these when the actual final figures are available and writing those in
ink. Every month you need to adjust your forward plans, altering the
pencilled-in figures to take account of forecast changes in opening stocks
and therefore orders, and of expected closing stocks. The line labelled
'adjustments' can take account of spoilage or other causes of leakage,
including post-entry adjustments when an actual inventory count differs
from the theoretical inventory shown in stock records. Example 14 has
assumed that we have actual sales, adjustment, stock and shipment
details up to June (in bold type); the light type indicates where we have

Example 13

Annual sales budget
Year: 1983
Market: Singapore
Unit sales

	Jan	Feb	Mar	Apr	May	June	July	Aug	Sept	Oct	Nov	Dec
Electric razors (men)												
Sales budget	200	100	100	100	100	200	100	100	100	100	400	600
Actual sales	220	90	70	110	105	160	80	85	90	120	410	640
% budget	110%	90%	70%	110%	105%	80%	80%	85%	90%	120%	103%	107%
LY actual	200	110	100	90	95	210	100	110	80	80	300	500
%TY/LY	110%	82%	70%	122%	111%	76%	80%	77%	113%	150%	137%	128%
Electric razors (women)												
Sales budget												
Actual sales												
% budget												
LY actual												
%TY/LY												
Electric toasters												
Sales budget												
Actual sales												
% budget												
LY Actual												
%TY/LY												
Electric irons												
Sales budget												
Actual sales												
% budget												
LY actual												
%TY/LY												

TY = this year.
LY = last year.

Example 14

Monthly stock and order control
Year: 1983
Product: men's electric razors
Market: Singapore

	Jan	Feb	Mar	Apr	May	Jun	July	Aug	Sept	Oct	Nov	Dec
Opening stock	300	227	275	305	290	235	165	265	265	265	565	765
Shipments received	150	150	100	100	50	100	200	100	100	400	600	200
Sales: budget	200	100	100	100	100	200	100	100	100	100	400	600
actual	220	90	70	110	105	160						
Adjustments (leakage)	3	12	0	5	0	10						
Closing stock	227	275	305	290	235	165	265	265	265	565	765	365

pencilled in our best forward estimates to balance stock and shipments against sales budgets.

Once you are in control of the sales budgeting, stocks and order planning systems in conjunction with the distributor, the next stage is to work with the distributor on the elements of market sales performance that you and he consider practical to measure and relevant as a control and future planning tool. It is usually beneficial to seek to tabulate some or all of the following:

- actual monthly sales this year
- cumulative sales this year to date
- actual sales for same month last year
- cumulative sales for last year to date
- moving annual sales totals (volume/value)
- comparison of sales performance against sales budget.

The last comparison has already been covered in one format in Example 13, which also incorporated a comparison with the same month last year to provide a basis for measuring growth and the direction of change in sales activity and results.

Monthly and cumulative sales data by product can be used, as in Example 15, to build up *moving annual totals* for each product that both eliminate seasonal trends by producing twelve-month rolling data and measure change. The trend underlying changes in the moving annual totals is often highlighted by transferring the data onto a graph. If there are known reasons for unusual peaks and troughs, such as promotions or shipping strikes, a note can easily be made at the appropriate point on the graph to remind you subsequently of the reason for unplanned or unexpected variations.

In my moving annual totals example of Example 15, where it has been assumed that 1982 was the first year of sales and provided the base year data, sales actually show a declining trend until the 1983 Christmas promotion, which began the start of the improvement and steadily rising trend. A table such as this should have prompted the marketer to be seriously concerned early in 1983 and to take corrective action. In my example, something happened to tie in with the Christmas promotion; possibly an advertising campaign for the first time helped sustain sales growth and consumer brand awareness.

The discussion and examples used in this chapter outline some of the basic information and controls that the export manager may work with his distributor to produce and use in monitoring performance and progressively planning for continued growth, and that will help to give the distributor confidence that his stock and ordering programme is in line with sales performance. Data on market returns, possibly

Example 15

Moving annual total sales
Product: men's electric razors
Market: Singapore

	1982			1983			1984		
	Month sales	Cum. sales	Moving annual total	Month sales	Cum. sales	Moving annual total	Month sales	Cum. sales	Moving annual total
Jan	200	200		220	220	1,995	250	250	2,210
Feb	110	310		90	310	1,975	130	380	2,250
Mar	100	410		70	380	1,945	100	480	2,280
Apr	90	500		110	490	1,965	120	600	2,290
May	·95	595		105	595	1,975	130	730	2,315
June	210[1]	805		160[3]	755	1,925			
July	100	905		80	835	1,905			
Aug	110	1,015		85	920	1,880			
Sept	80	1,095		90	1,010	1,890			
Oct	80	1,175		120	1,130	1,930			
Nov	300[2]	1,475		410[4]	1,540	2,040			
Dec	500[2]	1,975	1,975	640[4]	2,180	2,180			

Notes:

1. mid-year premium offer: discount travel bag.
2. Christmas offer: free cologne.
3. mid-year premium offer: beach towel.
4. Christmas offer: ½ price female cosmetic or male toiletry combination.

included under the 'adjustments' heading of the stock and order control sheet, may help indicate if the distributor is following your guidelines on market uplifts and returns.

The exporter should not make the distributor produce information and tables that will neither give any measurement of progress or marketing programme effectiveness, nor aid in future planning. Some of the foregoing may have a place in your information programme, if adapted to the specific product and markets you are developing. Only you, the exporter, can judge the need for and benefit of developing any data information systems to form part of the cross-flow of communication with the distributor in any market.

Summary

- Good record-keeping is essential to the smooth operation of an export department, and basic systems can beneficially include: a *shipping department log book*, recording summaries of all contact and discussions relating to production schedules, product movements and availability, requests for shipping freight quotes and verbal responses, etc.; a *quote book*, monitoring progress from first receipt of an enquiry to the provision of formal quotes, including notes on costing factors; an *order progress record*, noting each stage from issue of the quote or pro forma invoice to final receipt of payment.

- To measure progress and aid future planning processes, basic statistical analyses could include: comparison of company exports with national exports by product category and destination market; records of dispatches to each market monthly by product and pack size; comparisons of company performance both against the current plan and against performance to the same point in time in the previous year, monthly, cumulatively and on a moving annual basis; reports from distributors to cover sales and stocks, including monthly sales, annual sales to date cumulatively, and comparisons both with the current year sales plan and with performance over the same time period in the previous year; estimates of market share for each destination market.

10

Basic Export Documentation

A single export shipment can involve a mass of different documents to ensure that your goods reach the final consignee and that the exporter will receive full and timely payment for the shipment.

In this chapter I shall discuss some of the stages in issuing or preparing documents that form part of the process from request to quote to actual shipment. Because so many parties claim that they need a complete set of documents in order to handle their specific aspects of the shipment, the exporter may often have to produce from five to ten sets of full copies, each carefully checked to ensure that nothing is missed from the set. However, modern export documentation procedures can be labour saving in that every major document can be run off on photocopying machines from a master, including order confirmations, bills of lading, certificates of origin, customs and exchange documents, and final invoices. Attention to detail at every stage of the export documentation procedure is the key to avoiding problems and, as a general rule, no document should ever be issued until it has been checked for accuracy and compliance with rules, regulations and customer instructions by at least one other member of the export shipping department.

The flow of documents relating to an export order may be quite a burden on an inexperienced export administrative department, but each has its place in the total transaction. The customer should clearly specify the documents he requires, and the exporter can generally check the minimum or standard obligatory requirements of the importing nation by referring to *Croner's Reference Book for Exporters*, the bible of most export departments. Some of the usual documents are listed below and the major ones discussed subsequently:

- invitation to quote
- quote
- pro forma invoice and/or order confirmation
- product movement order (internal)
- bill of lading
- marine insurance policy or cover note
- commercial invoice
- consular or certified invoice

- certificate of origin
- packing list and weight note
- specification sheet and manufacturer's analysis certificate
- health and sanitary certificate
- quality inspection certificate
- certificate of free sale
- independent third party certificate of inspection.

The Simplification of International Trade Procedures Board (SITPRO) located in London has a range of publications on the standardization of administrative and documentation procedures, including complete systems that can be incorporated in the operations of most export departments. British exporters would be well advised to contact that body to review available material and for practical help.

Invitation to quote, and quote

The first paper work in the chain of an export order is the letter or telex received from the foreign party requesting the exporter to quote to supply a particular product or service. This is often an incomplete note, which necessitates a further exchange of communications to elicit relevant data and product specifications before firm prices can be prepared and quoted. Before making a firm quote or accepting an order, the exporter should identify all pertinent information to cover:

- product specifications
- quantities (units/weight/volumes)
- packaging (or quote own pack sizes)
- timing of shipment or delivery
- acceptable payment terms.

Agreement on these points generally enables an accurate price quote to be prepared and dispatched.

If the quote request or order comes on a written document, then check carefully that you understand any terms and conditions the buyer is placing on the purchase contract, and satisfy yourself that these are acceptable to you. In your quote, seek any clarifications or alterations and remove or reduce the risk of future disagreements. In your final quote, clearly state any limitations on the period of validity of the quote, and all other terms and conditions minimally imposed.

The following is an example of an exchange of telexes concerning a transaction to buy and sell cheese from Europe to the Caribbean:

Please give us lowest c.i.f. Trinidad for 1000 tonnes of Cheddar Cheese for delivery May through September.

[*Note*: this is a very general enquiry needing a more specific reply or clarification.]

RE YOUR REQUEST FOR CHEDDAR QUOTE, WE CAN SUPPLY AS FOLLOWS. 1000 TONNES CHEDDAR AGED THREE MONTHS AT TIME OF DISPATCH, MAX. 39% WATER CONTENT AND PACKED IN SOLID BOARD CARTONS AND BARRIER BAG LINING. SHIPMENTS CAN BE MADE 100 TONNES EACH MAY AND JUNE AND 200 TONNES EACH JULY TO SEPTEMBER. C.I.F. PRICE $1750 PER METRIC TONNE IN REFRIGERATED CONTAINERS. TERMS OF PAYMENT IRREVOCABLE L.C. [letter of credit] CONFIRMED ON U.K. BANK FOR WHOLE CONTRACT PERMITTING SHIPMENT AS SPECIFIED AND PART PAYMENT AS SHIPPED. OFFER VALID UNTIL CLOSE OF BUSINESS HERE FRIDAY, AND ACCEPTANCE SUBJECT TO RECEIPT OF L.C.

Acceptance – order confirmation

The buyer's offer or order may be accepted on an *ORDER CONFIRMATION*. Alternatively, a *PRO FORMA* invoice may be issued to assist the buyer either in deciding whether to accept the quote or in obtaining import licences or foreign exchange approvals prior to contracting; the pro forma invoice will be reviewed separately.

As illustrated in the last section, frequently in international commodity transactions the order, acknowledgement and confirmation may all be handled by brief telexes, if that is the practice of the trade, and these telex exchanges may have legal standing in the case of a dispute. Hence, they should be both explicit and retained as part of the documents in the appropriate order file.

As the buyer's order may detail a number of conditions of buying, some of which, if it is a standard form, may not even apply to your product, the exporter's order acceptance and confirmation should, in fact, be designed to state quite clearly the seller's terms and conditions, warranties and limitations of liability that may apply to the product or transaction. Terms of sale generally appear on the bottom or back of the acceptance note, and should both be approved by your corporate lawyer and be clearly legible in any photocopy of documents used, to avoid future claims that the buyer could not read them. If on the reverse of a form, then the front side should contain a bold reference to 'SEE TERMS AND CONDITIONS OF SALE AND WARRANTIES ON REVERSE SIDE OF THIS DOCUMENT'. A phrase in an order confirmation or acceptance clearly stating 'ORDER ACCEPTED ONLY SUBJECT TO OUR CONDITIONS OF SALE CONTAINED HEREIN' can generally be considered as a rejection of terms the buyer has included in his purchase offer if the buyer proceeds to buy the merchandise. If you feel that the buyer does not realize that you are imposing new or different conditions on a sale, then check with him to avoid future disputes. It is often a good strategy to have the buyer sign and return a copy of the acceptance or confirmation slip as acknowledgement of agreeing to your terms and conditions of supply.

The *order confirmation* should incorporate the following information:

- selling company's full name and address details
- buying company's full name and address details
- full details of product to be shipped, including product description, pack sizes, quantity/volume per pack unit and in total, weights and dimensions of each piece and total shipment
- mode of transportation
- port of origin and destination, and any transshipment points, if sold c & f or c.i.f., or note of point where ownership transfers if sold on other basis, e.g. ex-plant or f.o.b.
- terms and conditions of sale
- terms of payment
- value per shipping unit and in total for consignment; consignment value should include any freight or other agreed charges incurred to transfer point
- expected shipping date including vessel details if available (noting if this is after receipt of letter of credit or other relevant factor)

Pro forma invoice

In practice this document can include the same basic information listed above for an order acknowledgement, but, as mentioned, many importers require a pro forma invoice prior to confirming placement of an order, to assist in assessing the final costs of the goods delivered to the handover point, say the foreign destination port in a c.i.f. contract, or so that they can obtain the necessary local approvals and documentation that may be required to import the product, such as import licences and foreign exchange, or to arrange letters of credit or other negotiable payment documents.

The pro forma and final invoice must both clearly comply with every special instruction from the buyer. For example, he may want freight costs and insurance, or even a packing cost, separated out, even though you may be selling on a c.i.f. basis. This could occur if the destination country did not charge certain taxes or duties on such elements of a transaction. The final invoice should match the pro forma invoice in every respect if the details of the pro forma are incorporated in payment documents, such as a letter of credit.

If the importer has unusual requests either that you cannot understand the need for, or that involve false statements or information being included in any shipping document, then you must raise questions with the importer to establish the need or to explain your position in respect of inaccurate declarations. It is very unwise ever to issue documents that knowingly contain false statements, because that may cause your company to run foul of foreign authorities in the event of investigations.

Product movement order

This is an internal document, not normally forming part of the set of shipping documents, used to advise the factory or warehouse of your specific requirements and instructions relating to the preparation and packing of an order ready for shipment. It is best not to assume that the plant manager can read your mind on special requirements by a telephone comment such as 'Can you get ready for me a hundred electric razors for Nigeria by next Thursday?' Such a basic request, even if shipments to Nigeria are a regular event, will lead to errors, and the Nigerian importer may receive razors set at the wrong voltage.

The product movement order (PMO) should detail:

- the specific product, including size, model number, type, quantity of units, and variations from standard noted
- packing required, e.g. special packing may be needed for certain climates
- date collection due by carrier
- any factory certification or documentation required.

The plant should confirm back to the shipping department, possibly by returning one part of a multi-part PMO, that the consignment is correctly packed and labelled and ready for collection.

Bill of lading

Bills of lading are the shipper's contracts with carriers to move the merchandise from one point to another, and can involve inland, sea or air freight movement. Here I shall mainly address the sea element of an international transaction.

The bill of lading (often abbreviated to B/L or B of L) forms part of the shipping documents along with the commercial invoice, certificate of insurance and other required documentation for any one market. The bill of lading is generally a negotiable document, in that an original gives title of the goods and lets the consignee dispose of the goods by endorsing and delivering the B of L to another authorized party. Goods can therefore be sold in transit and a new owner take possession at the destination port. The buyer may specify that he requires a certain number of sets of documents. Customarily one set will go with the goods and the originals go via the banks if payment is by means of a letter of credit or other bank negotiable document, such as sight or term drafts. Other sets, non-negotiable copies, may be sent by post direct to the consignee so that he is fully aware of details of the dispatch and the consignment's scheduled arrival.

If goods are accepted by the shipping line on a *clean bill*, then there can be recourse by a buyer against the shipping line or under an insurance policy if the merchandise arrives in a damaged state. However, some shipping lines have the practice of only issuing a *shipped bill*, indicating that goods were shipped on a specific vessel but without reference to the condition of the product. This may be acceptable to the buyer under the terms of the transaction. A *received for shipment bill* may occasionally be issued, and the exporter must establish if that meets the buyer's stipulations, because clearly it is not committing the shipping line to actual shipment at the time they received the goods.

A shipping line may also issue a *claused bill* if it finds anomalies in the documentation or that the product is received by the shipping line in apparently less-than-perfect condition, and this can and usually will cause difficulties when presenting documents through the respective banks for payment by the consignee, who may require some form of indemnity from the shipper before clearing goods.

The shipping line may hand over goods to a person presenting an original negotiable B of L, but may not transfer a consignment to a consignee named in the B of L unless that consignee produces evidence of title in the form of an original of the B of L.

It is essential to ensure that sets of shipping documents and particularly the bill of lading reach the consignee before the arrival of the vessel, in order that the consignment be promptly claimed and transferred through the customs clearing procedures to the importer's warehouse, especially if the merchandise is of a perishable nature. Delays in clearing goods can result in penalties and mounting demurrage costs. Exporters frequently complain at delays in transferring documents via the banks under a letter of credit or other documentary payment process. If goods arrive before the bill of lading, the importer may ask for release of the goods under an indemnity to the shipping line. The exporter should resist this, as it may prejudice his ability to enforce payment on the agreed terms, such as a sight or term draft, and the consignee may not feel pressured to honour his payment terms once he has possession of the merchandise.

There is no substitute for careful attention to detail and rapid processing of documents to reduce the risk of problems caused by delays in receipt or errors.

At this point of the discussion on bills of lading, it is perhaps worth raising some basic matters concerning freight rates. Customarily, freight rates on shipments quote a volume or weight-related price, and the shipping line will elect to use the rate that gives them the highest revenue. In addition, an *ad valorem* rate may be in effect on some routes or product categories. The rates on a particular route may be fixed by a *shipping conference* − a consortium of shipping lines operating over the same routes. They will seek to protect the volume of freight on the routes they cover by exclusive shipping contracts with the shippers in exchange for discounts or deferred rebates. The party with the conference contract will not be free to ship with the often more competitive but smaller lines that are not part of the conference on that route. If the exporter is a party to a conference agreement but the importer is not, then the importer may prefer to buy f.o.b. and organize his own sea shipment, giving instructions to the exporter where and when to deliver the merchandise at a port or inland container point.

If the exporter is responsible for consigning goods to a foreign inland destination, then a *through bill of lading* may be arranged with the shipping line for onward consignment of goods once they reach the foreign port. This is easier than organizing a separate series of contracts. The first carrier, the shipping line, will organize the onward carriage as the agent of the shipper, and his contract will normally have a clause exempting the shipping line from any liability in connection with the merchandise or shipment once the goods are delivered to the on-carrier for inland transmittal. The shipping line will also normally only deliver the goods to the on-carrier when that party presents a copy of the bill of lading that the shipper has sent ahead to the consignee.

Problems occasionally arise over bills of lading. For example, where a bank making finance available in connection with the transaction considers the documents as presented so late as to put the buyer in a position of risk in respect of the consignment, as might happen if a perishable product arrived at the destination ahead of the documents, then we have a *stale bill of lading*. This situation must be avoided because the buyer's bank may refuse to accept the late documents on behalf of the buyer unless the shipper issues an indemnity in favour of the bank or consignee for resultant losses or problems.

Indemnities are frequently asked for where there are special conditions attached to the transaction, such as a stipulation that a clean bill of lading be provided, but a shipping line issues either a claused bill or other variant. In some instances it may be the shipping line that requires an indemnity if it could be held responsible for potential non-compliance with contract terms. In other instances it may be a bank seeking an indemnity before releasing documents where there is a situation of non-compliance with terms or conditions of the agreed payment documentary terms.

In preparing the B of L, the basic information that should be incorporated covers:

- name and address of the exporter/shipper
- any booking reference number
- cross reference to importer/exporter reference numbers, such as order number
- person to be notified at foreign port on arrival
- vessel name

- origin and destination ports
- number of cartons, description of products, weights and measurements of consignment
- shipping marks (usually consignee's identification markings)
- vessel departure date
- details of freight and related charges.

Waybills

Now that more goods are moving over land, the ocean bill of lading would not apply to such shipments, but other transport documents are required, such as *road* or *rail waybills*, which show that the goods were taken into the charge of the carrier for export. These documents may be perfectly acceptable in connection with documentary credits unless excluded in the buyer's stipulations.

Although currently only a small proportion of world trade moves by air, this is becoming increasingly important where speed or the lower risks of damage or loss are factors. Goods of high perishability or value often are very well suited to movement by air. An *air waybill* is issued for such consignments, which is basically a consignment note, detailing conditions of carriage, but not a document of title or a negotiable instrument.

Marine insurance policy

Insurance will be the subject of further study in Chapter 13, but it is the practice to provide a certificate of insurance with goods shipped under a c.i.f. contract, so I shall deal with that here. Under a c.i.f. contract it is customary to insure for obvious perils the consignment may face in transit; this may include 'war risk' if the vessel sails through troubled regions of the world, or damage from heat or humidity if the product is subject to deterioration when exposed to those factors in transit through the tropics. Other special factors should be taken into account because distressed goods traditionally have a low value if presented at a forced sale or auction in a foreign market in poor condition.

Cover should always be to the point where ownership transfers, or as otherwise agreed with the buyer; in addition to the physical risks, it should also cover the financial risks of such non-recoverable expenses as freight, insurance and any element of the foreign duties or taxes, handling or clearing charges that may be incurred before a claim is identified. Frequently importers specify cover at 'c.i.f. plus 10%' as a standard to give a margin to claim such sunk costs as the clearing and transit to their stores, where the goods are finally examined. If your terms of sale specify a normal level of cover, such as 'insurance will be arranged at 110% of c.i.f. unless otherwise notified by the buyer', then the buyer is responsible for advising you of other factors to incorporate in a higher rate of insurance cover.

Commercial invoice

The set of shipping documents could, of course, not be complete without inclusion of the shipper's final commercial invoice. If you have a standardized procedure for administration, this should be virtually a copy of the original order confirmation or pro forma invoice, simply photocopied using a stencil or overlay saying 'commercial invoice', and should contain all the final and accurate details in the list given under the section on pro forma invoices.

The price must agree with the contract (i.e. f.o.b. or c.i.f.), but it is not uncommon for the buyer to request that the freight, insurance or other sundry charges such as for consular documentation, be separated out as he may have a specific reason, such as a lower duty base, to want these itemized.

If the terms of sale are f.o.b. but the buyer requested the shipper to organize freight and insurance on his behalf, then the invoice should separate out those items and related charges.

Consular invoices and certified invoices

Consular invoices give the government agencies of the destination country the opportunity to seek out anomalies in transactions and monitor movements of goods into their country. The information on the consular invoice is generally exactly the same as that contained on the commercial invoice, but some countries provide special forms for use in submitting a consular invoice to an embassy or consulate for verification. The certifying party will be concerned to ensure that the declared value of the shipment and the merchandise description are correct. The invoice may be required in multiple copies and must be absolutely accurate and honest in its content.

In addition, a number of developing nations require the physical inspection of all merchandising being shipped to ensure that declarations are accurate and that contraband is not being consigned. This helps such countries control problems such as underdeclaration of values or overstating of quantities – commonly used techniques to circumvent exchange control regulations. Such inspection results in the issue of an *independent third party certificate of inspection.*

If the issue of a *Certified Invoice* instead of or in addition to a consular invoice is a requirement of the order, specified either by the customer or by his import authorities, then the exporter should ensure that the signed certification complies with the specified requirements, which may be that: goods are in accordance with the customer's order and specifications; goods are not from a particular source or country of origin; or they do not incorporate certain ingredients in the product or packaging.

Certificate of origin

This document basically serves the same purpose as a consular invoice, in that it enables the destination country to confirm the source of origin of merchandise. Such a certificate is particularly relevant if there are any preferential duty rates applicable to the source country when the goods are imported into the destination country. Standard approved forms or formats may be specified by the destination country along with the system for obtaining authorized certification. It may be that a local chamber of commerce can authorize a certificate of origin, or possibly a consular office of the destination country.

Information provided in obtaining a certificate of origin must, as with all documents, be true and accurate in all respects.

In some cases a country may require only a *declaration of origin*, not requiring authorization by an independent authority. In such cases the declaration will usually only require the original producer, who may not be the exporter, to provide and sign the declaration. This could upset the exporter if he did not wish an importer to identify his direct source, so many non-manufacturing exporters may have reason to prefer the more formal certificate of origin.

Health or sanitary certificates

In the case of food and other agricultural exports, some countries require certification of the sanitary production conditions of exporting manufacturer's facilities. Such certificates may be authorized by a consul of the importing nation on production of accepted evidence such as approvals of the plant by the appropriate authorized government agencies. Concerns here generally relate to risks of transfer of pestilence or diseases affecting animals or agricultural products.

Certificate of free sale

In addition, a country may occasionally require a certificate of free sale, in order to satisfy itself that merchandise exported is freely on sale to consumers or end users in the exporting nation, and that the exporter is not just dumping an inferior and unsafe product on unsuspecting purchasers in the foreign market.

Other documents

Customers or import authorities may require other sundry documents, such as:

- *packing lists* and *specifications*, setting out the details of the products or the packing of the goods;
- *weight notes*, issued by the seller or a third party indicating the weight of goods shipped (which should tally with other documentation);
- *quality certificates*, issued by the manufacturer;
- or possibly an *analysis* carried out by an independent organisation.

These are the main documents that your importer sees in connection with a consignment. From time to time someone will request additional certification, and it is the exporter's responsibility to comply with the request accurately and honestly. Truth and correctness are fundamental criteria in the preparation of all export documentation. While legitimate requests from your buyer must be complied with, and all the destination country's rules and regulations pertaining to imports must be adhered to, caution must be your approach to any request to complete any item of documentation with anything but strictly correct information. Fines can and will be levied by many destination authorities if errors are identified.

Because many smaller exporters feel unqualified to handle the paperwork associated with export documentation, shipping forwarders will often undertake all the documentary aspects of a shipment for reasonable fees, and advise you of the regulations particular to any country.

In addition to the documents to effect import at the destination, the exporter generally has domestic control documents to complete to comply with relevant export regulations, such as the *Shipper's Export Declaration* required from US exporters by census and trade bureaus, or British *customs and excise export entry forms*. Customs authorities may require other special documentation to be provided, such as *export licences*, and the exporter needs to establish all such documentary needs.

Dangerous goods declarations are required for a range of specified products. Goods moving through EEC countries may require suitable movement documents such as EUR 1 or T forms. Other requirements or systems may involve provision of additional paperwork or checks, such as the need to check that the importer has a current *import licence*, or that documents relating to payments (*letters of credit* or *drafts*) are received. Some exporters send a *dispatch advice note* when goods are shipped, either separately from the documents being transmitted via banks or as a practice where goods are sent on open payment terms. Export agents may sometimes request a *commission advice* note to be sent after each consignment is dispatched or payment received. All these sundry documents should be completed accurately and diligently.

Summary

- The main documents that result from a request to quote generally are: the telexed or written quote; a pro forma invoice; customer's written formal order; order acceptance and confirmation. Terms of sale and warranties should be clearly communicated to the buyer with any of these documents, and also be printed on commercial invoices.
- The set of shipping documents consists primarily of: the bill of lading (acknowledging receipt by the shipping line of goods for shipment on a specific vessel); marine insurance certificate; commercial invoice; certificates of origin, free sale or sanitary certificates as required; consular invoices or other documents required by the buyer, his agents or import authorities.
- Information included on all documents should be consistent between documents, accurate in all respects as regards product descriptions, values, volumes or quantities, markings, packaging descriptions, and comply with the requirements included in a customer's order or letter of credit.
- Presentation of a clean bill of lading is normally an essential requirement of customers under their terms of ordering and arranging payment by drafts or documentary credits.

Checklist

- invitation to quote
- quote
- pro forma invoice
- order confirmation/acknowledgement
- bill of lading/short form bill of lading
- air waybill
- road/rail waybill
- marine (other) insurance policy
- commercial invoice
- consular invoice
- certified invoice
- certificate of origin
- certificate of free sale
- packing list/weight note
- specification sheets
- manufacturer's analysis certificate
- health/sanitary certificate
- quality inspection certificate
- independent third party inspection certificate
- dispatch advice note
- dangerous goods declaration
- shipping or export consignment notes
- documentary credit or payment drafts
- export licences
- import licences
- exporter's commission advice to agent
- customs & excise export entry forms
- EEC movement documents: EUR 1
                                    T Form
- other specifically requested documents: ....
                                                              ....
                                                              ....
                                                              ....

N.B. A number of exporters find it more convenient to control the volume and variety of paperwork and related matters by designing a file folder that has printed on the covers the entire control procedures covering documentation, production of goods, payment, shipping instructions, and so on. Each separate transaction is then allocated to a numbered file folder.

11

Credit Control and Payment Terms

The fundamental rule of export credit is not to extend credit if you cannot control or enforce payment according to the agreed terms. In many instances where a relatively unknown customer in a developing nation, and even in a number of developed nations, requests extended payment terms or an open account arrangement, the exporter finds he has little practical recourse upon default. To conduct litigation in a distant market and unfamiliar business environment, probably against a financially unsound party, will be a costly affair with quite possibly very little of the debts and costs being recovered.

When opening up a new business relationship with a new customer or market, the exporter should set the ground rules for credit and payment at the outset. If there is unlikely to be effective recourse against customers who default, then you would be advised to operate on a letter of credit basis, or possibly request payment with order. Of course, most importers will resist either of these, but particularly the latter because then the customer feels at the mercy of your honesty.

If satisfactory credit checks on the customer can be obtained, then the risks may be assessed as worthwhile, and perhaps terms such as cash against documents or sight drafts can be introduced. The same applies if you can enforce payment, as when the importer has a party or associate company in your home market who undertakes to indemnify you against non-payment. For normal trading purposes, credit extended beyond the time the goods arrive at the destination port is not to be recommended, unless payment is secured or guaranteed by government agencies, banks, or an export credit insurance scheme such as those operated by some governments as part of programmes to encourage the development of trade.

If your credit checking does not support terms other than letters of credit or negotiable drafts at sight, and if the customer rejects these means of payment, then another alternative is to advise the customer to place the order through an export confirming house or similar company involved in extending export credit. These specialist export financial institutions often have much greater market knowledge and customer knowledge than a smaller individual exporter, and are spreading their risks across a multiplicity of importers and markets.

Banks can often provide the newer exporter with practical leads on where to seek aid in financing exports and customer credit, or discounting a negotiable draft to raise funds before the draft matures in order to finance the production of the goods for export.

In addition to consideration of the risks of default by the individual importer, attention should also be given to the stability of the importing country in meeting its obligations with foreign exchange as they mature. Government-backed export insurance programmes are available in many countries (such as that of the Export Credit Guarantee Department in Britain) to cover the risk of default in payment arising from political factors or certain commercial factors that develop in countries approved for trade as part of the particular insurance programme. As the rules and availability of such programmes vary from country to country, little space will be devoted to the subject here except to make the exporter conscious that he should check with a chamber of commerce, department of trade or commerce, or bank both to familiarize himself fully with all the exporting country's legal requirements for the conduct of foreign trade and to establish what services and support are available to exporters.

Credit checking customers

There are several standard procedures that the exporter can use to establish the financial status of prospective importers.

Credit questionnaire   First, the new customer may be requested to complete a brief questionnaire on his company's financial and trading status, ownership, paid-up capital, assets, and recent accounts and balance sheets. Some customers, notably private rather than public concerns, may decline or resent this. Others may feel that they are too powerful in a market to need to complete any questionnaire. However, in your efforts to establish if potential customers are soundly managed and financially strong, a cooperative response will speed up the credit-checking process, and your letter accompanying a credit questionnaire should aim to motivate cooperation.

Trade references   The second avenue to explore in credit checking is to ask for trade references. Ideally, these should be companies that have supplied the new customer with goods or services for a reasonable period of time, such as at least a year continuously, rather than firms that have performed a one-time service or shipment. The trade references will be especially valuable contacts if the importer claims any agency or sole distributorship, as a discussion with your opposite number, the export manager of those companies, will not only elicit credit and payment information, but help form views on the importer's sales distribution facilities, capabilities and aggression in tackling market development opportunities. A trade reference should be asked very specific questions on the amount of credit extended or involved in shipments, the frequency of late payment and length of delays, and the importer's reaction to and handling of specific problems that may have arisen in connection with any shipments. It is useful to know if the importer has a cooperative attitude when the inevitable problems of exporting do occasionally materialize. It is easier to contact nominated trade references in your home market initially, but a phone call to some suppliers in other countries, or even a telex, can still elicit relevant and informative trading background data.

Bank references   The exporter and importer normally exchange names and addresses of respective bankers early in communications, as both parties will need such information if payments are to be effected by bank drafts and the shipping documents are to be remitted from the seller's bank to the buyer's bank. Both the exporter and the importer can seek bank references on each other to establish their respective stability and maintenance of adequate balances and payment records. The exporter is usually the more concerned and nervous, since he may be scheduling shipments on extended credit terms.

The exporter should therefore give the name and address and foreign bank account details of the importer to his local bankers and request that a bank-to-bank reference be taken on the importer. A response will generally come back through your bankers within about two weeks, and it is most helpful to the banks if you can give an estimate of the expected value of shipments being discussed and planned.

Embassies   The commercial sections of your embassy in the destination country often try to keep basic data on local importers, or may attempt to obtain and collate such data on request. The exporter can either write directly to the appropriate embassy, or submit such a request through the local commerce or trade department, providing full known or claimed information on the company. The embassy commercial staff may have access to local company data or credit agencies, or may call or visit the firm to establish basic commercial data on size and financial stability. The constant problem faced in obtaining any meaningful credit data or information on company structure and financial performance is that often the available data are a result of self-reporting by the company in question rather than independently established. If the company is publicly held rather than a private entrepreneurial operation, information is more likely to be available from published accounts.

Credit agencies   Companies such as Dun & Bradstreet, which specialize in providing commercial credit reports on public and private companies, may have a branch in the foreign market and be able to provide summary information. A review of the scope of operations of the agencies through your own financial department will enable you to establish exactly which markets are covered by any credit-checking agency, and you can obtain their comment on the depth of information they can normally provide for any market. The weakness in using such specialized credit-reporting agencies is that they, too, often have to rely to a large extent on self-reporting by the party under investigation.

Government departments　If any governmental or quasi-governmental organization or agency is involved either in extending any credit or providing any level of insurance to an exporter, then it is likely that they will have some system of approving credit. For example, the Export Credit Guarantee Department in Britain insures many shipments for a wide variety of exporters to almost every country and, as a result, has significant historical information on both companies' and countries' payment performance. If you are exporting from Britain, and are covered for credit insurance by that agency, then they will advise you – upon your notification of the importer, destination and estimated shipment value – whether that is a risk they accept to cover. If they will not give coverage for the requisite amount for any customer, you would be unwise to ship on any terms other than an irrevocable confirmed letter of credit or payment guaranteed by a domestic party to the transaction, such as a confirming house.

Export associations　Contacts made through an export association may aid in obtaining credit comments on an individual company. Some export organizations have an export credit or finance committee that will meet regularly to discuss problems that members have experienced with either companies or countries, including the cause of problems, such as those arising from inaccurate documentation.

Chambers of commerce　Once again these all-purpose service agencies, either at home or in the foreign market, may have a system for providing or obtaining comment on a potential customer.

Because the basis for reports on any company outside your home market may be very weak or sketchy at best, the final responsibility rests with you, the export manager, to recommend the extent of latitude you should exercise in shipping orders to foreign customers. The safest approach is to start with strict payment terms, and ease these as the customer builds a good payment history with you.

The destination country

Many developing countries have chronic balance of payment problems, in recent years frequently arising out of fluctuations in energy costs either reducing an energy exporter's earnings as demand and prices fell, or increasingly draining the limited foreign reserves of energy-importing nations as energy demands rose and worldwide recession set in. In the early 1980s, a host of third world countries have found themselves unable to meet foreign loan repayment schedules and have had to impose import or exchange control restrictions on many or all products.

Many third world nations rely heavily on exports of one or two commodities to provide most of their foreign exchange earnings. In a period of recession in major markets, prices for these commodities will generally fall, further weakening the currency strength of the commodity exporter.

Import licences Before accepting an export order, check through agents, banks or embassy commercial services what, if any, import restrictions apply to that market, particularly in respect of import licences or foreign exchange regulations. If import licences are in operation, before you allow goods to be shipped, establish that the importer either has his own import licence with current validity, or has guaranteed access to an import licence before the merchandise lands. Some markets will actually require the licence details to be entered on certain documents related to the transaction. If the importer is buying against a confirmed irrevocable letter of credit, then your payment is assured, and he is unlikely to agree to such terms if there is any risk that his consignment will not be allowed to enter.

Exchange controls If there are foreign exchange controls in effect, then seek to establish if funds are allocated on a product priority basis or some other system. It may be that the exchange is guaranteed to the importer or his bank once the importer applies for it in relation to a specific order. If an import licence is issued, that sometimes also assures that the currency will be made available to effect payment. However, a number of countries have in the past issued an import permit but, when the goods arrive and the importer locally pays his draft to his bank, the central bank then holds up foreign exchange to complete the transfer of funds back to the exporter. Such action in Nigeria has resulted in exporters waiting months and sometimes over a year to receive their remittances. Problems like these just push up export prices as exporters seek to recover financing costs, and push up retail prices in the foreign market as imports become scarcer and stockists profiteer.

Deposits against imports Another system used by some central banks to limit imports to require an importer to deposit a significant portion of an order's value with the banking system when the order is placed. Since most importers have limited capital, this puts great strain on their financial resources and on their ability to develop a market for their principal's product, even where the principal provides extended payment terms.

Devaluations Any exporter who sells goods in terms of a foreign currency faces the risk of a devaluation and consequent loss of revenue in equivalent home market funds. The general rule to follow in the export department is to leave currency speculation to the banks; if you quote on c.i.f. terms in any foreign currency, then establish the definite date when receipt of payment is due and sell the currency forward.

At the time of quoting you should have built in a fair profit margin to allow for minute variations in currency, or your quote may include a clause to the effect 'Prices based upon an exchange rate of 150 pesos to the US dollar, and at the time of order acceptance adjustments may be made if exchange rates fluctuate'. Of course, a buyer will not be happy with any such phrase because he, like the exporter, has budgets and dislikes uncertainty in costs and prices.

Stability If you constantly hear of problems involving payment from certain countries, even if the importers are paying drafts when due, discuss any risks of possible government-imposed action with your bankers. If there is any risk of a moratorium on debt payments, then you will not be thanked by the accountants for continuing to let shipments go on normal bank drafts or open account. At that point the importer must be persuaded to use irrevocable confirmed letters of credit, if these can be secured, or to buy through a middleman, such as an export finance agency, who will be responsible for payment as a home market transaction.

Payment for exports

The various manners of payment customary in the export trade are combinations of the factors:

● method of payment
● time of payment
● place of payment
● currency of payment.

Merchant practices have developed over the centuries and generations of traders have been exchanging goods with the aim that the exporter may retain title to the goods until he either receives payment or has his drafts drawn on the buyer accepted. The buyer, of course, would like the opposite, namely to obtain possession and title before being obliged to pay for merchandise, thereby using supplier credit to finance his growth.

Custom has led to the banks and banking system serving as the conduit for documents, acting on instructions from the parties to the transaction. In the following sections I shall examine aspects of a number of methods of payment.

Open account This traditionally domestic system of payment is rarely used in international trade except with long-established agents and distributors where there is a strong feeling of security based on the relationship, or in exporting to associate or affiliated companies or branch operations, or between member nations of an economic group such as the EEC. Open account, such as payment being due ten or thirty days after shipment or receipt of goods, is subject to enough abuse in the domestic market, where it may be easier to enforce payment. In a foreign market it may cost more to seek litigative recourse than the consignment value.

Payment with order Cash before the shipment is the exporter's dream, but it rarely occurs, although in certain circumstances it is wise and even customary to ask for it. Transactions that warrant seeking this are orders from politically unstable countries or financially unstable customers, or where goods are specifically custom made for a new customer who has no long-term 'good faith' relationship with you and you know that there is no alternative market if the initial order is not either confirmed, collected or paid for. In addition, it is an appropriate method of payment for sales that may subsequently form part of an illicit operation, such as, say, cross-border smuggling. Your contract to supply goods may be legitimate, but if subsequently goods are seized by customs a smuggler will not feel obligated to pay.

Sight drafts and term drafts It is frequently agreed between the parties that the buyer will pay for the merchandise immediately on *sight* of the documents of title, or effectively on first presentation of the title documents to him by his bank.

This method of payment, and the term draft variations to be subsequently discussed, is generally only wise when you are well acquainted with the buyer and his reliability and credit status; the prospect of easier payment terms is often used as the proverbial carrot while initial shipments are made against letters of credit. Buyers have been known to leave goods uncleared at the foreign dock for some period of time if they do not have the funds to enable them to accept a sight draft. If the goods are of a perishable nature, then this could be catastrophic. In fact, some exporters have had experience of buyers who have failed to clear goods against sight drafts immediately in order to use that as a pressure point to obtain additional price concessions.

Many buyers who are short of capital to import and develop new lines, seek a *term draft*, such as one that gives 30, 60 or 90 days from sight to pay for the merchandise. If you approve this kind of credit in order to develop your market, remember to include your financing costs of the extended credit. You may base those either on your own borrowing rate or on another criterion, such as your company's internal rate of return on project investment, depending on what the market and buyer will absorb. But remember that one of the main reasons a foreign buyer often looks to the seller for credit is because either he cannot obtain local financing or his effective local interest rate would be higher than that included in supplier credit.

Problems will arise if there are financial upsets in the foreign market, such as a devaluation before the term of the draft is reached, because if the sale was denominated in the exporter's home currency the buyer may then argue that he cannot afford to pay the supplier at that time as it will cost him more. If the sale was denominated in the buyer's currency, then the exporter should have covered devaluation risks by selling the foreign exchange forward.

A draft is a negotiable document, which you may want to consider discounting with your bank or other financial institution to raise funds for working capital. It is similar to a cheque, and can be drawn in any currency. It may have interest accruing at an agreed rate if it is a term draft, and if the seller preferred not to incorporate the extra financing costs within the price quoted.

The elements of a *draft* or *bill of exchange* can be considered as:

- being an unconditional written order
- addressed from the seller to the buyer, and signed by the seller
- requiring the buyer to pay at sight or on demand or at some future fixed point in time stated on the draft
- stating the sum of money with any other charges or additions or deductions clearly specified
- requiring this sum to be paid to the seller or the party specified in the draft to receive it on behalf of the seller, normally a bank.

See Example 16.

The parties to a draft or bill of exchange are:

- the drawer: who is the exporter/seller
- the drawee: who is the importer/buyer

● the payee: the person to be paid by the drawee, often the bank
   acting for the exporter in arranging the collection and remittance
   of funds.

The inexperienced exporter can greatly benefit by spending time with
the international section of his bank to obtain advice on the mechanisms
of drafts and the preparation of such instruments, including a briefing
on any banking or legal technicalities. Local regulations may limit what
a draft may say or charge, especially if you, the exporter, want a bank
to accept the draft or letter of credit and release funds to you early
to have working capital. A time limit on the credit extended to the buyer,
such as 180 days, may operate for acceptances.

Example 16

Drafts or bills of exchange

Sight draft

£10,000	London, 1 January 1984

At SIGHT of this First of Exchange pay
British Bank Plc or order the sum of
Ten Thousand Pounds Sterling
currency for value received.

To: Philippine Imports, Inc.   All Products Exports, Ltd
    Box 1   Box 1234
    Manila   London

Term draft with clauses

£10,000	San Francisco, 1 June 1984

Sixty days after sight of this First of
Exchange (Second unpaid) pay American Bank
Inc. or Order the sum of Ten Thousand Dollars
in United States currency payable at the
collecting bank's selling rate for sight
drafts on San Francisco, with interest at
fifteen per cent per annum added thereto
from date of issue of this instrument to the
due date of arrival of the remittance in
San Francisco, for value received.

To: Hong Kong Imports Ltd   West Coast Exports Inc.
    Hong Kong   San Francisco

Some points worth making here on negotiable instruments are:

- Acceptance is normally signified by the authorized signature of the drawee (the buyer), given when he calls at his bank to collect the original shipping documents in order to take title and effect clearance through customs.
- All obligations of the draft or bill of exchange must be expressed in writing on the draft and signed by the party liable.
- All obligations of a bill of exchange are transferable by 'negotiation' of the bill, which usually means actual delivery of the bill and an endorsement.
- If a bill of exchange is transferred to another party, that party may acquire stronger rights because he can enforce the bill on prior parties and hold himself free from any defect in title.
- Drawers as endorsers can negate their liability by signing their signature alongside the phrase 'without recourse'.

If a bill or draft is not accepted by the drawee when first properly presented, it is considered dishonoured, and the presenting party should revert to the drawer for instructions. The drawee has the primary liability to pay a draft, and only on his default are the subsequent endorsers or drawer held liable by the holder of the draft. A term draft not paid on the due date is equally considered dishonoured. A draft is normally made payable at a bank, but most bills are not exclusively due to be paid only at the one place.

Customarily a draft is not as simple as the first example in Example 16, and may contain several clauses. For instance, a common clause may refer to the payment of interest by the buyer to the seller to cover the extension of credit from the date the draft is first drawn to the date when payment is due or received. The transfer of funds and the buying of the appropriate currency all have a cost, which may or may not be included in the bank charges connected with the transaction. A clause may be inserted to identify who is responsible for any charges (e.g. 'payable with collecting bank's charges', or 'payable without loss in exchange'). The second clause can protect against any loss resulting from exchange rate variations between the time the buyer deposits his payment at his bank and the time the conversion is made and released to the seller. A draft expressed in foreign currency need not have an exchange clause.

Again, you will be well advised to discuss each early shipment in detail with your bankers to ensure that you understand the documentary payment nature of the initial export transactions, and cover all those elements that might cause you to face unexpected costs or receive less than you expected when preparing the draft.

It is the general practice for the seller to attach the original bill of lading to his draft or bill of exchange sent through his bank to the buyer's bank for payment or acceptance upon presentation. This protects the seller from losing control of the goods before acceptance of the draft by the seller.

As it is also customary for several sets of shipping documents to be prepared for the buyer, some sets may bear a stamp saying 'non-negotiable'. Copies of the sight or term draft may be attached to every set of documents, but would bear the phrase 'first of exchange', 'second of exchange', and so on, and the buyer should only sign one draft on acceptance, generally the 'first of exchange' passed through the banks with the original of the bill of lading.

When you pass your draft to your bank to negotiate through the buyer's bank and present, along with the shipping documents, for acceptance or payment, your bank will also want clear instructions on the required action in the event of any irregularities or eventualities. Copies of your instructions will go from the remitting bank to the collecting bank – for example, that you want immediate advice by air mail of any failure by the buyer to accept the documents and draft on first presentation and failure to clear goods. You may also give instructions on warehousing or other storage of the merchandise on non-acceptance, or an instruction to advise your sole agent if you are using an agent to solicit orders rather than operating through a sole importer. In practice, the exporter often learns of problems more rapidly through the shipping line, because they have a vested interest in a smooth transaction to clear goods from their charge. The shipping line may also seek instructions on action they should take in an emergency, such as arranging storage. It is known that in some developing markets the banks are slow to advise of non-acceptance of documents, especially if the importer has some connections with bank personnel to encourage a few days delay in communications.

Documentary letter of credit   Most exporters would ideally like to receive payment guaranteed by a bank, at a point in time when the documents relating to the shipment are delivered, or at an agreed point in time later, such as 30, 60, 90 or 180 days from the time of delivery of the relevant documents. With a *letter of credit* the buyer is arranging with a bank, normally his own bank in his home market, to provide the finance for the exporter on delivery by the exporter of all shipping and title documents. The buyer's bank may work through a *correspondent bank* in the exporter's country, which will actually receive the documents and make the payment. The buyer's bank then has as its security for payment by the buyer either the title documents for the shipment, or advance funds already paid by the buyer to his bank, or an undertaking from the buyer to reimburse the bank at an agreed point in time all the funds remitted to the seller plus agreed charges and interest.

The procedure leading to opening a letter of credit starts with the foreign buyer agreeing with the exporter that payment will be by a documentary credit. The buyer then instructs his bank at his place of business to open a documentary credit for the exporter on the terms and conditions specified by the buyer, and agreed with the exporter, in his instructions to the *issuing bank*. The issuing bank, not being experts in the product, will require very detailed instructions covering product descriptions and specifications, quantities, agreed prices per unit and total shipment values, terms of trade (e.g. f.o.b., c.i.f., etc.), date payment is due after presentation of the correct documents, packing, shipping period (vessel goods should sail on, or the period the exporter has to complete shipment). It is very common for a buyer clearly to specify a period of validity of the letter of credit, and this could be important to both parties if the goods are required for seasonal sales or promotions.

The issuing bank arranges with the correspondent bank in the exporter's country to negotiate, accept or pay the exporter's draft upon presentation of all the correct documents specified in the letter of credit. The documents will include all those related to title transfer, supplier's invoice, bills of lading, required certificates necessary to effect export (if any are legally required by the exporter's country), and specified certificates needed to effect import in the buyer's country.

If the seller requires a *confirmed letter of credit*, then the correspondent bank may be asked to confirm the letter of credit opened by the issuing bank, and a fee will be charged to the buyer for this service, or the correspondent bank may act without any engagement on its part. Confirmation of the letter of credit by the correspondent bank in the exporter's country is often requested by a seller who does not know the buyer or his bankers, or where there are any fears of default by the buyer, his bankers or the importing country. The confirming bank is underwriting the payment and guaranteeing payment if all the buyer's terms and conditions are being complied with, and it will clearly only confirm a letter of credit if it is satisfied that the issuing bank is reliable.

In each and every transaction involving a letter of credit, the utmost care is needed to ensure that every detail required by the terms of the documentary credit is fully complied with, or the bank may justifiably refuse to honour payment. The bank is only acting as agent for the buyer with limited authority, and cannot make decisions that may subsequently be rejected by the buyer, leaving the bank with the commercial risk of the transaction.

If in any way you find you will not be in total and strictest compliance with each and every stipulation of the documentary letter of credit, then you should promptly communicate the problem area to the buyer so that he may advise the issuing bank of any changes or amendments to the documentary credit, or, if changes necessitate it, to issue a new letter of credit. Alternatively, the buyer could indemnify the issuing bank specifically for that item of non-compliance. The issuing and confirming banks will particularly want to ensure that all required documents presented are in good order and consistent with each other and the buyer's specifications. They will certainly not want to accept a claused bill of lading if a clean bill is specified. They will also reject part shipment or transshipment if these are not approved in the terms of the letter of credit agreed with the buyer.

Once again, a new exporter will find it especially beneficial to spend time with the international department head in his own bank to supplement any reading on the subject with practical experience. Because banks have a vested interest in avoiding problems, they are generally most cooperative in providing assistance in arranging terms of sales under letters of credit. The exporter should also obtain and study the International Chamber of Commerce document No. 400, *Uniform Customs and Practice for Documentary Credits*.

The exporter should never release goods from his control or ownership on the promise that the letter of credit is in the pipeline. Buyers may pressure for release with a plea of an imminent vessel sailing date. The letter of credit should have been received by the confirming or correspondent bank and passed to the exporter for study prior to release of the goods, because it is always possible that the actual written form of the letter of credit may contain terms and conditions other than those the seller thought he had agreed to accept. Even if you, the exporter, have a legal claim against the buyer for failing to open a letter of credit as agreed, that is still an insecure basis for releasing goods, because there is always a cost to enforcing a contract, especially if action must be taken in the foreign market.

In talking about letters of credit, terms such as 'confirmed' and 'unconfirmed', 'revocable' and 'irrevocable' are frequently used. These do not have the same meaning. The correspondent bank, in communicating with the exporter, will advise if the letter of credit is 'confirmed' or 'unconfirmed', either by the correspondent bank or other bank. However, it is the issuing bank, when communicating with the correspondent bank, that will say whether a letter of credit is 'revocable' or 'irrevocable'; in other words, whether the buyer may subsequently change his mind and cancel the letter of credit.

A correspondent bank will obviously only confirm a letter of credit that is irrevocable. An exporter who suspects the reliability of the buyer, his bank or the banking system in the foreign country should insist upon letters of credit that are both *irrevocable* and *confirmed*. In dealing with Europe, North America and a number of developing nations with strong financial centres, it is generally less common to insist upon confirmation of a letter of credit, provided it is irrevocable.

Revolving credits   Where an exporter is making regular shipments to a customer in a foreign country, the answer to the ongoing inconvenience of opening new letters of credit for each shipment may be to have a revolving letter of credit. The issuing bank would have standing instructions from the buyer to arrange for credit, subject to limits, in favour of the seller. No renewal would be needed for each separate shipment. The limits might include quantities or values.

Standby letters of credit   A standby letter of credit is raised by a bank on behalf of a buyer. The bank would effectively stand behind the buyer's credit as a guaranteed line of recourse available to the seller if the buyer defaults on a direct payment. Of course, there is a charge to the buyer for this supporting line of credit guarantee, but it is less than the cost of opening a separate letter of credit for each transaction. The buyer would be responsible for payment of each separate invoice as due, normally with the supporting bank being made aware of the transactions. Only if the buyer failed on a direct payment at the due time could the seller turn to the issuing bank for recourse.

Commodity traders frequently operate a system of *back-to-back* letters of credit, where goods are sold through several middlemen before reaching an ultimate user. Each middleman will issue an identical letter of credit to the one he receives from the ultimate buyer, thereby fully protecting himself, but the value attached to the letter of credit will vary according to the margins applied by the middlemen.

Transferable credits   A letter of credit does not authorize a bank to make payment to anyone satisfying the basic conditions of the letter of credit; it authorizes a bank to make payment only to the named beneficiary, and as such it is not a negotiable instrument. Assignment of the debt can only be made with the prior knowledge and permission of the debtor (that is, the bank), and can only be conditional upon the assignor (the seller) fully discharging his responsibility to the debtor by supplying the documents proving completion of the transactional responsibility between the seller and the bank. The seller cannot assign his responsibilities to another because that would make the debtor bank in default of instructions from the principals, who are the issuing bank or buyer.

If a transferable credit is required, this must be arranged with the issuing bank and buyer at the outset. A credit is transferable only if it is specifically designated as such. A transferable credit is where the beneficiary has the right to give instructions to the confirming bank or bank responsible for payment to the beneficiary to make whole or part payment available to one or more third parties, sometimes referred to as 'second beneficiaries'. Transfer can be specified only once, on terms and conditions stated in the original document, and fractions are transferable only if the original letter of credit does not prohibit partial shipments. The first beneficiary has the right to substitute his own invoices for those of the second beneficiary up to the original value and quantity stipulated in the original credit document. Transferable credits are commonly used where the first beneficiary is a middleman between the producer of goods and eventual user, who may not want the producer to know who the end user is; in transferring the credit, he may be free to substitute his name in addition to altering the value. Customarily the banks charge the first beneficiary for their charges in connection with the transfer of the credit to the second beneficiary.

Indemnities No matter how careful you are as the exporter selling merchandise to foreign customers, there will be occasions when you fail to comply in every respect with the instructions of the buyer transmitted to you in the stipulations of the documentary credit. Normally the correspondent bank will insist on an indemnity from the seller before it makes credit available. Discrepancies are usually in details of the documents, possibly resulting just from a typing error or a late shipment, and if a bank requests an indemnity the exporter should request a letter that will specifically identify the irregularities for which an indemnity is requested. Since the bank can and will hold the exporter liable under an indemnity, the exporter is best advised to communicate on the problem with the customer and reach an agreement on how the irregularity should be handled.

Negotiation and discounting of credits An exporter who needs finance, possibly for work in progress on an export order going to the customer opening the documentary credit, may seek to negotiate his documentary credit with his bank. If the documents required under the terms of the credit have not been presented for acceptance, then the bank *negotiates* the credit in providing an advance. If the supporting documents have been accepted in a transaction and an advance is required by the beneficiary, such as with a 90-day term letter of credit, then the bank is *discounting* the documentary credit. Whether or not the bank providing finance in advance of it receiving funds has a claim against the beneficiary should the customer eventually default on payment depends on whether the bank confirmed the credit. Clearly, if the bank providing the finance confirmed the letter of credit, it is liable to itself in the event of a default if the documents presented comply with the terms of the documentary credit.

The exporter should review with his bankers the ways and means of obtaining bank finance for exports, including the negotiation and discounting of term drafts and documentary letters of credit, as this is a subject beyond the scope of this book.

Summary

- Exercise great caution over credit matters. All new customers should be subject to extensive credit checking, including taking trade and bank references, requesting response to credit questionnaires and copies of audited accounts, and seeking comment from contacts in export associations, government commercial services concerned with exports, and credit-checking agencies.

- In considering terms of payment, attention should also be given to the stability of the foreign economy and its currency, and an assessment made of likely risks of devaluations or exchange control restrictions that may reduce the value of the proceeds upon receipt because of delays in remittance or other factors. Terms of payment may include provision for interest resulting from delays in receipt of funds.

- The main methods of payment used in international trade are: payment in advance; confirmed irrevocable letters of credit; sight or term drafts; or open account.

- Drafts and documentary letters of credit may generally be discounted at a bank or financial institution to raise funds in advance of the payment due date. The draft is commonly attached to the original bill of lading and sent to the consignee through the banking system for acceptance.

- Under a letter of credit the buyer is arranging with a bank to provide the finance to the seller on agreed terms and conditions and provision of requisite documents demonstrating shipment and compliance with the terms of the letter of credit. The seller should seek an *irrevocable* letter of credit (one that cannot subsequently be cancelled arbitrarily by the buyer), and normally request *confirmation* by a correspondent bank in the exporting country. Where a seller fails to or cannot comply with the terms of a letter of credit in each and every respect, he may seek amendments to the letter of credit, issue of a new letter of credit, or issue an acceptable indemnity to the bank.

Checklist

CREDIT CHECKS

- credit questionnaire
- importer's accounts and/or financial status reports
- current suppliers ....
  ....
  ....
- other trade references ....
  ....
  ....
- bank references
- government export agency
- embassy status report
- credit-checking agencies:
  Dun & Bradstreet
  others ....
- ECGD
- chamber of commerce
- export associations

IMPORT RESTRICTIONS

- import licences
- import quotas
- foreign exchange controls
- foreign exchange available
- deposits against imports
- other ....
  ....

AGREED PAYMENT TERMS

- payment in advance
- irrevocable confirmed letter of credit
  - demand
  - extended terms
- revolving letter of credit
- sight draft
- term draft
- cash against documents
- open account
- standby letter of credit
- confirming house
- other ....
  ....

12

Finance for Exports

Finding available finance to cover the costs of working capital needed by exporters is a continuing problem facing businesses both small and large. The larger businesses with a more established track record of domestic sales achievement and profit performance will find it easier to obtain such finance as may be made available. The small business and new exporter will find it harder to tap sources of funds. However, there are always avenues to be explored.

In seeking to expand exports that put a strain on internal resources the exporter should consider: whether external finance can be obtained at all for his products or projects; and if so, at what interest rate and for how long; will the interest rate fluctuate over the period and can it be passed on in the pricing or terms of sale to the customer whilst remaining competitive; is finance needed just for work in process or also to extend customer credit? It is a basic rule in extending credit to a buyer that the time period of the credit should not be greater than the useful life of the product or longer than the time it may take the customer to resell the product and receive his payment from users. Assuming that the exporter has considered all his options and can still profitably export if finance is made available, then we should look at some potential sources.

Export Credits Guarantee Department

Traditionally, most exporters in Britain see this body as one that provides a degree of insurance on exports leaving the country, but it can also assist exporters in matters of finance. In the insurance role, ECGD can provide cover for a range of political, economic and credit risks to approved customers in many countries. Transactions are generally insurable under comprehensive short-term cover where credit terms are no more than 180 days. Pre-credit cover from the date of contract may also be available, but this is generally worth the extra premium only if the goods were a special consignment with no ready alternative market and where there was a risk that the buyer might cancel the contract prior to shipment. Cover can be for such eventualities as insolvency of the buyer after shipment; a buyer failing to honour payment within six months of the due payment date; failure by a buyer to take up goods dispatched to him; foreign government actions, including those preventing remittance of payments; disruption of trade by political actions and war; repudiation of contracts by foreign government-controlled organizations; frustration of contracts by UK actions relating to licensing and exchange control restrictions. The ECGD, like any other insurance company, spreads its risks across many markets, and cover does not remove from the buyer the need to be commercially responsible in entering supply contracts, since potential compensation is frequently for less than the full contract invoice value.

In providing finance, a commercial bank may take an assignment over the seller's ECGD insurance rights in connection with a particular transaction, but in this case a bank's security in the policy is actually no stronger than the seller's, and depends on the compliance of the seller with the terms of the supply contract and the accurate provision of information under the ECGD cover.

Additionally, however, there are provisions and facilities for ECGD *direct bank guarantees*, for short-, medium- and longer-term credit. Under these schemes, banks agree to provide finance at a small premium over base rates. The ECGD charges a premium for providing the guarantees. If finance is being advanced under the *comprehensive open account guarantee*, the bank has recourse to the seller in the event of default in payment by the buyer. Where bills of exchange are involved in the transaction, while the bank may retain the right of recourse to the seller prior to acceptance of the bill, once the customer has accepted the bill the bank providing finance only has recourse to the ECGD.

For major overseas capital projects, specific bank guarantees can be arranged through ECGD, enabling the buyer to obtain bank financing. Also the overseas customer may be able to arrange finance of his purchases through a British bank that has a buyer credit guarantee arrangement with ECGD. In this case, the UK supplier receives his payment at the appropriate time and the bank's credit arrangement is solely with the buyer.

The facilities of ECGD are quite complex and comprehensive, and the exporter should familiarize himself with these by making contact with the Export Credits Guarantee Department and in discussions with his bankers.

Similar programmes exist in a number of other countries, and readers outside the United Kingdom should check with their banks and local department of trade.

Discounting drafts

The previous chapter dealt at some length with the methods of payment generally associated with export transactions. From the small exporter's perspective, the more secure the method of payment, the greater access he will have to raising funds for working capital or providing customer credit. An irrevocable confirmed letter of credit is, of course, the most secure instrument if correctly drawn up, and if complied with by the exporter. The exporter's bank may be approached for an advance against this instrument. Sight and term drafts may also be used to raise cash in advance of receipt of funds by *negotiating* or *discounting* the draft with a financial institution, when an amount less than the face value may be made available, the difference being the charges and interest associated with the advance. If the draft is discounted, the drawer is still liable to the bank for the advance should the drawee for any reason subsequently fail to honour his obligation to pay (except where ECGD bank guarantees are in force by arrangements discussed above). Financial institutions do not normally want to be involved in extending credit against negotiable instruments maturing in anything over 180 days.

Finance houses

A finance house may be in a position to fill a role as a middleman between the exporter and the importer, and may undertake to pay the exporter the full value of the goods shipped, subject to the required documents being provided. The finance house is unlikely to want to be involved in the actual shipping or insurance aspects of the transaction, beyond checking that all documentation is in order. Hence, the finance house may raise a contract with the seller, but will not normally accept any liability for commercial claims between the buyer and seller relating to specifics of the merchandise such as quality. The finance house will then enter a second agreement with the buyer on agreed payment terms and conditions, with the buyer paying such charges and fees as are agreed. The buyer usually accepts drafts drawn on him by the finance house, enabling the finance house to grant credit or payment by instalments.

If government export insurance programmes exist, such as the British Export Credits Guarantee Department programme, that cover either commercial or political risks, the export finance house will generally have recourse to that programme to insure its involvement, but without the buyer knowing. In fact, the exporter should bear in mind that it may be difficult to bring pressure to bear on buyers to meet payment commitments if they realize that the exporter has a back-up insurance programme limiting his exposure to loss in the event of default.

A finance house will want its own study done on the creditworthiness of the buyer and the reputation and ability of the manufacturer to meet his commitments related to the transaction. The financing institution will clearly also want evidence that the buyer has all necessary licences and authorizations to import the merchandise, including the requisite foreign exchange permissions to effect payment according to the agreed programme. In this kind of transaction the financial institution has no recourse to the seller provided the seller has complied with the terms of his supply agreement.

International hire-purchase

Relations between financial institutions in the seller's market and the buyer's market may make it possible for the importer to find a local source of 'hire-purchase' finance, whereby the seller is paid in full by a financial institution providing some form of hire-purchase finance, and the importer then pays locally under the transaction terms he agrees with his local hire-purchase institution. The seller should be clear about any ongoing commitment he may have in respect of performance of the item supplied and warranties the exporter may be required to give. The fundamental rule is always to give the minimum warranties necessary to achieve the sale, and not to give any warranties if the use of the product or the conditions of use will not be in accordance with those recommended by the manufacturer. For example, even a piece of capital equipment may not perform with the same effectiveness in high heat and humidity as in the cooler temperate climates of the exporting country. Forms of hire-purchase will be unlikely to apply to consumer goods.

   The importer of plant and capital equipment may also make leasing arrangements to gain access to the equipment without the full outlay of the funds initially, and financial institutions in either the exporting or the importing country may be willing to enter such arrangements, paying the seller in full his moneys due under the contract.

Factoring

Where goods are of a standard type, not requiring complicated negotiations on specifications and payment terms, the exporter may avail himself of a factoring service. A factor may select his clients so that he knows both the buyer and seller with whom he is dealing, and handle the collection of funds from the overseas buyer without getting involved with the shipping documents. The overseas buyer may be notified that he should pay the sum due under the invoices to the factor, who will charge a commission to the exporter in exchange for making the funds available. The factor may handle the mechanical functions of credit control, invoicing and collection, and may agree to make an initial non-recourse payment to the exporter before collection from the buyer. Such a non-recourse payment is generally for an amount less than the full invoice value, often to a maximum of 90 per cent of the invoice total. The fees the factor charges the exporter will vary according to the specific services provided by the factor to the exporter.

Generally the buyer knows when a factor is involved in the transaction, but there may be occasions when the seller does not wish the buyer to be aware of his private financial dealings. In such a case the exporter can 'sell' his goods to the factor but, acting as agent on agreed terms for the factor, ship and invoice for them direct to the buyer, and remit proceeds to the factor.

Export banks

It is a common practice for governments to encourage the development of export trade by introducing a system of export banks to make finance available on special and favourable terms to exporters. Frequently this is seen in countries with a heavy dependence on exports of agricultural commodities. The interest rates charged to the exporters by such institutions are generally well below the commercial market rates. Such a benefit amounts to a subsidization of exports by the authorities of the exporting country, and arouses much complaint and criticism from less-advantaged exporters of similar products in other countries. The government banking agency involved in providing the export finance will set the terms and conditions and product categories for which it will make finance available, and the net result may be that the exporter can effectively pass on a reduced rate of financing to the foreign buyer, thereby having a commercial edge in quoting to supply goods or services. The export bank will expect to have knowledge and probably the right of acceptance or rejection of any transaction, but if funds are available for, say, capital equipment, then the exporter may be able to line up a contract to supply his equipment exclusively because he alone can provide medium- or long-term financing to the other party, who perhaps was unable to find a satisfactory source of local finance for the project.

This kind of programme is of major benefit to companies or consortiums bidding to supply equipment, plant or machinery, or to tender for an all-inclusive construction programme to design and build a foreign plant using domestic components. The government-backed export banking agency may also have an insurance programme to remove the risk or minimize the exposure of the sellers of goods and services, possibly taking the rights to direct recourse against the buyer, which may even be a foreign government agency.

In the USA, the Small Business Administration may make loans available to companies needing finance to develop exports; such loans generally would be secured against firm export orders rather than for speculative development projects.

Supplier credit

If the individual exporter trying to win a contract uses ingredients or components supplied by other, perhaps larger, domestic manufacturers, then it may be beneficial to discuss any problems relating to the short-term financing of the export contract with those other suppliers. They will have a vested interest in making additional sales, particularly if their own plants have spare capacity. If fully briefed on the terms and conditions of the supply contract, and satisfied as to the security of the method of payment, they may agree to cooperate by extending credit beyond their normal time periods to enable the exporter to obtain the contract.

Finance available to the importer

It is natural for the buyer or importer to seek credit from the exporter as his first approach to funding a transaction. However, if the products or services being sought by the importer in the foreign market are in any way considered essential to the development of that market, then the importer may have access to local sources of funds that he has not fully explored. Particularly in respect to major capital projects, such as constructing new industrial facilities or services (like hospitals) that contribute to the community, the local government or some of its agencies may either make funds directly available, at preferential interest rates, or underwrite the commitments of the project. Similarly, international agencies may also have a role in underwriting major projects in developing countries.

The exporter should therefore seek to be as familiar as the importer in such situations with what other avenues of finance or financial guarantees are available to the parties contracting. The project can therefore be beneficially discussed confidentially at an early stage with persons or agencies who may specifically know of available support, such as the commercial banks, central banks, trade departments and respective embassies of both the importing country and the exporting country. Major projects may take many months or years of planning before they even commence supply or construction because of the intricacies of securing finance for the parties involved.

This chapter has given an initial introduction to some of the avenues that may be open in seeking to finance exports if the supplier does not have sufficient internal resources. Your own bank is always the starting point in seeking finance, and the more it knows of your business, programmes, success and aggression in seeking new opportunities, the more time it will give to aiding your search, whether for working capital or venture capital.

Export trade organizations and chambers of commerce, as well as local offices of government agencies such as trade departments or commerce departments, may all have specific ideas and contacts. The complications and many varied aspects of exporting and opening new markets, in terms of documentary requirements, legal or financial matters relating to each and every transaction, make it impossible for the export manager to be up-to-date or expert in all aspects of constructing deals. But he should have a vast network of contacts to whom he can turn for specific and accurate advice when problems or new situations arise.

Summary

- Exporters frequently need access to financial resources in order to progress export orders. Loans may be available from a commercial bank or financial institution or governmentally sponsored agencies such as the Small Business Administration in the USA. Such loans normally relate to financing connected with a specific export contract. Suppliers of raw materials and inputs may also be cooperative in extending additional credit where they can be satisfied on the viability of a project.

- In addition, finance for goods sold may be raised by discounting drafts or documentary credits with commercial financial institutions, or by interposing into the export transaction the services of another factoring institution, finance house or credit institution extending credit for exports. Such financial institutions may advance funds to the seller, and also extend credit to the buyer if they take possession of merchandise.

- Importers may find credit sources such as for purchasing heavy plant and equipment through leasing or hire purchase companies in the importing country, or by purchasing through an export confirming house or other export financing institution in the exporting country. Additionally, government agencies in the exporting country may underwrite credit where they have a specific export promotion programme.

- Commercial banks and government export promotion agencies can give specific current advice on the potential sources of finance available to assist an exporter conclude a supply contract.

13

Insurance

It is very unwise to ship without adequate insurance, since merchandise transported long distances utilizing several modes of transport, and out of the direct physical control of both the buyer and the seller, faces greater risk than similar merchandise shipped within the home market, often on trucks belonging to either the seller or buyer.

Most exporters negotiate a *marine* insurance policy that can be operated for all their export shipments and will extend to cover such overland or other modes of transport utilized while the goods are in transit from the premises of the exporter to those of the importer. In addition, coverage may be extendable to cover reasonable periods in store, or to cover specific product risk factors, such as heat and humidity damage, by negotiation with the insurers.

Insurance is a complex subject, and in this chapter I seek to review those general aspects the exporter should consider and be familiar with if he is to ship goods internationally without undue exposure for resultant claims.

The insuring party

The contract of sale negotiated with the buyer will normally stipulate which party is responsible for effecting the insurance cover on the shipment. If this point has not been discussed, do not assume that the buyer is accepting responsibility; seek confirmation in writing from him to that effect. A c.i.f. contract by definition assumes that the buyer is accepting to take the cover arranged by the seller, which is included in his delivered price. A c & f contract assumes that the buyer is accepting to organize insurance cover, but does not state that. The c & f contract should, therefore, specifically incorporate a clause stating that the buyer undertakes to effect insurance cover, and may even specify that the cover be for not less than the c & f invoiced value, to protect the buyer's interest in the goods while in transit.

If goods are sold on terms other than a confirmed irrevocable letter of credit, then it is important for the seller that the goods be insured. Some sellers seek to protect their interest by including a charge for insurance in all price quotes, particularly if the goods are perishable.

If the seller organizes the insurance as part of a c.i.f. contract, then a copy of the insurance certificate must form part of the complete set of shipping documents transmitted to the buyer, generally through the banking intermediaries. If the seller has taken insurance to protect his interest independently of the buyer's request, then a copy of that certificate may not be compulsorily included.

Much of the world's shipping insurance is placed through underwriting members of Lloyds of London on marine insurance companies. The exporter will normally work through a broker to effect the insurance coverage; once the broker has placed the insurance, he will issue a cover note. The cover note may be an open cover note if the insurer expects to receive more specific details on a particular shipment, or where the insured party has a general or floating policy negotiated under broad parameters and requiring specific details to be filed for each separate shipment prior to the shipping date.

The party taking the insurance cover should ensure that the broker has been promptly advised of all details relevant to a specific shipment and the value and extent of cover required, including the sailing dates and additional cover such as for heat and humidity damage if that is a risk either en route or at the destination. Notice of claims or potential claims must also be notified promptly to the broker or his agent or to the insurer or his agent in writing. The policy may give a time limit on such notification, and the insurer may wish to inspect the cause of the claim immediately at the site of the goods. The broker is responsible for paying premiums to the insurer and for collecting his commissions from the insurer; the service of a good broker is therefore not a direct charge on the exporter.

Main types of policies

A policy may state a finite value of the merchandise insured, and this is generally referred to as a *valued* policy, or the policy may be less specific, for example placing a maximum limit on the sum insured, and as such is termed an *unvalued* policy. The insurable value may subsequently be ascertained on the basis of ascertainable costs and invoices and other documents relating to costs of the shipment such as freight and insurance. A valued policy may give a higher level of recoverable insurance than an unvalued policy, because the anticipated profits of the importer may be included. Most buyers prefer to have cover of the valued type that identifies very clearly their expected level of reimbursement in the event of any claim being filed. Goods that may rise in value while in transit could be covered under a policy that recognizes the possibility of a rise in the value of the item or increasing cost of replacement.

Variations in insurance cover may specify cover for:

- a fixed time
- specific voyage of unspecified duration
- a combination of the above.

Cover extensions may operate for goods delayed prior to shipment or on arrival at the destination port before clearing customs. Cover may also operate for an unspecified time while the goods are in transit from the seller's warehouse to the buyer's warehouse. If goods are of a perishable nature and will have less or no value after a period of time, then, if the insurer will give cover for delays in transit, this may be an important protection to both parties. Even after the arrival of goods at the buyer's final warehouse, some policies will permit an extension of cover of certain or all risks, possibly dependent on the nature of the product being insured, for a limited period, often up to 30 days. If foreign buyers feel that they cannot obtain adequate local insurance cover on the goods in store, yet expect to sell them within the period of any extension of the shipping cover, then they may request the seller to arrange such an extension of his policy. Care must be taken that cover is in effect for the full period the goods are at risk and outside the control of the seller prior to receipt of payment or transfer of title under the terms of sale.

Floating policies are commonly used in the export trade, whereby a seller has general conditions of insurance agreed with his insurer for regular export trade but also has to advise the insurer of particular details for each consignment as soon as such specifics are known and available. The floating cover may set a limit on the number of annual shipments, or on the amount at risk on any one vessel (say, £300,000), or on the total risk outstanding at any one point in time (say, £1 million), including a number of consignments on several vessels or in transit, or at any insured locations. The exporter who has such a policy needs to be aware of his outstanding risk at any point in time, because occasions may arise (for example, if several vessels are delayed in transit or offloading) when the insurer may need to be notified that the limit is being approached or exceeded. Generally an insurer will cooperate to give a temporary increase in the level of cover.

Accuracy and honesty are essential when completing any documentation related to insuring merchandise or any resultant claim, or the insurer may subsequently refuse a risk or reject a claim. If a claim arises at the destination, it is normal for the insurer to have a local agent to inspect the goods to assess the extent of damage or any recoverable element. Some policies will entitle the insurer to take title and salvage any goods when a claim is settled. If the nature of your goods is such that your market reputation would be harmed by damaged goods being sold at 'salvage' prices (as would be the likely case with heat-damaged confectionery), then your policy could be negotiated to include a clause for total destruction of such goods.

Open cover policies are similar in principle to floating policies, and may have time limits applying to the open cover or be perpetuated subject to a period of notice by the party wishing to terminate the policy. Open cover will also normally contain limits on 'any one bottom' (the maximum at risk on any one vessel in transit), or at any one location. While a floating cover fixes the absolute amount of cover that may be in effect or available over a finite period of time, an open cover will cover each and every shipment made during the agreed time period and within the other terms of the cover.

The terms of insurance cover should be studied and carefully understood by both the shipping manager and the export sales manager, in order both to communicate to buyers and to prepare correct declarations.

Normal insurance documents

When the exporter is responsible for organizing the insurance cover, he normally provides a certificate of insurance along with other shipping documents to the buyer. The certificate acknowledges that insurance cover has been obtained, but does not carry the same weight or detail as the actual policy document. The buyer may choose to insist on a copy of the policy. Also, instead of the insurance cover note, it may be that either the supplier's certification that insurance is in effect or a cover note from the broker will suffice, and the exporter may wish to clarify this with the buyer, especially if the letter of credit makes a specific request for an insurer's cover note. Where a seller has an open policy, the certificate of insurance is the normal instrument to summarize the insured risks and the nature of the goods insured, normally giving summary details of consignment value, markings, quantities and any other data relevant to the consignment.

Contract clauses and issues

Any unusual aspect of the consignment or its voyage must be notified to the insurer, particularly if any element of risk might be considered greater than normal. For example, the insurer may require that goods be stowed below deck if they risk deterioration from exposure if stowed on the decks.

A *held covered* clause may be inserted in the policy to cover the eventuality that an oversight or innocently erroneous description or omission might increase the risk for the insurer, but oblige him to accept the insurance at an additional premium. An exporter or insured party must always notify the insurer immediately he notices any mistake, omission or error, or cover may be rejected or reduced in the event of a claim, depending on the terms and conditions of the policy.

Goods can only be insured in transit if the party seeking insurance can demonstrate an interest in the property of the goods, such as the producer, exporter or importer. The exporter selling on a c.i.f. basis clearly has an interest until the title to the goods transfers under the terms of sale when goods arrive at the agreed destination. If the sale is on an f.o.b. basis, the buyer has an insurable interest once the goods are loaded on the vessel, and an exporter assisting by organizing insurance at a buyer's request is really acting as an agent for the buyer. Difficulties arise if an exporter is selling on f.o.b. terms but against extended payment, such as a 30-day draft. A policy can usually be negotiated by the seller to cover the seller's interest contingency, which gives cover to insure the goods against damage in transit or the buyer's subsequent refusal to accept the documents. Many exporters feel more secure to have covered their *seller's contingency interest*. The seller's interest in the property is more strongly demonstrated if the sales contract contains a clause reserving the seller's right to the property in the goods until goods are paid for under the agreed terms.

It may be that the insuring party might inadvertently over-insure or have more than one policy in effect covering all or part of the risk associated with a consignment. In the event of any claim where double cover is in existence, it may be that one insurer undertakes to assess the loss and settle and then negotiate the adjustment of the losses with the other insurers. The insuring party will not find the separate insurers each willing to accept and pay the same claim in full to a party who has over-insured. However, if the goods have been separately insured by more than one party, each with a demonstrable interest in the property, then each could claim separately and expect settlement from his insurers. For example, the seller, the carrier and the buyer could insure separately under different policies, each to protect his interest.

A policy taken out by one party with interest in the property is not customarily assignable to another party (such as the seller assigning the policy to the buyer or vice versa) when interest in the property transfers, unless such a clause is contained in the policy enabling assignment to be effected upon endorsement by the first insuring party. If the policy is assigned from the seller to the buyer, then the buyer has the right to claim the full sum insured if a claim arises subsequently, even if the sum originally insured by the seller under the policy was for more than the price the buyer was paying for the goods. The seller does not have the automatic right to claim the difference.

Insurable risks

The insured may have to give certain warranties as a condition of insurance, for example that goods are free 'from inherent vice' or are 'packed in suitable export cartons'. If an insurer inserts 'warranted free' as part of a clause, that normally indicates an exemption from coverage, such as 'warranted free from loss or damage resulting from riots or civil disorder'.

The marine policy will, like any normal household policy, summarize the risks against which the insurer will cover loss or damage and negotiate claims. It is important that the exporter consider any special risks his particular products may face, such as damage from heat, humidity or infestation, and seek cover extensions against these risks. The insurer may be quite unwilling to give cover against some specific risks, such as 'inherent vice', for example – a particular problem facing exporters of dairy products who may find mould rapidly developing on cheese shipments.

Many clauses are written in standard form, such as the standard clauses of the Institute of London Underwriters. Some of these 'institute' clauses cover theft, pilferage, non-delivery, riot, strikes, lock-outs, civil commotion, change of voyage, general average, seaworthiness, and transit.

Under transit clauses, the cover can often be extended beyond the sea journey to include cover from warehouse of the seller to final destination warehouse of the buyer, usually requiring a declaration of exactly where these locations are. If for any reason goods are not delivered according to the scheduled voyage plan – for example, they are offloaded for any reason at another port en route, possibly because of congestion at the correct destination – the insurer must be notified and may hold the goods covered for a limited period of time subject to certain conditions, including satisfactory storage or resale within a certain period of time. This can be a problem if the goods either are perishable in nature, or are not an importable item at the offloading port, and a solution would have to be discussed between the insured and the insurer to minimize the loss factors while protecting each party's interest.

Degrees of cover

The exporter will normally find any cover will fall into one of several degrees of comprehensiveness, such as:

● 'free from particular average'
● 'without average'

- 'all risks'
- 'all loss or damage'.

Particular average is where some damage is caused under an insured risk, but the damage is partial and only affects an individual insured party's cargo. For example, water may damage a perishable commodity on deck but not affect other parties' products also stowed in the same location. The loss must be borne by the individual insured party or his insurer.

Where cargo is deliberately jettisoned, perhaps to save the vessel from a temporary risk, or to save the balance of cargo from a risk related to the jettisoned cargo, then a *general average* clause will normally operate. Here, each shipper, or his insurer, who has goods on that vessel facing the same risk is expected to share in the loss of the party whose goods were jettisoned, and the vessel owner can take a lien on all cargo in his possession until owners of the saved cargo contribute to the losses incurred by the owner of the jettisoned cargo.

The policy may have a clause exempting the insurer from liability under particular average where the loss or damage is less than a certain specified percentage of the whole. If the loss were more than this percentage, the insurer will normally be exposed for the entire loss, not just the excess over the exempted percentage. This type of clause is often found where a particular cargo has an inherent risk of a certain degree of damage of a certain type, such as heat or water. A package may be covered if totally lost or destroyed, yet not covered if only partially damaged.

All risk cover will protect the insured against all risk of loss or damage to the goods shipped except for any specified exemptions in the policy, such as inherent vice, delay, wear and tear.

A cover against *all loss and damage* does not generally contain exemptions, provided that the insured can demonstrate that he has both suffered loss and not been instrumental in causing that loss.

Claims

As soon as an insured party identifies either a loss or likely cause of claim, the insurer or his appointed agent must be notified. He may have a view or advice on particular action that could be taken, such as salvaging any part of the product subject of a claim. The insurer will normally have his local representative examine the goods promptly to assess the degree of damage and any potential sale value of the distressed consignment. If goods are claimed lost in transit, the insurer's agent will seek proof of the delivery of the full consignment to the care of the carrier at point of departure and compare this with the actual quantity of product delivered to the buyer. A buyer should not sign a receipt of delivery without actually taking an accurate inventory of what he receives and recording any discrepancy on the documentation involved. The insurer's agent will write a survey report on the extent and likely cause of damage and potential salvage value.

Both the insured party and the insurer, as well as the agents and representatives of the concerned parties, have the duty and responsibility to work to minimize any losses, and to issue claims against any other parties contributing to the loss or damage, such as the carriers.

A claim always involves a lot of paperwork, and usually delays of several months before any settlement is received by the insured. Close cooperation between the insured and the insurer will reduce delays and facilitate settlement.

The claim may involve total or only partial loss. A total loss would occur where the goods were actually lost or damaged beyond the point of repair, or where repair would cost more than replacement of the product. If the goods are not destroyed and the insurer pays a claim of full value for the merchandise, then clearly the insurer has the right to take the goods and dispose of them for salvage value, unless a clause in the policy provides for total destruction of damaged goods. This type of clause is quite common in the case of shipments of foodstuffs.

The sum recovered will relate to the degree of damage, and reimbursement may only cover repair to the item or reduction in market value. No doubt a person importing a brand-new automobile would be most upset if his new vehicle arrived all dented and the insurer just said, 'Take it to your local repair centre'. But that is the right of the insurer in most cases. With a total loss, the level of reimbursement will depend on whether it was a 'valued' or 'unvalued' policy. Partial loss on a 'valued' policy entitles the insured party to claim proportionate reimbursement of the total insured value of the item. On an 'unvalued' policy, partial loss or damage entitles the insured only to the insurable value of the lost or damaged portion of the whole consignment.

Once the insured has been paid his claim by the insurer, the insurer assumes the right to sue such persons who may have caused or contributed to the loss or damage to the consignment, such as the carriers, to the extent he provided cover and compensation only. If the insured goods are sold at some salvage value, the benefit of the sale goes to the insured party if the insured was only partially compensated for loss, or to the insurer if the total insured value was paid to the insured.

Overseas buyers frequently request that insurance be taken out by the seller on behalf of the buyer if the cover is better than what the buyer might otherwise obtain, or if it is less costly. The claim could be payable in either the exporting or the importing country, and in either currency, according to the agreement in the policy.

The insurance broker will be the expert adviser to the exporter on the types and levels of cover available and preferable for any product type or destination, but the exporter should be familiar with the terms and conditions of any cover or master policy, as well as the meaning and limitation of clauses and exemptions.

Summary

- The merchandise in transit can be insured under a marine insurance policy to cover likely and insurable risks in transit (normally excluding inherent vice) between agreed points such as the seller's warehouse and the buyer's final destination.
- The terms of sale generally dictate who has responsibility to effect insurance cover, but a seller is wise to ensure that the buyer understands his responsibility if sale is on other than c.i.f. terms. Sellers may cover their contingency interest.
- Insurance should cover the cost of goods and shipping charges, and generally an additional margin for sundry or non-recoverable costs. The policy may state the actual value of goods covered or simply fix a limit on the sum assured on any one consignment. Generally buyers and sellers fix the assured sum ('valued' cover).
- Floating policies fix the absolute amount of cover that may be available over a time period; an open policy covers each and every consignment during the agreed time period.
- The insurer or his agent must be notified immediately a potential claim is identified, and will assess the degree of damage and any likely salvage values.
- Where the seller is responsible for effecting insurance cover, a copy of the certificate of insurance goes with the shipping documents.

14

Carriage of Goods to Foreign Markets

The large manufacturer shipping to several export markets or shipping inter-company to overseas branches or affiliates can probably afford his own export shipping department, including professionally trained shipping clerks and a qualified shipping manager. The smaller exporter, with limited experience and resources, is better devoting his financial resources to achieving actual sales. He can employ the services of a forwarding agent, and acquire skills gradually through the consistent liaison with that agent. In selecting a *forwarder*, it is essential to identify who will give you the time, attention and level of service you require. Depending on the type of products you are offering for export, you will need varying degrees of speed in quoting, freight rate competitiveness, and aid in documentation. For example, a commodity trader needs both the very best freight rates, from conference and non-conference shipping lines, and very rapid response to enquiries because the basic commodity prices fluctuate with great frequency and margins in the business are traditionally slim. A manufacturer of a specialized consumer product may not be under the same pressure for 'instant' quotes, and may equally not be concerned over the last few pence of a quote, but he may have complicated documentary requirements relating to duty drawbacks on incorporated components that were previously imported. Even if a particular forwarder cannot provide every aspect of service you need, it is likely that he can take much of the administrative load off the exporter, and even provide some internal training for the exporter's staff on other procedural aspects of administration.

The exporter needs carefully to weigh the merits of a larger, long-established forwarder versus a newer, smaller and more hungry company. A larger forwarder may not be as attentive to special requests, but may offer more established systems for support documentation such as consular invoices and certificates of origin and even, possibly, the insurance aspects.

Because the international movement of goods is such a wide subject, in this one chapter I can give only an introduction; I would refer the reader who needs in-depth knowledge to the reading list at the end of the text and invaluable discussion with experts such as freight forwarders.

Major modes of transport

Ocean freight is still the main mode of transport used in moving goods internationally, although air, road and rail all have important roles between certain markets or for certain goods.

In reviewing the mechanics of moving goods I shall concentrate on the more traditional ocean mode of transport.

Air freight offers speed, security, low damage risk, simplified documentary requirements, often reduced packaging costs and reduced ordering lead times. It is particularly ideal for smaller and more valuable consignments. The higher costs and space limitations reduce its attractiveness and suitability for lower-value and high-bulk items.

Road transport offers greater flexibility in collection and delivery, is often more rapid than rail or combined transport systems, is generally secure and reliable, and transit documentation under TIR (Transport International Routier) bond conditions is minimal. It is especially growing within the European Common Market, to the Middle East, and in the Americas.

Rail freight is only practical to the extent that railway systems are developed. While there may be relatively low risk of loss or damage, goods may need delivery to or collection from depots. Modern rail freight systems can utilize multi-mode containers. Transit documentation can be relatively simple, and there may be no need for any handling of goods between consignment points. This mode is frequently attractive for bulk commodities using specially designed containers.

Containerization is the modern preferred system of most exporters, including consolidated containerized shipments where one consignment alone would not fill a container. This permits door-to-door uninterrupted service with no handling in transit, a high degree of security, low damage risk (with probably reduced packaging and insurance costs), reduced transit times (also giving a cost saving to buyers who may order smaller, more frequent consignments). Containers are, of course, particularly ideal for goods requiring temperature or other controlled shipping environments.

Documentary payment terms can take account of shipping documents other than the traditional ocean bill of lading to effect payment, even though these may not give title to the goods, where it is arranged as part of the payment terms that such documents consigning goods to a carrier are to be accepted as proof of export.

Mechanics of arranging carriage

On the starting assumption that you, the exporter, have received an order requiring the shipment of a consignment on c.i.f. terms to the buyer's destination port, the first stage is to contact either a shipping forwarder or a shipping line directly to obtain both freight rate quotes and the available vessel details and sailing times to comply with the buyer's delivery specification. Just as the shipper normally uses a forwarder to handle his freight movements, so the shipowner normally uses an agent to handle the booking of available space. The forwarder receives his commission from the shipowner or his agent, but may levy other agreed charges according to the level and complexity of services he provides, such as obtaining necessary certificates connected with the transaction.

In most cases the exporter is not in the market to handle an entire charter contract for a vessel, but seeks space only for a container load or perhaps less. Goods shipped in sealed containers are generally considered more secure from potential damage and pilferage, and often attract both lower freight costs, because of the easier handling and storage, and lower insurance rates, because of the reduced exposure to risks. Sometimes space in a container is available on a 'less than container load' basis if two or more parties are shipping goods to the same destination from sources in close proximity or from the same container loading point. The main problem with shared containers is that the parties sharing may have incompatible products: one item may be heavy and crush the other if wrongly loaded, or one may give off strong odours that are damaging to the other if it is a food item. The exporter should seek to share a container with compatible products if possible.

The shipowner will advise the shipper of the delivery point for the consignment, latest acceptable time for delivery, and scheduled sailing time and date for the named vessel in advance. It is the shipper's sole responsibility to deliver the consignment to the vessel on time. Late arrivals may be locked out.

The shipper should dispatch the merchandise in good time to the vessel, along with his shipping note advising the nature of the goods, quantities, identifiable shipping marks and any other relevant details. In general, the shipping marks stencilled on cartons shipped as a less than container load shipment (palletized or loose) will be the marks given by the buyer and used by him to identify his consignment quickly at the arrival port.

When the merchandise is actually delivered to the ship, the shipowner will issue a bill of lading, acknowledging receipt for custody and shipment. The shipper wants a clean bill of lading, showing that his goods were accepted in undamaged condition, because that may be a stipulation of payment terms. A claused bill, indicating some identifiable aspect of apparent damage or deterioration, will generally cause a problem over acceptance by the buyer or obtaining payment under a letter of credit.

If containerization is the agreed mode of transport, then the container is either loaded at the shipper's premises, or goods are sent to a container loading point, and the container shipping line issues the bill of lading.

Several originals of the bill of lading are customarily issued, and the goods can be delivered against the first original presented, which immediately negates the value of the others. The shipper may dispatch non-negotiable copies of the bill of lading to the buyer, sending the original via the bank system along with the drafts for payment. All goods on a vessel are recorded in the ship's manifest.

It is the general practice of shippers to send parts of the set of bills of lading by different means to ensure that at least one set is with the buyer prior to arrival of the vessel at the destination, and thereby facilitate prompt clearance of the goods through the importation formalities. One set could go with the vessel master, another by air mail. The exporter must decide how many sets and by what means to transmit them in order to ensure that he receives payment promptly and that the buyer clears the goods promptly. With a documentary letter of credit or draft, it is more likely that the exporter will initially send documents only through the bank to ensure acceptance or payment, but if goods are being sold on cash against documents or other open credit terms, or to associated companies, then originals of the bills of lading may be dispatched directly to the importer.

The shipowner is responsible for the goods until they are delivered to the consignee in the correct manner and place specified in the carriage contract, which may only require delivery to a dock company or warehouse at the destination port. However, the shipowner is responsible for delivering the goods to the named consignee only upon presentation of an original bill of lading showing entitlement to collect the goods. If, as sometimes happens, the vessel arrives before the original bill of lading is transmitted through the banking system, then the importer may pressure the shipper to agree to release the goods without an original bill of lading. To comply with that request, the shipowner would require an indemnity, and if the consignee did not then accept the draft at the bank, the shipper has a serious potential payment problem.

There is no substitute for ensuring that the bill of lading is both received back from the shipping line promptly by the shipper after dispatch of the goods to the vessel, and transmitted by the fastest means through the banking system in the case of payment by letters of credit or drafts.

Freight charges

Payment of the freight charges to the shipowner are technically due on delivery of the goods to the consignee or on arrival at the destination port as per the contract of carriage. If the vessel or goods are lost in transit, freight is not normally due unless other contractual terms incorporated in the bill of lading apply. Most shipping lines do put a clause in the bill of lading requiring that freight be paid in any event.

Freight is normally calculated on one or more of these three criteria: (a) value, (b) volume, or (c) weight. The shipowner will choose the freight cost calculation most advantageous to him.

The cost of freight varies according to whether *conference* or *non-conference* shipping lines are used. The shipping conferences are pools of shipowners who maintain regular sailings and shipping space on certain routes or to certain parts of the world. Frequently a shipper is encouraged to ship exclusively with a shipping conference on a particular route or region in exchange for freight rebates or discounts. Deferred rebates are offered to limit defection to the often cheaper non-conference lines operating over the same routes. Sometimes a shipper may contract to take an immediate discount off the freight invoice in exchange for exclusively using a conference line. Some shippers treat the rebate as theirs, to partly offset administrative costs, and others automatically pass it on to customers.

Although the exporter may be contracted to a shipping conference, the importer may not be so contracted. If a customer is quoted f.o.b., then he can seek his own freight quotes and perhaps arrange his own shipping through a forwarder in order to benefit from the lowest freight quote. Alternatively, a customer may specify that the exporter use a non-conference line. The exporter may not be considered as in breach of his conference contract if the buyer pays the freight or it is clearly established that the exporter is arranging the carriage of the goods only as agent for the buyer (more easy to demonstrate on an f.o.b. contract than a c.i.f. contract).

If a bill of lading is made out in the name of a freight forwarder, then the freight forwarder will normally receive the rebate. Therefore, if forwarders are used, the exporter should ensure that the bills of lading are made out in the exporter's name, or agree with the forwarder to reflect rebates in freight quotes.

The bill of lading will customarily include a clause holding the shipper responsible for freight. It is therefore necessary for the exporter to satisfy himself on the financial stability of the shipping forwarder if moneys for freight are being paid to the forwarder, because the shipowner will claim freight from the shipper if the forwarder defaults.

The consignee is not liable for the freight unless it is clearly demonstrated that the shipper was only acting as agent for the consignee, or unless the consignee has taken title to the goods under the contract of sale and the bill of lading has been endorsed to the consignee. If the consignee or endorsee re-endorses the bill of lading to yet another party, who acquires the property in the goods while they are in transit, the new party is liable for unpaid freight. If transfer of goods in transit is stopped for any reason by the seller, then the seller is again liable for any unpaid freight.

If the shipowner has a clause in his bill of lading stipulating that freight is due on shipment and is not rebatable even if the consignment is lost or not delivered, then the shipowner is entitled to retain prepaid freight or to sue for it if it has not been paid, unless the vessel never sailed or the goods were lost before shipment commenced or advance freight was due.

The shipper can insure for freight losses if prepaid freight is not recoverable from the shipowner. If the shipper failed to deliver a consignment to the vessel according to a contract, and did not cancel the contract by a specified time, then the shipowner can claim the lost freight from the shipper if the space was not filled. If goods are rerouted in transit on instructions of the shipper, then the shipper is liable for any supplementary freight charges. Also, if the shipowner considers that it is in the interests of the shipper to deliver goods to another destination, possibly because of strikes at the original destination, then the shipper, once again, is responsible for additional freight and other related charges.

The shipowner can take a lien on goods in his possession to cover:

- any unpaid freight due
- any general average contributions
- expenses incurred by the vessel master in protecting the goods.

Bills of lading

In Chapter 10, we looked at the bill of lading as a shipping document, but because it is such a vital instrument in the shipping transaction it bears some additional study and repetition.

The *bill of lading* does three things:

- It confirms the receipt by the shipowner or responsible carrier of the quantity and type of goods bearing specified shipping marks.
- It summarizes the terms and conditions of the carriage contract.
- It acts as a documentary title to the goods, enabling the shipper or owner of the goods to endorse title to other parties, sell goods in transit, and present to banks with other documents in seeking payment under documentary credits.

The creation of the system of bills of lading reportedly dates back to around the sixteenth century. A small individual shipper has no bargaining power to negotiate individual clauses under bills of lading, but the charterer of a ship may be able to do so. The Hague Rules, dating from 1921, and subsequent modifications of those rules, have been adopted by most countries. They clarify certain minimum responsibilities of carriers and certain maximum exemptions. The shipowner is fundamentally responsible for exercising due diligence to provide a seaworthy vessel, to load, handle, stow, carry, keep and care for goods in his custody and to discharge them safely at the destination. He should issue a satisfactory bill of lading to the consignor.

Bills of lading may be issued as *shipped* or *received for shipment*; the latter may not be acceptable under the terms of some documentary credit arrangements since it does not actually show that goods were on board the vessel ready to sail.

Container companies may issue a bill of lading for a container full of merchandise loaded and collected from the shipper's premises, and for delivery intact to the buyer's premises, as *received for shipment*. A bill of lading issued by a container company will contain clauses clearly stating the container company's accepted responsibilities for each stage of the various sections of the journey to the final foreign destination, whether inland or ocean. The shipper should ensure that a container bill of lading is acceptable under the terms of any documentary credit.

If a party charters a vessel and accepts consignments, issuing its own *charter party* bills of lading, once again it must be established with the buyer and the banks involved in documentary credits if the terms and conditions of the charter party bills of lading are acceptable.

Where goods must go beyond the initial destination port to another inland point, a *through bill of lading* can be issued whereby the primary carrier (the shipping line) arranges onward carriage as agent for the shipper or the consignee of the goods but without liability. Transshipment is customarily an additional risk that the owner assumes. Goods will be handed over at the final destination upon presentation of a set of the through bills of lading.

A bank acting for its client (the consignee) can reject a bill of lading as *stale* if the document is presented so late that it may involve the consignee in additional costs resulting from the delay in presentation. In situations such as these, an indemnity may have to be sought from the consignee that he accepts the late documents and releases the bank from liability.

The description of the goods contained in the bill of lading is especially important if the goods are to be sold in transit, because the potential buyer is not in a position to inspect the goods. The bill of lading therefore normally notes the main markings shown on the packaged goods, declared weights, product descriptions, and the apparent condition of the goods when received by the shipping line.

The bank responsible for making payment on the consignee's behalf and the consignee are both entitled to expect the goods to be presented for shipment in perfect condition under a *clean* bill of lading, and not indicating some irregularity under a *claused* bill. Frequently a shipowner will seek to provide himself with some element of protection by using such phrases as 'said to contain' and 'quality and condition unknown'. The shipper is considered as indemnifying the shipowner against inaccuracies in the shipper's declarations, but the consignee may still seek to hold the shipowner liable as a party in any claim involving the description, quantity or quality of goods received.

Many exporters will have encountered situations where a consignee obtained access to or delivery of goods without presenting a true original bill of lading, usually under a bank indemnity that the bill of lading would be presented in due course. This assumes that the bank trusts the importer to accept a draft upon its receipt, if that was the agreed method of payment with the shipper. If the consignee subsequently does not accept or pay the draft, the shipper may enter a claim against the carrier for releasing goods without a bill of lading. Exporters should be wary of countries that have practices that bypass traditional systems in the handling of documents, and should satisfy themselves on the status of importers who are expecting shipment on payment terms other than irrevocable letters of credit.

Alternative shipping documents

With the development of more sophisticated transport modes, such as containerization and air freight, new forms of documents are developing or are used that may not have the same title rights as the ocean bill of lading.

Air waybills act not as title documents but as a consignment note and receipt for goods shipped. To retain some control over merchandise prior to payment, the goods could be consigned to the care of an agreeable correspondent bank for subsequent release to the buyer. However, many banks do not wish such involvement.

Road waybills or CMR (Convention Merchandises Routiers) consignment notes are non-negotiable transport documents used particularly in cross-border European trade, where much of the business is conducted on open account terms.

Rail consignment notes can be controlled in a similar fashion to air waybills. This mode of transport is more common where bulk products are being shipped without the time benefits usually offered by road transport.

The terms of payment and documentary credits need to clarify what shipping documents are acceptable to effect payment. Freight forwarders frequently issue their own *house bills of lading* where they consolidate shipments for several clients, and a *container bill of lading* is usually issued as a receipt by a container company accepting goods at its depot for delivery to a final foreign destination with shipment by several modes of transport.

Carrier's liability

The carrier may have clauses in his contract limiting his liability for loss or damage. Apart from such stipulations, common law would generally hold the carrier responsible unless loss or damage resulted from an act of God, war, inherent vice or shipper's negligence. The shipowner must ensure that his ship is seaworthy, properly manned and equipped, and that the goods are safely stored as per the contract (e.g. refrigerated, stowed below deck). Negligence by the shipowner leaves him open to a claim.

Rules relating to bills of lading will normally excuse the carrier from responsibility for loss or damage resulting from:

* fire, unless the fault of the carrier
* act of God
* acts of war, riot, civil commotion or public enemies
* arrest or seizure under legal process or by others able to prevent delivery because of their status as rulers, people's government, etc.
* strikes or lock-outs
* attempting to save life
* inherent vice in the product or wastage
* insufficient packing or inadequate markings
* accidents at sea
* errors in management or navigation of the vessel
* any other cause not specifically the fault of the carrier.

Although this kind of list makes it look as if the shipowner has no liability, it should be compared with the risks for which insurance coverage can be obtained. Because a shipowner may have a maximum limit on liability fixed by local statutes where goods are not specifically valued, shippers customarily seek to hold a shipowner liable for the value of goods shipped by inserting the value of a consignment on shipping documents, including the bill of lading.

If there is any likelihood of a claim against a carrier, the carriage terms will generally specify a time limit, such as three days after arrival of the vessel, to enter a claim. The shipper should always follow the stated claim deadlines to avoid disputes.

Summary

- A new exporter without the resources of an internal shipping department would benefit from working through a shipping forwarder to handle the carriage of goods and related export documentation.
- The shipper is responsible for delivering goods to the vessel or receiving point by the scheduled date, along with a shipping note describing products, quantities, shipping marks and other relevant data. In return, the shipper should receive a bill of lading acknowledging receipt for custody and shipment.
- The bill of lading acts as a receipt for goods received by the shipowner or carrier, summarizes terms and conditions of carriage, and is a documentary title to goods. If on-carriage is being arranged to an inland destination by the original carrier, a through bill of lading can be issued. The original clean bill of lading is generally sent with other shipping documents and invoices through the banking system if payment is by draft or letter of credit.
- Freight charges are based on factors such as volume, weight and value of a consignment. A shipper can apply for special consideration and rates if basic quotes are excessive in relation to a product's value (i.e. commodity-related products). Shipping conferences fix rates on certain routes and offer shippers incentives to use the conference exclusively. Non-conference lines may be cheaper but have less regular sailing schedules.
- Liability of the shipowner is often very limited under his terms of carriage, but many shipowner's exceptions may be insurable risks under a marine policy.

Carriage considerations checklist

In considering the mode of transport to be used for the carriage of goods the matrix below may help.

	Ocean	Air	Road	Rail	Containers
Space:					
limited		−	−		−
unlimited	+			+	
Cost:					
higher		−	−		
lower	+			+	+
Speed:					
faster		+	+		(1)
slower	−			−	
Security:					
more secure		+	+	+	+
less secure	−				
Damage:					
higher risk	−				
lower risk		+	+	+	+
Documentation:					
more simple		+	+	+	(1)
more complex	−				
Value of goods:					
higher	−	+	+		+
lower	+	−	+	+	+
Temperature controlled	−	−	+	−	+
Container facilities	+	−	+	+	+
Payment receipt (c.i.f.)					
faster		+	+		
slower	−			−	(1)
Transshipment (ease of)	−	−	+	−	+

Notes
+ = an advantage in respect of this factor
− = a disadvantage in respect of this factor
(1) Depends on container mode of transport: road, rail, ocean

PART FOUR

LEGAL AND REGULATORY CONSIDERATIONS

15

Contract Performance

Performing contractual obligations

Your main obligations as exporter under the contract to supply merchandise are to complete the three functions of:

- delivery of the goods
- transferring the property of the goods
- transferring the risk associated with the goods.

These three phases may not all occur at the same time or place, as should be evident within the differences of f.o.b. and c.i.f. contracts.

Delivery normally takes place when the buyer or his agent takes custody and control of the merchandise. In a c & f or c.i.f. contract, that would be when the bills of lading pass to the buyer. Under f.o.b. terms, delivery passes when the goods are loaded at the vessel or other agreed loading point specified in the f.o.b. contract.

Passing of the property in the goods can be a legal problem if the goods are considered as 'unascertained', and the buyer has paid for goods but the seller declares insolvency before delivery. For example, the buyer may have ordered and paid for 500 cartons of canned soup from an exporter. If the exporter has 500 cartons of the specified soup in his store room but declares bankruptcy prior to effecting delivery, the buyer will not be able to claim that stock of soup as his property, because property in the soup has not been transferred and the buyer is left as just another creditor seeking redress.

If the goods are very specific and 'ascertained', the seller may impose conditions under the terms of sale agreed with the buyer whereby the property does not pass until certain conditions are met, for example full payment has been received by the seller. If the seller has drawn a bill of exchange transmitted along with the bill of lading to the buyer through their banks, but the buyer has not yet either paid or accepted the bill of exchange, then property still has not passed to the buyer. For example, the exporter may already have dispatched the specific 500 cartons of soup under a sight or term draft, but the buyer has not accepted or paid the draft because the merchandise is still in transit.

If the buyer declares bankruptcy prior to the draft's acceptance, the soup still belongs to the seller. Alternatively, if the seller declares insolvency prior to accepting the draft, the seller does not have title to the merchandise, and the buyer can seek to dispose of the merchandise to another party.

With an ex-plant, free delivered or strict f.o.b. contract, delivery of the goods to the buyer or carrier occurs when the property in the goods transfers to the buyer, along with the associated risks. The time when risk passes can be very important in the event of subsequent loss or damage before the goods are received or used by the buyer. Risk traditionally passes when property in the goods passes, which, under modern practice and terminology, means when delivery is effected under the agreed terms of sale. For example, in an f.a.s. contract, risk passes when goods are delivered alongside the vessel. In an f.o.b. or c.i.f. contract, risk passes when the goods are placed on the vessel in the care of the shipowner, because the buyer thereafter has recourse against the shipowner in the event of any loss or damage.

If the goods are of a perishable nature, the buyer may seek an undertaking under his supply contract that, even under an f.o.b. contract, the goods are merchantable upon receipt at destination, and may have a claim against the seller for a deteriorated product.

The whole area of international sale of goods laws is both complicated and specialized; this work is not intended to make the exporter his own lawyer, but only to alert him to some potential problems and thereby encourage thoroughness and caution in negotiating terms of sale to ensure that the exporter can comply with his resultant obligations.

Bank guarantees

On occasions you, as the seller, may feel you want a back-up guarantee of payment if you are not shipping under an irrevocable confirmed letter of credit. It is customary in such situations to request a guarantee either from a bank or from a parent or affiliate company of the buyer in whom you have more confidence or feel you may have more strength in recourse, perhaps because the associate company operates from your home market too. In this situation, the back-up guarantee is less strong than a documentary credit, because the guarantor can be called upon to honour the obligation to pay only if default can be proved against the contracting purchaser, and that may take both time and expense to demonstrate or prove in a legal action.

Performance clauses

In the case of supply contracts to government agencies in foreign countries or even in connection with major tenders, especially connected with construction and capital projects, it is common for the seller of goods or services to be requested to provide a *performance bond*, or other guarantee through a third party, such as a bank. Frequently the level of the performance bond may be set at about 10 per cent of the value of goods or services being provided. If you are ever required to put up such a bond, great care must be taken to ensure that the bond cannot be called unjustifiably on pretext, as has been commonly known in many countries. Do seek thorough advice from a bank and lawyer on the terms of a bond. The buyer generally seeks very loose conditions applicable to making a claim under the bond, invariably favourable to the buyer and often extending the validity of the bond way beyond the conclusion of the supply contract. For example, on a construction contract, the buyer may insist on having a 10 per cent performance bond valid for three years after completion of construction as a security that the contractor will make good any problems arising within those three years. However, in practice, the beneficiary of the performance bond could still claim the entire value of the bond one day before its expiry, with little recourse from the supplier. Performance bonds connected with the supply of perishables are also very onerous, for example guaranteeing the quality of cheese supplied under a tender. Who is the arbiter of quality? In some instances a party placing a contract has insisted on such vague terms to a performance bond, including who is the potential beneficiary, that in reality the supplier must consider that the bond will be called on some pretext. (Avoid a 'bearer' bond where the unnamed person with possession of the bond has all rights as a beneficiary!)

Quite apart from specific bonds on performance, the parties to any contract may mutually agree such *penalties* as they find acceptable for non-performance for any reason. Penalties are often imposed for late delivery or completion of a contract, where the buyer can charge a sum or deduct a sum from a contract price for inconvenience caused by late delivery. This is common where the late arrival of certain goods does impose a cost on the buyer, either because it causes a hold-up in other related work, or, if the goods are mainly seasonal and they arrive after the seasonal sales period, the buyer may subsequently have to discount the local prices to sell them off.

Quality certificates

Frequently buyers either require for their own peace of mind, or are required by authorities concerned with regulating aspects of importing to provide, certificates attesting that the merchandise will perform satisfactorily in the manner claimed by the seller and comply with agreed quality or analytical standards. If this is a stipulated term in the contract or the letter of credit, then the seller must comply. The buyer may specify the acceptable manner of compliance or authority that may certify the quality. This may either be the internal production or research department of the supplier, or require an external certificate of analysis from independent experts such as a public analytical laboratory.

Additionally, it may be a stipulation either of the importer or of the importing country that an independent inspection of the merchandise be conducted prior to loading of shipment for the purpose of verifying the nature, quantity or quality of goods and the compliance with the order specifications or invoice details. Several specialist organizations will conduct such impartial surveys, such as: Superintendence Co. Inc., Cargo Superintendents Ltd, or Société Générale de Surveillance.

Warranties

A purchase or supply contract may frequently contain a clause requiring or giving a condition or a warranty, such as a guarantee that the product will perform in a particular function or fashion or that the product will match either samples or specifications. If the contract is so strongly worded that a performance in respect of an aspect amounts to a *condition*, then non-performance is a serious breach of contract, and the buyer can reject the goods and refuse payment. This will leave the supplier with a serious problem if the goods are already in the foreign market before they are subject to inspection or testing.

If the supplier is in breach of a *warranty*, then the buyer is less likely to reject the goods outright, but may take possession and sell them off at the best realizable price, and claim damages from the supplier for any resultant shortfall. A buyer who does not fully exercise his rights to reject goods if a contractual condition is not clearly complied with may subsequently find that he can enforce a claim only for partial damages if he belatedly pursues a claim.

Acceptance and examination of goods

Whether a buyer is purchasing on ex-plant, f.o.b., c.i.f. or any other terms, it must generally be accepted that the buyer cannot practically examine the exported goods until the order is received at his destination warehouse. The contract will normally request 'export packing', and if the supplier complies it may fairly be assumed that the merchandise will be in the same condition when it arrives as when is left the supplier.

The buyer will be unlikely to have access to inspect goods at the customs warehouse, and so will also be exposed to paying import duties prior to having his first inspection opportunity. Therefore, if, at the first point where the buyer may reasonably make an inspection, and on inspection at that point there are elements of non-compliance with the order's terms and conditions, then it is reasonable to assume that the buyer has an enforceable claim not just for the value of the product, but also for all costs incurred up to the time and place of first inspection.

Examination must take place within a reasonable time, which may be specified in local laws at the destination. Alternatively, the seller can, and ideally should, put pressure on the buyer to conduct an early inspection by a stipulation in the contract that the buyer must examine the goods and file any claims by notification to the exporter within, say, eight days after arrival of merchandise at the final delivery point.

Receipt and approval of the goods may be quite independent of 'acceptance'. Goods can be 'approved' without being 'accepted', and vice versa. Goods can be 'received' without being 'accepted'. Goods may be 'accepted' when the buyer indicates he has accepted them, or when he received them and takes any action inconsistent with the seller's ownership rights, such as using them in a further production process or construction, or selling them to another party. Or they may be considered 'accepted' if there has been no official notification to the seller of non-acceptance or rejection within a reasonable period, perhaps specified in the supply contract.

If a buyer chooses to resell goods to another party without inspecting them or notifying the seller of grounds for non-acceptance, and if subsequently the sub-purchaser finds fault with the product, the original buyer's only valid claim against the exporter is on matters of warranty. A buyer may accept or reject less than the full consignment if there is a consignment of mixed goods, but if all the goods are identical on any one shipment then the buyer must accept or reject the entire consignment. If the wrong quantity of merchandise is shipped for any reason, the buyer can accept and pay for only that part of the order actually received.

Rejection of goods

Rejection can be effected only by a buyer specifically communicating back to the seller that he is rejecting a consignment. Both prior to and subsequent to that communication the buyer must not act in any way that is prejudicial to the seller's right to ownership of the rejected merchandise, such as reselling it or using it in further processing (perhaps with the hope that the seller would offer a discount). The buyer is not bound to ship the goods back to the seller or necessarily to accept any cost connected with the goods, but he is obligated to take care of the goods in his custody.

Legal cases have upheld that buyers have two rights or opportunities for rejecting goods:

- first, the right to reject the documents if they are not correct
- second, the right to reject the goods if they do not comply with the purchase contract specifications.

The seller, therefore, should learn from this section that the sale contract should be specific in respect to product specifications, and contain a time limit for the examination and rejection of goods to reduce exposure in any claim. If samples are sent for inspection, ensure that these are very clearly marked so that the buyer may not claim confusion subsequently.

If the buyer rejects the goods and the seller accepts that position, the property in the goods reverts to the seller, and the buyer does not have a lien on the goods for repayment of any prepaid invoices or expenses.

If the supply contract calls for several shipments under separate bills of lading, then each and every shipment can be treated as a separate contract.

It is very common, in the interest of goodwill, for either the buyer or seller to request minor changes from the original order or contract. For example, the buyer may request delayed delivery or an alteration in the product mix in a shipment so that he can balance inventories. Whatever the reason for change, you may wish to check with your in-house lawyer to ensure that you are not waiving any rights to enforce a contract by a voluntary change. Your initial sales contract may include a clause to the effect that any mutually agreed alterations or modifications will not be considered or be a waiver of any duties, rights or obligations enforceable under the original contract. As a contract customarily requires a consideration if the contract is effectively being changed in any respect to protect the rights of either or both parties to treat the modified terms as an enforceable contract, then it may be considered necessary by your lawyers to include a consideration for changes in the terms.

Seller's rights to the property

The seller is generally more exposed to risk than the buyer in an export contract. The goods normally leave his physical control long before he receives payment, and once the goods are en route to the foreign market there is little the exporter can do to stop the movement. The foreign country could introduce exchange control regulations or devalue its currency, or the buyer could declare himself insolvent, sell out to another party, or find himself unable to pay for the goods for a variety of reasons.

The first responsibility of the export manager is to sell on the most secure terms he can obtain, ideally an irrevocable confirmed letter of credit, before parting with ownership of the goods. No number of legal 'ownership' technicalities in international law substitute for discretion, and any legal claim will have a substantial cost factor.

The seller's terms of sale should specifically retain the property of the goods vested in the seller until the seller actually has receipt of all payments due. When the buyer is in default of his obligations to make payments or becomes insolvent before payment is received by the seller or the bank acting for the seller, then the seller is normally entitled to stop the delivery even if the bills of lading are with the buyer or his agent. The exporter should act to stop delivery the moment he learns of any reason to suspect that payment for his goods is at risk.

If the seller has not parted with the goods when he learns that he cannot expect payment because of default or insolvency, the normal first course of action is to take a lien on the goods. If the goods are somewhere in transit between buyer and seller, and not actually in the possession of the buyer, then the seller can exercise his right of *stoppage in transit* only if the buyer is insolvent.

It will normally be the case that goods will have left the seller's possession before any payment default becomes imminent or known. If the goods are sold on credit terms, the seller cannot claim any lien on the property during the credit period except in the event of the buyer's insolvency. If the goods have passed into the hands of agents acting for the buyer, then they cannot be stopped in transit because they are then seen as being in the possession of the buyer. They can be stopped in transit only if they are still in the seller's hands or with a neutral party such as a carrier. Notice of stoppage in transit must be given promptly to the carrier or his agent or principal, and can be effected only if it is reasonable for the carrier to effect stoppage, for example if the shipping line principal or office can actually communicate with the vessel master or agent to prevent delivery.

Even if the bill of lading is made out in the buyer's name, the right of stoppage can still be invoked. If the buyer has acted without the seller's consent in any resale or disposal, the seller can still seek stoppage in transit or a lien, unless the buyer endorsed the bill of lading to a third person for fair consideration, giving the third party a valid claim on the goods.

If the seller manages to exercise a lien to hold the goods or regains possession of them by exercising his rights of stoppage, his contract is not automatically cancelled and he is not free to dispose of the goods unless such a condition was stipulated in the original contract. If the goods are perishable or the seller gives fair notice of his intention to sell to the buyer, and the buyer does not pay for the goods within a reasonable period, then the unpaid seller may reasonably be considered as free to dispose of the goods, minimizing any mutual losses.

Frustration of contracts

There may be occasions where either a seller or a buyer is 'commercially frustrated' in completing a contract because of a major or significant change in circumstances affecting one or both parties. A contract may be frustrated if the specific goods are destroyed prior to delivery. War may break out between the countries of the contracting parties; a ship may sink in transit; an export embargo for political reasons may restrict exports of goods such as capital equipment or defence-related products. Clearly, an event that might have been foreseen at the time of contracting, even if that event was not considered likely, should not give rise to a claim of commercial frustration by either party. For example, a commodity trader can and should expect reasonable fluctuations in market prices for his commodities. However, the magnitude of what may be reasonable may be a matter of debate and arbitration may occasionally be necessary. The trader would normally cover forward for any contracts, but if some external action, such as a major crop failure resulting from pestilence or a government action restricting exports, increases prices to the extent that completion of the contract was not a reasonable act, the seller might claim *frustration*. However, frustration would and should be upheld only if the contract could not subsequently be completed in a reasonable time period. Moreover, if either the buyer's or the seller's government imposes licensing controls or foreign exchange restrictions, the parties must use every reasonable and practical endeavour to obtain licences or foreign exchange before there is any claim of frustration. Closing of a shipping route, such as the Suez or Panama canals, need not be a cause to frustrate performance of a contract, because there are alternative, if more expensive, routings.

If either country requires an import or export licence or any other compliance with a specific rule or regulation restricting or controlling trade, then the parties to any contract should satisfy themselves prior to contracting that each can expect to obtain the licences or otherwise comply with regulations and fulfil the order requirements. If either party did not put a stipulation in the contract, such as 'subject to obtaining all requisite import licences and foreign exchange permits', then the party that fails to obtain the requisite authorities can be held to have absolutely contracted to perform the contract. If there is a 'subject to', and the contract is not performed for a reason relating to that clause, then the non-performing party needs to demonstrate when claiming frustration that every reasonable and timely effort was made to comply with the terms of the contract.

When frustration does occur, one party may have a claim on the other for partial reimbursement of expenses and costs incurred to that point. For example, the seller may be holding a deposit from the buyer, against which he may be entitled to charge any demonstrable expenses or outlays incurred in connection with the particular contract claimed as frustrated. Where a buyer requests that goods be specially made or designed or modified for an export order, it is quite common to request partial payment in the form of an advance deposit, particularly to cover any one-off expenses related to the special order, such as specially designed packaging.

It may be useful for the buyer and seller, prior to contracting, to consider likely factors that could frustrate performance of the contract, and to agree to defining mutual rights and duties relating to these possible problems. A *force majeure* clause may generally define frustrating causes as

riot, civil commotion, acts of war or terrorism, fire, strikes, lock-outs, government restrictions on imports or exports or foreign exchange availability including the imposition of licensing requirements or quotas, accident to plant or machinery, or any other contingency beyond the control of the seller.

The *force majeure* need not specify that the contract is automatically cancelled, but only that it may be cancelled at the option of either or both parties.

Rights, duties, obligations and commitments under an export supply contract are not only more complicated than those applicable to a domestic sales contract, but also more difficult to enforce. The desire of the buyer and seller to perform, and mutually and satisfactorily to resolve actual and potential problems in the interest of goodwill, is important, because both know the difficulties and costs of litigation. But the exporter would be well advised to work with his lawyer to produce standard terms and conditions of sale, and to have these clearly printed on order confirmations and all relevant invoices and sales documents. Prevention is much less costly than resolving a dispute.

Summary

- The exporter has the responsibility to the buyer to deliver the goods and transfer the property and the risks of the goods. The terms of sale may give the seller retention of the property in the goods until payment is received. Risk generally passes when property passes according to the terms of sale, such as when goods are delivered to the named destination under a c.i.f. contract.

- Some contracts require performance bonds to give a buyer assurance that the supplier will honour commitments to provide goods or services or honour warranties. Performance bond conditions should be reviewed by bankers and lawyers in an effort to agree on terms that minimize risk of abuse.

- The sales contract should require prompt inspection and acceptance of goods by the buyer, generally on receipt at his warehouse, or notification of any grounds for non-acceptance. The buyer may have rejection rights if documents are not correct or goods do not meet agreed specifications.

- If it becomes apparent that the buyer will not meet obligations, particularly in respect to payment, the seller may have stoppage in transit rights to prevent delivery, or rights to take a lien on goods.

- Commercial frustration should only be claimed if problems making completion of a contract difficult or impractical could not reasonably have been foreseen, and if subsequent completion of the contract terms is impossible within a reasonable time period. Contracts frequently contain *force majeure* clauses to cover likely disrupting eventualities.

16

Regulation of Trade

In spite of the efforts by governments to encourage and increase international trade, they do tend to place certain barriers in the way. Both exporting and importing nations generate a host of rules and regulations pertaining to the conduct of trade. Those that only involve reporting the numerical details of transactions are a limited inconvenience, and one that can equally benefit the exporter when he comes to do desk research. Export or import licences or quotas or other specific restrictions impose additional rules on the game of international trade, rules that are not interpreted by independent referees. Some of these restrictions are examined here.

Export licences

Many governments impose requirements for export licences for certain categories of goods or for goods intended for certain destinations. These regulations will vary from time to time, and it is essential that you obtain full copies from the government trade or external commerce departments, or through your export trade association. Non-compliance with any special export regulatory requirements will probably carry fines or other penalties, and you, the exporter, will not be able to claim ignorance as an excuse. If forms are required, the appropriate government trade or regulatory department will have these. If an export licence is required, then the forms should be returned and approved prior to your acceptance of a firm order. Otherwise, provision should be made in your offer by a clause such as 'subject to receipt of all necessary export permissions'. Banks and chambers of commerce are also generally very familiar with export documentary requirements, the banks especially as they may have reporting requirements, particularly in respect to foreign receipts of funds.

Typically, goods of a military or defence nature, possibly including communications equipment, may require export licences, along with items of unusual artistic or historic value, such as artwork, antiques, precious metals and jewels. Certain agricultural commodities or live animals may also require export permits.

It is essential that all applications and certification supplied as part of the licence application are accurate and truthful. False applications or breaches of licensing regulations are generally treated very seriously.

The export licence may not be transferable from one party to another, or from one destination to another, and may only be valid for a limited period. In addition, it may restrict transshipment or shipments that the seller has any reason to know or suspect are going to be reshipped to an unapproved destination.

Some regulatory bodies require an export licence application to be made only by a direct manufacturer, and may choose not to grant licences to export forwarding agents or other middlemen. Frequently there will be a requirement for subsequent proof that the merchandise licensed for export went to the specified customer and destination, and was not just held in bond for later onward shipment to unauthorized destinations.

Export quotas

Quotas on exports of a product will normally only be introduced if the authorities see it as a scarce resource, and possibly a non-replaceable resource. A global quota could be allocated, or a specific quota by destination. The quota could be open for any person to make application, or it could be limited to manufacturers or other registered exporters.

Import licences

A great many countries, both developing and highly developed, operate a system of import licensing, particularly for products seen as nonessential to the economy. This is usually a means of controlling imports in relation to several factors:

● the importing country's ability to meet its commitments to provide the necessary foreign exchange for imports in a timely and orderly manner;
● the importing country's assessment of its import priorities (for example, basic foodstuffs will generally be high on the list and luxury items much lower);
● exercising control of legitimate imports in order to identify, reduce or eliminate illicit imports resulting in black market transactions;
● restricting imports of products that are freely available from local sources or production;
● limiting imports of products where there is a local fledgling industry seeking protection in order to build its market and acquire production skills.

Import licences may be issued in any of several ways, depending on the preferences of the issuing authority or the strength of any special interest or lobby group that can influence the method of issue. Some of the most common allocation systems are:

● First come, first served. This literally means that applications are accepted and processed according to the date of receipt in strict order, and licences are allocated accordingly until the quota, if one is in force, is fulfilled.

● Licence issued to historical importers. By this method, long-term special interest groups, such as a wine importers' association, may be recognized, and those importers who were in the business prior to the introduction of a licensing system would be protected by having first access to licences, with an allocation of any quota according to some formula worked out with the importers to give each a quota share relating to the existing level of business in an agreed base year. This system has been strongly operated, and equally strongly protested by potential new importers, by the United States Department of Agriculture in allocating import quotas for cheese and dairy products.

● If licences are issued for the import of any raw materials, then it is common practice to issue the licences only to the legitimate end user of the raw material. This lessens the risk of exploitation of a legitimate user by inflated prices imposed by middlemen. However, if the end user holding licences actually does not utilize his imports or allocation, but has the right to resell any surplus, once again he can take advantage of any competitor who is short of his requirement. Some countries attempt to counter this problem, but all too often with limited success.

Many developing nations that choose to exercise exchange control and import licensing procedures also have a priority list both of importable products and of who obtains the available import licences. Licences are frequently allocated to persons with connections or influence with government officials, and the person who may be allocated the licence as a favour may have no real interest in handling imports. It is of fundamental importance in appointing an importer or agent in any country with any form of control on imports or foreign exchange to satisfy yourself that your appointee can obtain all the necessary permissions governing importation of your products and in sufficient quantity. This may mean you need an importer with demonstrable political connections as well as the financial strength to pay for goods ordered and shipped. In such a situation it is also necessary to form a view of the longevity of your secure operations, because a change in government may mean your favoured importer is no longer favoured. Your agency contract may beneficially contain a clause that the contract may be cancellable if the importer fails to obtain necessary licences within an agreed time period.

If licences are transferable from the original holder to others, then there will probably be a market value to the licence, and persons may be persuaded to sell their licence for a fee or share of profits on goods imported. If licences are transferable under any legal arrangement, then both the exporter and importer should establish who holds licences and for what values or volumes so that, if business develops, attempts may be made to 'purchase' additional licences.

Other rules may also apply to the issue of licences or exchange control, such as limiting an application in one year to the actual value or volume allocated or imported in a previous year. If any rules such as that operate, then a licence holder, even if he has the right to transfer a licence, in reality will want imports in his name so that he has the right to re-apply the following year.

Import quotas

In general, allocation of quotas and licences go together, and much of the preceding section applies. If a quota is going to be issued, it is better for the exporter that it be issued to specific persons or companies, with whom the exporter may then seek to develop a good working relationship to supply a quota holder's requirements. However, occasionally a situation arises where a global quota is allocated, and the only rule is that anyone may import against the quota on a first come, first served basis. This system has been known to result in vessels lined up to off-load before a quota is filled; once it is filled, the remaining goods are refused entry, with someone (the exporter) bearing the costs of shipping the merchandise back home. Exporters really should avoid participating in such quota races, and limit activity to situations where the risks are calculable, such as where a specific importer has a known quota or licence, and fulfilling it comes down to good old-fashioned price and quality competition matched by prompt delivery.

Exchange control

Either or both the exporting and importing nation may have regulations pertaining to exchange control.

The *exporting* nation is not likely to discourage exports, except of scarce resources, but may require that:

● all foreign earnings be reported

- foreign exchange earnings be 'exchanged' at official banks and at official exchange rates
- no foreign exchange may be held in offshore accounts.

Exchange control in the exporting country also helps authorities ensure that exports are being paid for in a timely fashion according to contractual payment terms. Authorities may even limit the time period of payment, say to less than 180 days, to balance inflows of foreign exchange with outflows required for imports. Additionally, the central bank of the exporting nation may be seeking to satisfy itself that any reported commissions and fees to foreign concerns are strictly for legitimately supplied services, and not just a ruse to bank funds offshore in a stronger currency.

Exchange control in the *importing* country will aid in restricting the importing nation's indebtedness, and reduce the volatility of exchange rates. Frequently regulations may operate that require the importer to deposit a portion of the value of any specific licence issued or pro forma invoice, so that the central bank can aid in controlling the money supply by ensuring that the importer is not entirely dependent on foreign credit sources for expansion. The length of credit terms or the portion of the invoice value that may be on extended terms may also be limited. Some nations impose regulations that, prior to importing certain goods, the importer must either pay by letter of credit or deposit part or all of the full invoice value in the banking system, thereby restricting to some degree increases in the supply of international credit putting pressures on the domestic money markets.

Exchange control and licensing requirements, and the presentation of acceptable import authorizations or documentation to customs authorities, may also help reduce illegal imports or illegal currency transactions in a country that does not have strong domestic currency, and that needs strict control of imports and exchange transactions.

Customs controls and reporting

Most exporting nations have very strict regulations on reporting exports by volume, value, product type and description, and destination, with penalties for false declarations or non-compliance with the rules. The exporter requiring specific information on reporting procedures and documentation for his products should contact initially the local office of the customs authorities, whose personnel are always most cooperative, especially in aiding the new exporter to understand the procedures and practices. In the USA, a Shipper's Export Declaration must be completed and filed with customs. In the UK, Customs and Excise forms C273(1) and C273(4) may suffice.

Exporting customs authorities will normally require information covering the value of the consignment, and the product description or specific formulation or composition of a product if it is open to interpretation as to which customs category the export could be allocated. Importers will often ask the exporter for the customs category under such conventions as the Brussels Tariff Nomenclature, so that the importer may assess duties or licensing requirements prior to placing an order. The exporting customs can provide full lists of the various classifications, and may assist in deciding which is a relevant reporting category if they are provided with a sample and formulation for any product. Product descriptions on all documentation should match up with each other and with product labelling, and the export declaration will require the shipper to note the appropriate export numerical classification agreed with customs (such as the Schedule B number from the 'Statistical Classification of Domestic and Foreign Commodities Exported from the United States').

The customs authorities of the importing nation have the principal duties of ensuring that:

●   import duties and taxes are paid at prescribed levels
●   requisite licences and permits are correctly available and applicable to the specific consignment
●   merchandise reported on the shipping documents is the actual merchandise in the consignments, i.e. that contraband or goods of more value than those on the invoice are not contained in the consignment, possibly in fake packaging.

If there is a *duty drawback* system in the exporting country applicable to the element of a formula or consignment that is re-exported, then the exporting customs records by category and product formulation will be supporting evidence for the exporter to reclaim previously paid duties. Similarly, if there are any other systems of subsidy on certain categories of exports, the export customs documentation will provide the basis of proving a claim for reimbursement under the export subsidy programme operated in the exporting nation, for example with system of subsidies operated within the European Economic Community for various agricultural products.

In most instances the product classifications of the exporting and importing nations used on their respective customs declarations will match if the two countries use standard nomenclatures such as the Brussels Tariff Nomenclature. The USA has developed its own classification system, but this can be cross-referenced to the major international systems in lists available either from the customs authorities or from the department of commerce offices in major cities. The exporter should obtain these cross-reference sheets so that he is familiar with both major nomenclatures, particularly in reference to codes applicable to his own products.

Goods that are held in a *BONDED* warehouse by either an exporter or importer may require different documentation. It is a common practice to hold goods in a bonded customs warehouse if the level of import duties or other excise taxes is high in relation to the value of goods. The costs of storage may be less than the forgone interest on the duty outlay, or the importer may simply not have funds to pay all duties and taxes at one time, preferring to make payments as withdrawals are made relating to the market sales levels. Liquor is an instance where most importers leave their imports in bond until actually needed for imminent sale.

It is a constant frustration to exporters that they often need to comply with the customs documentation procedures even for smallish samples dispatched to potential customers. In fact, the recipient of the samples historically has much more trouble clearing small volumes of samples through customs, especially if the goods normally required an import licence. Therefore, before complying with a foreign sample request, do establish with the recipient the best method of dispatch to minimize delays in clearing through customs and to reduce the resultant paperwork. Very often the importer will advise that parcel post is quicker than air freight for samples because the customs authorities attached to the post office are more willing to accept the straightforward exporter's declaration of 'samples for research evaluation – no commercial value'.

Goods shipped on a *through bill of lading* are normally treated as in transit, and may be held in bonded warehouses or other specially designated areas until shipped on to the ultimate destination. They do not normally incur any import duties or related taxes at the transit points so long as no customs import entries are filed. Control of goods in transit is very strict to ensure that there is no tampering with the product or falsification, and containers are normally custom-sealed.

Sales and value added taxes

More and more countries are developing systems of either sales or value added taxes. On the other hand, goods exported do not normally have to pay the domestic taxes operating in the exporting nation or, if these have been prepaid, then claims for relevant rebates may be filed according to the local practice and procedures. Without a system of rebates, the exporter would be at a competitive price disadvantage with exporters quoting from countries without a sales or value added tax structure.

The need to report exports or file claims for rebates will again add to the administrative burden of the exporter, or, more specifically, his shipping department. However, a little practice in the completion of the forms, and the introduction of a standard administrative system to prepare claims as each shipment is effected, will aid in avoiding the task becoming a problem, which often happens if preparation of claims is left until a much later time, when all the relevant documents must be retrieved from files. As the department can become computerized, it is an easy matter to prepare a program that calculates the relevant rebates relating to each formulation and shipment. It may be that the procedures specify that only a certain group can file for rebates, for example manufacturers rather than export traders (since the manufacturer is the person who actually used the taxable ingredients). Alternatively, there may be a registration procedure, as with the European dairy exporters, whereby a licensed trader can register to be eligible to file export subsidy claims. The exporter should ensure that he has filed any registrations applicable to him subsequently being eligible for any export rebates or subsidies, and, as previously mentioned, the export customs entry documentation will normally be a requisite in filing such claims.

Some importing nations require a proof of *FAIR MARKET VALUE* to establish that the product is not being dumped cheaply in their market, thereby undercutting local producers. In such situations the exporter should seek the authorized certification to be exclusive of any local sales taxes. The importing nation may even have a system of charging duties on the basis not of the actual invoiced value, but of the exporting nation's fair market or other value. This is a practice adopted by some nations that have ongoing problems of either under-invoicing, in order to pay lower duty, or smuggling. Indonesia is a case in point. While not having other exchange control restrictions at that time, she did have high import duties with the aim of limiting imports, and was for many years plagued with false documentation on re-exports of products from neighbouring Singapore. Their answer to the under-invoicing (where the importer really paid not just the face value of the invoice included with the consignment, but also the requisite difference against a separate invoice) was to establish duties based upon arbitrary sales values of similar products on the Singapore wholesale market. This is a cumbersome system, but may be encountered from time to time in developing nations.

Proof of origin

The major reasons why an importing nation may require *proof of origin of merchandise are*:

- if there are any systems of preferential tariffs operating in favour of certain nations, such as the British Commonwealth preferential treatment of goods imported from other member nations, and those operated within the Association of South East Asia Nations or the Latin American Free Trade Association, and other regional political trade associations;
- where there are embargoes on trading with certain nations for political reasons; and
- where there are health restrictions on imports from certain sources, say because of fears of pestilence, including foot and mouth disease with cattle, associated with agricultural imports from a number of sources. In fact, products from sources not considered free of such risk will normally not be importable.

Under a preferential tariff system, goods that are simply re-exported, or where a large part of the components were from outside the region or association treated preferentially, may not benefit from application of the preferential import tariffs at the importing nation's customs, even though such goods may still be eligible for duty drawbacks in the exporting nation.

Once again, all declarations in certificates of origin must be accurate in all respects because they have commercial and legal significance in the importing nation. Usually a certificate of origin must be certified by an independent office, such as the local consular services of the importing nation, or a chamber of commerce may be authorized to sign certificates.

In addition, some importing nations request other certification under such headings as *certificates of free sale*, which are intended to show that the products are generally acceptable as safe and freely available in the exporting nation, and not an inferior product being 'dumped' on the importing nation.

Government involvement in regulating the flow, volume, value and nature of goods traded for export or import will not suddenly disappear; indeed, the trend has been towards more rather than less regulation, to the frustration of exporters. Therefore, in your role as export manager, you must not only become familiar with the applicable rules and regulations of all the countries with which you are trading, but also understand the interpretations put upon regulations. It is the manner of interpretation of rules and regulations that often enables trade to take place even in difficult circumstances. For example, if imports from country A to country B are restricted, could goods be first sold to a party in country C for re-export? That will depend on how imports from country C are restricted (e.g. will the exporter in country C have to show certificates of origin). Once again, to operate within the rules and regulations yet use them to your advantage wherever possible, flexibility and adaptability are key attributes in successful exporting.

Summary

● Government regulation of international trade has tended to grow rather than lessen. Exporters generally are required to complete documents for their customs authorities identifying many aspects of the export transaction, such as the 'Shipper's Export Declaration' required by US customs on exports.

● Certain classes of goods may require export licences, or export quotas may apply to certain scarce or valuable resources. Exporters may be required to report all foreign earnings and remit them into the domestic banking system.

● Exporters may also be entitled to duty drawbacks or the refund of prepaid sales or value added taxes on goods subsequently exported, and export documentation generally forms the basis for any rebate claim, including the subsidies on agricultural exports from the European Economic Community.

● Importers often require import licences to effect importation, and imports of some or all classes of goods may be subject to quotas. The exporter needs to be satisfied that his importer has access to all necessary permits to effect importation, and should be familiar with the licensing and control procedures of foreign markets.

● Less developed nations are particularly prone to using foreign exchange controls as a way of limiting imports of goods seen as non-essential, allocating scarce foreign exchange according to an internal import priority list.

● Importing nations may also require additional certification, such as of fair market value or free sale in the exporting country, or proof of origin, to aid in ascertaining that inferior or cheaper products are not being dumped or to assess any preferential import tariffs on goods from certain sources.

17

Industrial Property Protection

Protection of your company's trademarks, patents and copyrights is an essential step in preparing for international business opportunities. These may often be assets with vast immeasurable monetary and intangible non-monetary values. An internationally established and respected brand name should generally be protected in such markets as you already sell into or expect to sell into, or where there is a risk of another party registering and using your name. Similarly, patents on processes or designs should be protected in markets where you may aspire to license your product or know-how, or where there is a risk of a competitor applying for the patent, and copyright protection should be sought where music, films, literary and other creative works are concerned.

Such protection may not be possible or necessary if you are selling a bulk commodity or generic products such as industrial construction materials, but it is advisable for most consumer branded products or exclusive processes or technology. Occasionally a company may take the position that their process is better not patented as that will give competitors more information than they are otherwise likely to obtain. That is more likely to be the case with an exclusive formulation or processing technique rather than design of equipment.

Registration of patents and trademarks should advisably be in the name of the original owner, rather than a local agent, representative, associate company or licensee. It may then be sub-licensed to a foreign subsidiary or affiliate or licensee, giving maximum protection to the rights of the registrant.

Patents

Traditionally a patent is protected only in the territory where the letters patent has been filed and accepted. Therefore, separate protection by the necessary filing of registration documents is required for any country where it is felt protection may be required for either marketing or defensive purposes. Various degrees of protection are available, depending on whether a patent is applied for to protect an original invention or process, or whether protection for a design or technical improvement is being sought.

It is usual to seek the help of a specialist patent and trademark lawyer to assist in assessing the elements of a design or process that may be unique and protectable because of the degree of originality. Such specialist lawyers will normally have access to a worldwide network of associates to handle the registration mechanics of foreign patents and trademarks, estimate the likely fees and other costs, and organize a professional search of existing registrations in the territory that might conflict.

Under guidelines of an International Convention for the Protection of Industrial Property, a person filing in one territory may have a priority right in filing in another territory participating in the Convention and accepting its guidelines, but such a priority period normally only extends for one year from the date of application in the original territory. Some countries have rules that limit patent applications if there is publication of data or production of items prior to filing for the protection. Others allow for filing within a period of, say, one year from first publication or production or sale of the item, as in the United States. The one-year 'breathing space' during which a party can file a patent application in other countries after first filing in the home country gives the inventor or marketer time to assess the real commercial potential in markets before rushing off on an expensive mass registration process.

Apart from the rights and protection provided by the various patent conventions, major industrial countries have occasionally entered into bilateral agreements with other countries not members of an existing convention. Also, within Europe the members of the European Common Market have been moving away from the system of separate registrations in each member state to introducing a registration process covering the entire European Common Market.

Some eighty countries ratified the original International Convention for the Protection of Industrial Property of 1883 and the subsequent revisions. This Convention broadly offers the following protection:

● All persons and businesses having residence or commercial establishments in a country have the same rights as nationals without discrimination.
● Within twelve months of filing an application in one convention country, a business or person has priority to file applications in other convention countries; the priority date is the first date of application in the original country where an application was filed.
● A 'grace' period is granted for the payment of renewal fees by original registrants.

● Temporary protection may be granted to patentable inventions exhibited or demonstrated at international shows.

The right to apply for a patent rests either with the inventor or with the party who can claim ownership, such as an employer if the invention was made specifically in relation to the terms of employment. The patent application must give detailed specifications, and professional advice really is essential in filing for patent protection in order to reduce the risk of other parties subsequently 'designing round' the product or process. Because processing of patent applications takes so long, frequently several years, there is always the danger that another similar patent application is in the pipeline ahead of yours.

An invention or process not capable of being industrially exploited is unlikely to be patentable. Products or processes that are considered not novel or obvious, or where the specifications are inadequate, may not be patentable.

Many companies are nervous about patenting new processes that give them a technological lead over competitors because filing of the specification may simply serve to alert the competitors of research approaches to be considered to 'design round' the patent. Whilst a patent can be exploited by a licence, a product or process does not need to be patented for licences to be granted or sold. Many licensing arrangements nowadays are actually only licensing a system of conducting business – the 'business format' franchises offered by many small business franchisors.

Quite apart from the protection afforded to a design, product or process by a patent, the inventor may have other more basic copyright protection of his plans, drawings, designs and specifications.

Trademarks

As incomes around the world rise and more people have the opportunity to visit other countries for business or pleasure purposes, so the value of international trademarks becomes more apparent to the marketing men. Travellers may feel more secure buying a product they are familiar with from back home, and the youth of the world may wish to consume or wear the fashionable products seen in films and other international media. There has been much opposition in some developing countries to the spread of western youth culture to their own youth, but it is a trend that has not yet lost momentum.

Prior use of a trademark in a territory is often taken as giving a priority claim to protection and registration. In the United States, the user of a mark in one particular state may have protection without registration within that state by demonstrating an active sales history prior to another user of the same trademark or name offering the product for sale in the particular state. If priority of use is the accepted criterion in any market, and the exporter can demonstrate the first usage and regular use for a product freely sold in the market, he may have a basis for protection against infringement, even if no formal application for a registration is made.

In other countries, the basis for protection and ownership is the first application to register the mark. It is usual for trademark registrants to be required to prove continuing use to register and keep a trademark. Ownership may be based on uncontested use for a given period.

The system of giving a registration to the first applicant for a mark has proved detrimental to some multinational corporations with international brand names, who find a local person or company has already filed for their trademark in any market. The exporter could be forced to negotiate an agreement to use what he viewed as his own mark, or to find another brand identity that may take more time to develop. However, although it puts more cost on companies, this system does force the export and international operatives in corporations seriously to assess where they may expect to conduct business and sales over the foreseeable future, and develop with their trademark and patent lawyers an active approach to protecting such industrial property as trademarks and patents.

Both in the United States and in the United Kingdom the favoured system is one where ownership is based on uncontested use and registration for a period of time. Use of an unregistered mark by one party does become an obstacle to another party subsequently seeking a registration of the same mark.

It may be possible to seek registration for a mark purely for use in export markets, if no other party can show a prior proprietary right to that mark for those export markets.

The International Convention for the Protection of Industrial Property affords protection in the same manner as for patents, including:

- the right to equal treatment with residents and nationals in the foreign country without discrimination in registering and protecting trademarks;
- a six-month priority period after first registering in the home country to file for registration in the foreign country;
- the proprietor of a registration in one convention country in principal being able to seek the same protection in other covention countries in the registration's original form;
- registration not being cancelled for non-use until a reasonable time period has elapsed and a defence may be made of special circumstances preventing use;

- renewal in one convention country not obligating the mark's proprietor to renew the mark in other convention countries; and
- the possibility of claiming in another convention country that if registration were granted to another party it would cause real confusion with a similar or the same mark previously registered or used in a different convention country. Such a claim may have time limitations to proceed with a claim or attempt to block the foreign registration attempt.

Where a 'user agreement' is arranged in a foreign market, care must be taken over shipments into that market by registered users or other exporters in other markets, especially where the parallel imports are through a party other than the registered user. Proper arrangements that comply with local procedures and practice are essential to avoid invalidating a trademark or user agreement in the importing market. As a general guideline, where goods of the same brand or trademark are being imported from different sources, it is better for all imports to go through one registered user, but this can often only be practically organized if all the sources are affiliated.

I should mention in passing the general principles of what may be registerable and some potential problems. For a trademark to be registerable it must be distinctive and used in the course of trade and not be misleading. Countries may differ on what they will accept for registration. Most trademarks used as brand names are registerable because they are 'invented' words and not proper nouns, such as names of persons or places, or simply descriptive words or phrases.

Trade mark applicants traditionally seek registration for use in as many classes of goods as they can practically hope to justify, and wait for other parties to oppose registration in any particular class (perhaps for lack of use) subsequently. The applicant should be the person or company planning to use the mark. Applications may be opposed or rejected on the grounds of similarity or confusion with another mark, or because the mark or design is not sufficiently distinctive or original. If there are subsequent changes in ownership of the company that has registered trademarks and patents, then the new owners need to ensure that the acquisition includes the transfer of ownership of all such industrial property rights.

In some markets, situations may arise where the local population find a particular brand name difficult to pronounce, and give the product some locally acceptable name, which may perhaps be descriptive. The exporter should ensure that his trademark lawyer is aware of this and that consideration be given to potential registration of the 'local' product name as a protective measure. Also, the trademark owner needs to avoid risking the loss of a distinctive name as a registerable mark if that name becomes adopted as a common name for all similar products in the local vocabulary.

Copyright

This is perhaps the most difficult area of industrial property to seek to protect in an international context, probably because it is most obviously abused by infringements. Under traditional British practice, copyright in an artistic work is effective from the time the work is produced, not necessarily published, and for fifty years after the author's death. Most countries have basically similar protection. A 'work' need not be of demonstrable merit, but purely be the result of the originator's own effort and skill in producing something tangible. (An idea is not copyrighted.)

Generally copyright applies to such works as books, plays, poems and any other literary effort, music, songs, films and, nowadays, video games and computer software. Protectable works are usually considered as having artistic merit, skill and originality, and the criteria may be seen as rather open to subjective interpretation. Many reproductions may be legitimate and not infringements if they are demonstrably for personal use or research purposes. But work copied without the owner's permission for non-legitimate purposes will generally be seen as an infringement. Industrial designs belonging to companies may in Britain have at least fifteen years of initial protection.

Works may be protected internationally in countries that are signatories to copyright convention treaties under similar terms of protection offered to local originators. In seeking to enforce copyrights internationally, the exporter should bear in mind that he may have cause for action against both the actual persons making the copies and any persons who commission or knowingly market the copies. But it will be harder to enforce action against end users or distributors who unknowingly have purchased or used illegal copies, except perhaps by having any such copies that may be recovered destroyed.

As copyrights are separately protectable in each country, it could be that a legitimate copy in one country may be breaching the copyright elsewhere if it is sold into a market where another party has a right such as a licence on the copyright.

Under copyright laws, the benefit of protection is not so much to prevent others using the work as to ensure that the originator receives income in the form of royalties as his reward for his creation. Compliance with local market copyright protection procedures will make enforcement and control over potential royalty earning that much easier. Some countries, such as the United States, may wish a copyrighted work to be registered, and the appropriate lawyer should advise you on your own specific protection programme, particularly if you are likely to want to grant any licences in connection with copyrighted works. A copyright licence goes beyond just giving permission to use or quote a work or to perform a play, and may very likely transfer certain property rights in a specific market.

Infringements

If a trademark or patent is infringed, the infringer risks a suit for damages and an injunction to prevent further use or abuse of the registered mark, design or process. Even if the alternative design or mark is not identical to the registered and protected item, there may be a case of 'passing off'.

Most exporters of branded products to foreign markets have seen cases of copies based on their trademark or concept. Sometimes the forgery is very poor, and some persons may say there could be no confusion. From the marketing man's viewpoint, any copy can cause confusion and risk the loss of customers who become uncertain over quality. Copies particularly develop in those countries with less enforcement of some aspects of commercial law, and where they are developing an industrial base mostly of small, labour-intensive entrepreneurially owned manufacturers. The Orient is full of copies of designer leather accessories, watches and electrical sundries. Even books have been copied in total, ignoring international copyright laws.

The similarity between the real and fake item may be in such general matters as overall impact or image, pack shape or colour, or a local name in similar style to the foreign name, which causes confusion with persons of limited literacy. In a 'passing off' case it is not always necessary to prove either that fraud did take place or that particular consumers were deceived, but that deception might result.

The exporter must rely heavily on his agent or distributor to police the market for copies, and to try to identify the producer and distributor of the forgeries or other misrepresentations. Frequently exporters have found that a visit from the exporter's agent to the infringer can help in warning them of an awareness of their activities. Sometimes the copies will stop if the infringer fears legal recourse.

Defending a trademark or suing to prevent infringement in a foreign market is both costly and time-consuming, and the best approach is a thorough programme of trademark, patent and copyright protection, with an automatic system to alert you to renewals and defence procedures such as making regular deliveries and sales of registered items to avoid a claim of non-use. Your distributor will generally cooperate by receiving occasional small consignments even of products he does not normally distribute if that helps to demonstrate commercial activity.

The exporter should build a file record of all marks observed on his travels that closely resemble his, on both similar and different product categories. He should occasionally review his findings with the trademark lawyer in case of potential problems.

In many countries, ownership of a mark is limited to a particular product category. In the United Kingdom, for example, some thirty-four product categories are distinguished; the same name can be applied to different products in different categories, and the mark owned by different manufacturers. Once a mark is registered, its use must generally be demonstrated, and an unused mark may be protested by another party if it is blocking their use. As mentioned above, it is necessary, therefore, to introduce a programme to demonstrate occasional shipments and sales.

Licensing patents and trademarks

A proprietor of a trademark or patent may license its use to a franchisee in exchange for fees, royalties or other considerations. This is becoming particularly common with lower-value consumer items, such as beverages and fast foods, that would not bear the shipping costs or delays. A licence can also be issued to a subsidiary of a parent multinational corporation; in fact, the parent company is advised to own all its international marks in the parent's name and to create such sub-licence or 'user' agreements with associates, affiliates and joint venture partnerships in order to retain full control of the use of the mark or design. The registered user may have rights to defend the marks against local infringement. If you plan to license any trademarks or patents, then close attention to your registrations is fundamental for an international brand, because without the registered trademark you may have little of commercial value for either you or your franchisee to exploit.

To plan a realistic trademark registration programme, the exporter must realistically assess where he may expect to sell the product in the foreseeable future or have other sound reasons to seek protection. Then he should work through his trademark lawyer to commence the filing of registrations – but always remembering that with each registration come legal costs and the need to support an application at some time with proof of usage.

Patent and trademark law may seem rather complicated, but it is an area in which the exporter may have frequent cause for concern, either because of potential infringements or because of the need to obtain registrations. I would recommend that the reader not become his own lawyer but sit down with the company patent and trademark lawyer and obtain an understanding of the principles. In addition, he could beneficially obtain and read a copy of his national laws on the subject to expand on this summary chapter (In the USA see International Patent Act, U.S. Code 1964 Title 35, Section 102, and International Trademarks Act, U.S. Code 1964 Title 15, Sections 1057, 1091, 1092, 1111–1114, 1117, 1125, 1126.) (In the U.K. see: Patents Act 1977 Chapter 37; Copyright Act 1956 Chapter 74; and Application of Trade Marks Act 1938, and the Trade Marks (Amendment) Act 1984 Chapter 19. All are available through Her Majesty's Stationery Office.)

Summary

- Patents, trademarks and copyrights may have both monetary and non-monetary value, and should be protected at least by registration in those markets where either the item will be marketed or local conditions suggest that there is a likelihood of copies being produced that could disrupt marketing plans.
- Separate patent and trademark registrations are generally required in each market, but international patent and trademark conventions recognize a priority to file for registration in foreign markets within prescribed time limits from first application at home or first publication of data.
- Trademarks of internationally known products have great commercial value, and should be aggressively protected from infringement by recourse to legal remedies when necessary. Copies of simple-to-produce products are very common in some regions.
- Patents and trademarks registered in the exporting company's name may subsequently be licensed or franchised to foreign parties to develop markets where direct product export is not commercially practical.

18

Legislation, Litigation and Arbitration

An exporter and his merchandise are not excused from controls, laws, rules and regulations in either the domestic or the foreign country just because the merchandise crosses national boundaries.

Licences

Certain classes of goods will require an export licence, as discussed in Chapter 16, particularly if they relate to defence industries or scarce resources. The exporting nation may insist on an export licence for all goods or only those of certain categories that are destined to certain countries being the subject of export licences. Trade embargoes and sanctions imposed by the government will be monitored and enforced, and must be complied with by exporters. Products that might particularly aid in the industrial development of an antagonistic nation may be subject to export restrictions, either to that one destination and its allies and client states, or to any middleman who might transship goods. In the case of such products, the regulating export licence agency may require clear proof of the identity of the final owner, user and beneficiary of the products or services.

If the importing nation requires import licences for all or certain classes of merchandise, then the exporter should ensure that his customer has such valid documents prior to shipment. He may risk confiscation of goods or other sanctions at the destination or have problems obtaining payment.

The exporter should establish the licensing regulations of both countries, and ensure compliance with them.

International corruption

In many developing nations, to obtain business, especially government-related or approved contracts, it is necessary to have the right contacts, frequently connected with government departments and senior officials. Direct bribery has been a common and accepted practice in many nations to smooth the way to major contracts that involve multinational corporations and local officials. Incentives have been provided for such a range of services as approving major construction bids to just clearing a container promptly through a congested port. Pressure has grown within the major western countries to cease such practices used to obtain or retain foreign business. It has been considered socially unacceptable to encourage the accumulation of vast wealth by a few persons in power in nations that generally have intense poverty and inequality of distribution of wealth. This direct or indirect provision of benefits for favours received or promised is perhaps seen as the unacceptable face of capitalism, and may even contribute to the idealistic and socialistic oppositions to established power groups in some nations.

Governments such as those of the United States have tended to legislate against the provision of benefits to individuals, particularly those in government service in foreign nations, under threat of severe penalties on companies and individuals. The USA introduced and enforced the Foreign Corrupt Practices Act in the late 1970s and into the 1980s, with many senior industrialists arguing that the result was losing major contracts to other more liberal nations. European governments have tended to be less inclined to restrictive legislation.

While on the one hand it may be hard or impossible to change the cultural traits of officials seeking advantage in any nation, the international business executive must comply with the laws in both his own and the foreign nation in respect of conferring benefits upon individuals. Some exporters of goods and services have found that they were able satisfactorily to establish the necessary relationships by appointing or using the services of lobbyists, lawyers or other legitimate middleman services in the foreign market.

Restrictive practices

Many countries have legislation designed to prevent domestic monopolies or restrictive trade practices, such as price fixing or establishing geographical areas of exclusive influence. The exporter should establish the current state of legislation that may affect international trade, such as limiting rights of exporters to agree to export pricing structures, or export conditions of sale, or agreements to divide the world into mutually exclusive spheres of influence or trade.

Agreements that provide for exclusive selling, distribution or marketing rights in foreign markets are not normally in breach of domestic regulations. However, before granting any foreign party any special or exclusive rights in respect of products or markets, it is necessary to check with lawyers in that country about any future restrictions that the agreement may impose on the exporter's rights. For example, a number of countries require that, in the event of termination, a distributor or sales agent is entitled to compensation, which may include ongoing sales commissions from sales to customers he initially introduced to the principal, or compensation for other lost earnings or potential earnings, or for investments required to be made by the principal for the distribution of the products.

Local market laws may also limit the degree of exclusivity the principal can demand in an agency or distribution agreement. While it might be acceptable to restrict an agent not to represent any similar product directly competing with that of the principal (say, another electric toaster), it may not be acceptable to restrict the agent not to represent any other items in the general product category (say, electrical household goods).

Resale price maintenance agreements are commonly considered illegal if operating within a country, but export pricing agreements may not be included in such legislation. Manufacturers may, in any event, be able to demonstrate that exports would suffer without such cooperation, in either a formal or informal agreement. However, in the foreign market there may also be laws involving price-fixing agreements that the importers might be subject to.

Free trade agreements between countries may also include restrictions on monopolies or price fixing or other restrictive practices in trade between parties to the free trade agreement. Government trade departments will be able to advise on such matters. The old European Free Trade Association agreement in Europe contained provisions for governments to annul agreements offending the terms of the free trade agreement that ruled against restrictive practices.

The theory of trade within the European Economic Community has been that differences in offer price at the border should reflect only differences in cost structures, possibly related to marketing and distribution, local sales taxes or other distinguishable factors. However, there have been a number of complaints involving the same product being sold in two EEC countries at vastly different prices. For example, British customers for Jaguar automobiles found that they could order the domestic model in Belgium from the importer there, and return it to England tax and duty paid at less than the British market price. Of course, the manufacturer could respond that perhaps the Belgian distribution and marketing costs were lower, or simply avoid meeting orders through Belgium for the domestic model, but would be unlikely to admit that export sales were possibly on a marginally costed basis.

The European Economic Community does not sanction agreements that are likely to restrict trade. Such agreements would include:

● direct and indirect price-fixing agreements
● arbitrary division of the markets into exclusive spheres of influence for individual manufacturers

- supplying parties on unequal terms for equivalent products, putting some parties at a competitive disadvantage
- limiting or controlling of production, technical development, investment, or markets
- market sharing or sharing of supply sources, possibly to the detriment of other suppliers.

Laws governing contract and performance

Jurisdiction Since the agency or distribution contract between the buyer and seller may involve the laws of two countries, and any dispute may present serious difficulties in court litigation and resolution, avoidance of serious conflict is the first rule. Although a contract may state that the laws of one or other country will apply to litigation, that in itself may become an issue of dispute consequent upon any other disagreement, and a court in one country cannot practically expect to understand and interpret the laws of another.

Attempts to reduce conflict have been made in establishing Uniform Laws of International Sales. Generally a contract for sale of goods is governed by the laws of the country designated to hear disputes according to the contract. If no country is designated, then the 1955 Hague Convention recommended that the laws in effect in the country of domicile of the seller be used, unless the order was specifically received and accepted in the buyer's country, in which case a dispute should be heard in and according to the laws in the buyer's place of domicile.

Since there is no overriding international agreement on laws of trade, an agreement between parties should not only identify what laws will apply but establish the enforceability of any decision.

In many nations of the world the exporter will feel disadvantaged in any attempt to sue a national, who will possibly have local influence and connections and succeed in delaying proceedings through legal manoeuvres. That is a reason why many exporters seek to have their contracts of sale or agency interpretable by and under the jurisdiction of domestic courts. The clause in the agreement governing which laws should apply should clearly cover both the formation of the contract and all performance under it. Problems could arise if one part of an agreement is governed by one nation's laws, and another part or other clauses by a second nation's laws. In this situation, one or other nation's authorities might seek to demonstrate that more than a normal commercial interest is operating in the agreement, and perhaps there is an attempt to evade the law of one nation. Clauses should not be included in an agreement that are not in compliance with the laws of either country.

Disputes   Most agency and distribution agreements, and many other agreements of an international nature, have a clause or section dealing with arbitration, where parties to the contract seek to resolve a dispute without resort to litigation. That clause will normally show where and how such arbitration should take place, including reference to any standard rules of arbitration of a national or international association, such as an international chamber of commerce. If there is no clause to the contrary, then it might reasonably be concluded that the parties were accepting the laws of the country where arbitration was accepted to take place to apply to the overall contract, unless the arbitration was to take place in a third country purely for mutual convenience.

Illegal contractual terms

Many countries will not enforce a contract or contractual terms in the event of a suit where the court identifies that terms of the contract were contrary to the laws of one or other country. For example, the terms of the contract, perhaps relating to where and how commissions be paid, may deliberately be aimed at tax evasion by a party. In many markets with strict exchange control, importers and agents may face a regulation that all fees and commissions be reported and remitted back to the country, whereas the agent probably sees that as his secret retirement fund. A particular category of goods may be prohibited from import, such as firearms or material seen locally as offensive to public morals. Nations on friendly terms are not likely to encourage overtly illegal acts against each other's laws, if such acts come to the attention of authorities as a result of any suit, and may specifically frustrate or nullify a contract known to exist for illegal purposes.

While this spirit of cooperation may exist in principle, the courts of one nation are unlikely to enforce the foreign revenue or penal codes of another nation, even if that nation exerts pressure. A foreign government is not likely successfully to pursue a case in United States courts to recover import duties or taxes from an exporter or importer who it felt evaded them; it would have to sue the parties in its own courts.

Illegality arising after a sale contract is completed is not likely to receive attention from authorities or courts. Goods sold, say, ex-plant or f.o.b. Mexican border in the USA, and subsequently smuggled by the buyer or his representatives across the border, may not be seen as a breach of United States law and still give an enforceable contract. Also, falsification of import documents to the export market, or the issue of false documents by the seller may still not nullify the enforceability of the contract of sale in the seller's country.

The courts of one country will also not customarily enforce the criminal code of another nation at the second country's suit, or punish offenders of another country's laws. However, some countries do have statutes that if one of their citizens commits an act while in a foreign country that is a breach of the first nation's laws, that offence could be tried and punished when the offending party returns home. If a crime is committed in a foreign country that is on a list of extradictable offences in a joint extradition agreement, then the foreign country could sue for extradition of the offender.

An exporter or international contractor who suspects or knows that aspects of his contracts or business relationships may breach the law of his own or another country's party to the contract should seek advice from his lawyers on his risk and exposure. While the foreign country may have no direct legal recourse against the exporter or contractor, if they identify activities they consider illegal in their nation, they may take local action against any assets or investments in their country or jurisdiction, such as confiscating goods in transit.

The general rule is not to breach the laws of your own or another country that is party to your trading activities.

Litigation

As soon as the risk of litigation becomes apparent, the exporter should consult the company lawyer. If the litigation will take place in a foreign country, then clearly it will be necessary immediately to consult and retain a local lawyer to ensure proper drafting of pleadings, the taking of depositions, and the conducting of subsequent court cases. By consulting a lawyer early, the exporter may avoid the risk of unintentionally issuing any communications that may subsequently be used against him.

If proceedings can be taken in the exporter's own country, this will almost certainly reduce the likely level of legal costs, and the laws of the exporting country could be applied to the contract. A writ could be issued against the buyer in the exporting country, if litigation is contracted to take place there, and the buyer may choose to defend the case or simply not to put in an appearance and risk judgement against himself. If judgement is made for the exporter, whether or not it can be enforced against the buyer in the exporting country will depend on whether he has any assets there that could be attached. If there is an appropriate bilateral agreement on such matters with the foreign country, the domestic court judgement may be enforceable in the foreign court by taking that judgement to the foreign court for ratification or registration.

Arbitration

The normal international agency, distribution or other contract to supply goods or services will contain a clause or section covering rules and guidelines for arbitration and its venue in the event of a dispute not resolved otherwise between the parties. Arbitration will generally sour business relations to a lesser extent than litigation.

In disputes purely over matters of fact or clearly demonstrable factors, such as quantity or quality of merchandise supplied against an order, arbitration may be the quickest and cheapest route to settlement. If, on the other hand, the disputes arise over interpretative matters relating to contracts, then that will more likely require court proceedings and the resultant judicial rulings.

The American exporter will want arbitration in the United States, and the British exporter will want arbitration in the United Kingdom. The arbitration systems of both countries are held in high regard in general in international business circles, and, as English is a dominant language in international trade, foreign parties may accept a contractual clause that arbitration be conducted in either of those countries according to guidelines and rules of a neutral body such as the International Chamber of Commerce. The London Chamber of Commerce has an international reputation in arbitration matters because it administers the permanent institution of the London Court of Arbitration. A contract for arbitration in England should specify 'according to the rules of the London Court of Arbitration', and a contract specifying the United States should have a clause 'conducted under the rules of the American Arbitration Association'. Arbitration associations generally have panels of persons qualified to assist and act as arbitrators.

Occasionally a contract will nominate a party or persons other than a chamber of commerce if arbitration is to take place in a less developed market, where perhaps it would be easier to appoint a panel of professional persons such as lawyers and auditors. The contract could also stipulate that arbitrators be appointed by neutral parties such as the president of the local law society. If two arbitrators are to conduct the hearings, it may be that these are both neutrally appointed, or that each disputant appoints one. If there is to be a third arbitrator or umpire, then he can also be appointed by a neutral party, or by agreement between the two arbitrators nominated by the disputants.

The contract should stipulate a reasonable time limit for arbitration to take place to reduce the risk of one obstructive party using delaying tactics to his benefit. Both parties should be contractually bound by the decision of the arbitrators, who may hear evidence on oath and have powers to seek all necessary documentation. As the contract is a legal document, generally jurisdiction over the arbitrators and umpires rests with the courts in the country of arbitration. If the contract itself is the subject of dispute, then arbitration is unlikely to solve anything until a court rules on the validity of the contract. The arbitrator may also rule on costs, and either award costs against the party in the wrong or suggest a cost-sharing formula.

Where an exporter is dealing with a foreign government agency or state-controlled buying organization, local advice should be sought on how disputes can be practically and fairly resolved. A foreign trade arbitration commission may be constituted in a state-planned economy to hear disputes. Since a nation will wish to seem fair, it is likely that arbitration in a neutral country might be acceptable to hear disputes between state-controlled organizations and a foreign supplier.

The basis of international trade is goodwill; if arbitration and litigation must be resorted to, then there will be a loss of that goodwill. Incorporating a multiplicity of arbitration and litigation clauses into a contract does not absolve the exporter from his primary responsibility – to do his homework thoroughly. Research, study, preparation, negotiation, goodwill, mutual profit opportunities, are all key to the successful outcome of an international business relationship. A contract entered into by the parties without thorough preparation and mutual understanding of each other's business objectives, capabilities to perform and market conditions starts from a weak base.

Summary

- The legal requirements of the exporting country with respect to licences, export documentation and the conduct of international business, including anti-corruption laws, must be fully and correctly complied with. Domestic restrictive practice laws rarely apply to foreign transactions.
- The importing country's laws on jurisdiction and agency agreements, along with any other rules and regulations pertaining to imports, must also be complied with by the contracting parties. The exporter should not intentionally breach the laws of any trading partner's nation.
- Economic groups, such as the European Economic Community, frequently have laws governing restrictive practices on price fixing and monopolistic matters of trade on intra-community trade.
- Where it is feasible, the exporter will feel more comfortable with his own nation's courts having jurisdiction over agreements and disputes, providing decisions are binding on both parties and enforceable. Arbitration should take place under previously agreed standard terms and conditions and be conducted by neutral parties.

● Litigation should only be used as the last resort, and in foreign markets the exporter's local embassy may recommend reputable lawyers to act for the exporter.

PART FIVE

ALTERNATIVE MARKET DEVELOPMENT PROGRAMMES

19

Foreign Branches and Subsidiaries

As international business for an exporter grows and certain markets come to be especially significant, it is a natural progression to consider ways of increasing market penetration, distribution and effectiveness of management control. One logical option is to set up a local branch or subsidiary to manage the company's marketing and distribution directly.

The benefits of getting directly involved in the marketing are often more clear to management than the problems that will subsequently be encountered by the person charged with responsibility to implement the plan. Equally, there may be inadequate information on the respective alternatives of a branch, local distribution company, subsidiary company of the parent, joint venture, or franchise manufacturing. While it is not possible in a work of this nature to explore the problems and alternatives on a country-by-country basis, it is possible to raise some warning flags and discuss some issues. When considering direct involvement in any foreign market, it is essential to review your thoughts, objectives and alternatives with both a local lawyer and accounting firm. In fact, many auditing firms are multinational and will be able to give great assistance, even through the home office initially, once you discuss the matter with them. Some accounting firms, such as Price Waterhouse, publish excellent booklets on specific aspects of doing business in foreign markets, and you can obtain these by calling their local office.

Branches

Once the exporter's business to a market becomes significant and still demonstrates growth potential in a politically stable environment, he often envisages the idea of a foreign branch with his own resident representative as an attractive progression. The first approach is usually just to transfer a man from the home staff, give him a secretary and small office, and leave him to develop more effective and aggressive marketing programmes through a network of distributors. Usually the initial thought is that the branch should purely handle sales and marketing, and not actually take title to goods and subsequently distribute the merchandise. There may be local reasons why the company initially does not want to handle physical distribution. That would involve more than just a branch, large amounts of working capital and a significant level of staffing, with possibly a resultant differing tax basis than applied when there was just a resident representative covering, probably, the local region.

This branch marketing office system is a well tried and proven technique for increasing control over management and marketing of distributors with minimum commitment and investment by the parent company, and it should be considered as the first stage. A local representative will learn far more about his markets than the home-based representative can ever expect to learn with his perhaps twice-yearly trips to the distributors. There are also significant political benefits and business merit in recruiting some local staff to assist in the marketing aspects just as soon as the branch can justify expanding beyond the one-man, one-secretary level. Having local management employees demonstrates your commitment to training the local talent in your products and foreign management techniques, and adds to the effectiveness of the branch with the input of local cultural knowledge on business practices, language and local marketing.

The local branch sales and marketing office gives a breathing space for the manufacturer to work for greater market penetration without major commitment, while learning the mechanics and skills of actually running a business in that market. In any case, the original distributor agreement may still have some time to run before the manufacturer's branch could legally assume a role as distributor.

It would be common for the branch in, say, Singapore or Bahrain also to assume regional responsibility over, say, Southeast Asia or the Middle East. The costs of travel within the region would be far less than sending other persons out from the home office, and visits to any one market would become much more frequent, according to the estimated business potential.

In order for the branch manager to function independently in the foreign market, it is wise not to accept the kind offer of your local distributor to use an office at his facilities. Maintaining independence generally proves critical to developing and implementing programmes, or to putting pressure on a local distributor to perform. In most markets there is no shortage of office space, but if you feel the need to have shared facilities it would be better to, say, rent space from your advertising agent or auditor rather than your distributor, partly because such agencies are more used to client/agency relationships where there is both a closeness and a separation of interests. Working out of a distributor's office would greatly limit the privacy of communications with the home office, since customarily much of the communication is by telex.

Initially all the local office need be is one room, a couple of desks, filing cabinets, typewriter, telephones, telex, and a competent secretary to support the manager. To make it a plush, prestigious establishment in the first year of operations is unnecessary; the kind of man who is most successful at running such small-scale branch offices does not generally have the need to satisfy an ego with ostentatious trimmings, because he is usually a more down-to-earth, 'hands on' performer.

It is essential to study, understand and comply with all local laws dealing with establishing a branch in the foreign market. For example, the regulations applicable to obtaining a work permit may be much less rigorous if you are basing a regional representative in the market rather than a man with responsibility for only one market, where the authorities may feel you should exclusively hire a local person. It may be that the branch should not generate a local profit but should only be a cost centre; any other situations might involve compliance with numerous other legal and tax regulations and reporting formalities. Your accountant and lawyer in the market will be the keys to minimizing formalities.

Branch managers

A discussion of branches would be incomplete without a discussion of aspects of selecting and rewarding branch managers, since the man is the key to achieving the objectives. Before selecting and sending out a man to an alien culture, the exporter owes it to him fully to research local living conditions, including salary structures, taxation, schooling and medical facilities, fringe benefits, and to ensure that the selected branch manager has the independence of personality to survive the inevitable trials and frustrations that will be encountered, especially in the formative year. The family circumstances of the individual may have a strong bearing on his ability to perform. If he is married, then his wife will need to be equally independent in order to cope with the periods when he will be travelling within the region and with the other frustrations of living in a city where all the home comforts may not be so readily available, or where the climate may present its own adverse reactions.

The expatriate will expect to be on a clear contract specifying his terms and conditions while abroad, and protecting his position and rights within the home organization to give a secure future. Locally recruited staff need only be on local contracts complying with the practices of the market in terms of salary and benefits. The company that moves a man abroad has a strong responsibility for his welfare, career development and morale, because that man is outside the mainstream of company activity. Most companies with expatriate staff soon realize the benefit in terms of morale and performance of keeping very close liaison with the expatriates, and frequently a noticeably paternalistic approach to dealing with such employees develops. After a man has learned the workings of a market or region and the local language, it is expensive if he is poached away by a competitor, but fortunately that happens rarely.

Remuneration of the branch expatriate manager may be significantly more than for a similarly evaluated position back home. An expatriate sacrifices the home comforts to improve his financial position, after tax, and generally accumulate capital. The personal attributes and skills required in the man must result in a higher monetary valuation in the particular circumstances, because he must be decisive and independent, and able to cope with the most varied range of frustrations from the inability to get the telephones to work to threats that he will be imprisoned because the tax returns are late. Benefits to an expatriate branch manager will normally include company vehicles, possibly cost-of-living allowances, if that is not assessed in the basic compensation, free medical cover, contributions to the continued education of children of school or college age back home, continuity of membership of home company pension or profit-sharing plans, housing or rent allowances, disability or life assurance cover, bonus and incentive schemes, and home leave.

Surveys of the level of remuneration and benefits for expatriates in certain markets may be available through auditors, international management consultants or multinational banks, who generally have considerable experience in these areas of operation.

Do not send a man abroad until all the details are worked out and mutually agreed, otherwise you risk major morale problems while he feels he is being forgotten or exploited. In fact, it is wise to include a period back at the home office each year (say, one or two weeks), just so that he still feels an integral part of the team and no 'them and us' attitudes develop. Equally, there is a limit to the time an expatriate manager can be based on assignment in a market and still function effectively as an extension of the home team. Many companies have concluded that three to five years is the limit, and have developed policies of repatriation after a term overseas, with a home office assignment for a period before a further overseas posting. Some expatriate managers get to like the lifestyle overseas and perhaps resist coming home, but in general the company will benefit more in the long term from a clear and accepted rotation policy.

The contract terms should satisfy the man that the company is fair, generous and concerned over his well-being. The company should demonstrate sensitivity, professionalism and clarity of thought. Issues such as repatriation at the end of a contract period or on termination of a contract should be addressed. Also, corporate limits on the branch manager's authority and power should be identified, and any necessary local powers of attorney raised, such as to operate a local business bank account, or to commit to renting a local office or business or residential premises in the company's name. Various bonds, indemnities or insurance may be needed.

Apart from the earlier suggestion that advice relating to the specific employment of expatriates may be obtained via banks or international auditors, do not overlook the old standbys for general information such as your embassy or local branch of the American or British chamber of commerce. Your sources of useful information, in summary, are:

● international management consultant organizations
● the embassy
● advertising agent
● chamber of commerce
● multinational auditors
● banks, especially branches of international banks
● the personnel vice-president of any other company that you know has a foreign branch in the market.

People will be most helpful in assisting you to identify parameters for rewarding expatriate staff and with practical advice in establishing your local office.

Foreign legislation

Earlier reference has been made to the need to ascertain the legislation, rules and regulations applicable either to basing an expatriate branch manager in a foreign country or to opening and operating an office there. A regional office and staff may receive different treatment from an exclusively local market office, in terms of the issue of work permits or taxation of the individuals or operations. A number of questions should be put to your advisers, the lawyers and auditors you plan to use, including:

● How will income and associated benefits of expatriate staff be treated for taxation purposes?
● What restrictions may apply to travel in and out of the base market and region?
● What tax treatment will the branch attract? Will it be accepted as a non-profitable cost centre operating on remittances from the

parent, or will it be assessed in some way as if it generated local profit, possibly with home market dispatches to the market being assessed as if they were actually made by the branch at an arbitrary profit level?

- Does the expatriate need any specific licences or permits to open and run a non-trading branch?
- What local labour laws apply either to the expatriate or to locally recruited staff?
- Will there be regulatory problems in importing samples of merchandise or advertising materials for examination by the branch? (Although customs duties may be normal and acceptable, if other local agencies concerned with product approvals or censorship of advertising materials get involved, samples can sometimes be held up for months.)
- If the branch develops to handle distribution, what will then be the tax treatment, and is there any risk either of taxation on parent company profits or of an examination of inter-company pricing mechanisms and practices? (Some countries feel that they are exploited by multinationals that prefer to take the bulk of profits at home on exports and leave little for the locals to tax.)
- What regulations or restrictions apply to any management contract between the parent and branch or subsidiary where charges are levied for services provided from the home base? (Many countries have regulations limiting such activities, because they again may be seen as a way to repatriate profits.)
- What restrictions apply to royalties on trademark or patent user agreements between parent and subsidiary or branch operations? (The same comments as above apply.)

These are just a few of the most basic questions that need study. In the final analysis, the objective is to increase sales and profits when a branch or subsidiary is established; if the local laws are going to be so restrictive that there is no net benefit to the exporter, then the establishment of the branch must be questioned. The local legal and financial advisers should be clear that their roles are to assist with opening a branch geared to minimum local tax liabilities and impact of rules and regulations upon both the branch and the foreign parent, consistent with the company's objectives of increased sales volume, market share and penetration.

Subsidiaries and joint ventures

In order to achieve greater control over sales and distribution, and possibly to handle local manufacturing, assembly and packaging, some manufacturers set up a foreign subsidiary or possibly a joint venture operation with local interests if the rules of the country restrict foreign ownership of equity in local operations. Generally the manufacturer would prefer 100 per cent ownership, but many developing countries limit ownership to below 50 per cent. Therefore, the task of seeking a suitable local partner commences.

It is essential that the local partner be financially sound and generally able to make a positive contribution to the business, even if that is only in terms of political contacts, contacts who can issue all the relevant permissions needed to operate. The manufacturer should be wary if the partner does not want actually to contribute investment funds to the project but just receive his stockholding as a gift in exchange for the use of his name. Traditionally, such partners feel little commitment because they have little or no investment at risk.

Once again, the best advice on local partners and methods of operation may come from banks, embassies, accounting firms, other government commercial agencies, and possibly chambers of commerce. Extensive research is advised because, once the local company is registered and operating, changes in partners are virtually impossible.

Most foreign countries that have the objective of encouraging investment will have a specific government agency charged with providing advice and assistance to the visiting manufacturer. In fact, financial help may be made available either directly or indirectly, including reduced taxes or tax holidays for some finite period, land grants or subsidies, employment and labour grants to encourage training of local labour, foreign trade zones enabling the manufacturer to avoid local taxes and duties on goods destined for re-export, priority in obtaining import permits for essential plant, equipment and raw materials (it is vital that the manufacturer is fully satisfied that all plant, equipment and raw materials not locally available may be imported without undue delay or restriction).

Setting up a foreign subsidiary will involve considerable time and expense, and it is important fully to understand your own reasons for seeking to take this route, other than just a corporate ego trip to attach the claim 'multinational' to your operations. Some of the more common reasons for considering a foreign subsidiary include:

- When your domestic plant is operating at or close to capacity, and the options are to expand domestically at the existing site or to develop a new site, then consideration should be given to where the sales from the new facility will actually be made.
- Building a manufacturing facility in a foreign market may enable you to seek protective import restrictions to block out competitive products totally or partially through import licensing controls and duties applied to your product category.

- The foreign market may already have excessive and punitive import barriers, either to protect an already developing local industry or to limit foreign exchange outgoings. Market development may therefore already be hampered or at an impasse unless you do put up a local facility.
- Foreign trading subsidiaries may enable much greater market penetration than working only through a local distributor, partly because consumers may respond positively to knowing the manufacturer is there to stand behind his products with warranties.
- Certain basic ingredients or raw materials may be less expensively or more abundantly available locally in the foreign market, reducing the costs of the finished products.
- A plant in one foreign market that is a member of a regional economic association of geographically close or culturally similar nations, such as ASEAN (Association of South East Asian Nations), CARICOM (Caribbean Common Market), EEC (European Economic Community), may benefit from trade preference arrangements in shipping to the other members of the association. It is essential that the plant be established in the member of the trade association of nations that offers the greatest benefits to the manufacturer in terms of taxation, security and availability of materials and skilled labour.
- There may be pressure from the foreign country to aid the balance of payments and provide local employment opportunities.

In essence, the exporter seeking to set up a foreign branch or subsidiary or joint venture should satisfy himself that there are clearly ascertainable economic and political benefits to the home company in establishing the foreign operation. If the benefits are seen to exist, then the next stage is to consider the financing of the project. Some factors to consider in this respect are:

- Can some or all of the capital requirements of the foreign subsidiary or corporation be raised from sources in the foreign market; if so, on what terms and conditions?
- What maximum shareholding can the parent company hold; if it is less than 100 per cent, are there systems of pyramiding by inserting holding companies above the operating company in order to gain more effective control of assets and management and profits?
- Are any investment, land or equipment loans or grants available to induce the parent to enter manufacturing in the market?
- Will the foreign subsidiary or corporation receive all necessary permits to import needed plant, equipment and raw materials, and what ongoing guarantees are given in this respect?

- Will earnings from the subsidiary or joint venture receive any favourable tax treatment (tax 'holidays' may be available), and will earning be freely remittable to the foreign parent? Many corporations invest in a country only to find at some later time that regulations are imposed limiting their right to repatriate profits, such as that profits can be repatriated only to the level of the inital investment capital.
- Will plant and equipment (especially used plant and equipment from the parent) be eligible to be considered as the parent's contribution to the capital investment?
- Does the expected level of return on the foreign investment equal or exceed the level of return on capital being achieved in the home market, with any assessed adjustment for the higher risk factor?
- What local rules exist on the structure of management and boards of directors? The parent company will clearly want maximum management control to protect its investment, particularly at board and senior management levels.
- Will any rules or regulations in existence or planned in any way discriminate against wholly or partly owned foreign corporations, for example in tendering for government contracts?
- Can royalties and management fees be charged for provision of know-how and services from the foreign parent company and repatriated freely?

If the answers to these basic questions are favourable, and the financial and marketing considerations indicate that a subsidiary or other form of joint venture or foreign operation should be set up, then the next stage is intensively to study the local labour market and conditions affecting the recruitment, training and employment of staff, including all minimum wage laws and rules relating to unions or job security. In some markets, once you employ a person, that person has a high level of security and legal benefits, and it may be extremely difficult to terminate even the less-than-satisfactory performer. Also, a number of countries, such as some in the Orient and Mexico, have a practice of paying a thirteenth-months' salary to employees, and that should be identified before doing any costings, along with any financial obligations upon redundancy or for social security programmes.

The domestic legal and financial departments should be fully involved at every stage of a study on any foreign investment, because the formation of such a venture may have legal reporting requirements or restrictions on the activities of either the foreign or domestic corporations or on the management of either. The Foreign Corrupt Practices Act in force in the USA was, in the early 1980s, a major deterrent to foreign investment and marketing decisions of domestic United States corporations, which feared to operate in the accepted manner of many developing nations and were thereby disadvantaged compared to European or Japanese groups in many instances. Equally, if parts or equipment are being provided from the parent to the subsidiary in the foreign market, there is a strong likelihood that the internal revenue authorities in the foreign market will at some time investigate the inter-company pricing structures, possibly in an effort to demonstrate that these goods are being overpriced as a way of repatriating additional profits.

Most developing nations are actively seeking to encourage investment that creates employment opportunities, and discussions with your own country's international agencies concerned with aid programmes will yield considerable practical advice on both the climate for investment and the expected security.

Summary

- Exporting companies that develop significant sales volumes to certain markets or regions frequently consider expanding market control and penetration by establishing foreign marketing branches or subsidiaries to handle importation and distribution.
- Great care must be taken in the selection of key personnel to manage such operations because of the need for certain additional skills and particular personality traits not necessarily required within the larger home office environment. The comprehensive total remuneration package and contract should include provisions for repatriation and rotation programmes.
- Advice on matters relating to the formation of foreign branches and subsidiaries or joint ventures should be sought from banks, lawyers, auditors, government agencies and your embassy branch in the foreign market. A thorough understanding of the legal and tax treatment aspects of such alternatives is necessary to ensure that there will be tangible benefit to the exporting company.
- Joint ventures present a special problem in identifying suitable, financially stable partners that can make a positive contribution to a venture. Sources of local capital and finance that may reduce the exporting company's direct commitment also need to be identified and studied.
- Local manufacturing facilities may be a consideration if: home plants are operating at or close to capacity; import restrictions limit market development; local labour or raw material costs offer a cost advantage in production; a foreign operation would benefit from protection against other imports or have preferred access to other members of a regional trade association of nations.

20

Licensing Arrangements

An alternative approach to expanding international markets is to licence or franchise another party in the foreign market to manufacture, pack and distribute the product to the market in exchange for fees or royalties related to the volume of sales. There is a multiplicity of formulas for constructing licensing arrangements; in this chapter I shall review some of the factors a manufacturer might consider in seeking to assess if his product is suitable for such an arrangement. He will have realistically to identify unique attributes of his product, process or brand name, and the benefits to the licensor and licensee of a mutual agreement. The preparation of an agreement will finally rest with the lawyers for both parties; however, as always, it is preferable to see the first rough draft of general terms and conditions drafted by the company marketing manager responsible for the arrangement of licences, because that ensures that he is fully sensitive to all he is asking for in the face-to-face negotiations.

Why a licence?

A manufacturer may seek to license his product, technology or trademarks for a number of reasons that relate to his particular products and circumstances, including:

- insufficient capital to enter the local market with his own subsidiary or a joint venture corporation to handle any or all of the production, distribution or marketing functions related to the product
- import restrictions that either already have or subsequently would stop or prevent market development of the product, because either duties would result in unworkable market price structures, or imports were limited by quota or banned
- where the relationship of the cost of freight to the market value of the item would create an unacceptable price structure compared with other similar and competitive products already produced locally

- where the shelf life of a product is such that a product shipped into the market would have too short a balance of shelf life to guarantee requisite quality to the consumers
- where the product is of a delicate nature such that it might not satisfactorily withstand the rigours of shipment over long distances by several modes of transport
- where the product is not mutually exclusive but would necessarily form part of another complete or finished item, such as an accessory for other equipment, or process to be used in the production of another manufactured item
- where there is benefit from linking with a corporation that has an existing and effective distribution network serving the same potential users, or that produces or sells similar or complementary products
- where one party controls or has special access rights or privileges to essential ingredients or raw materials that would be needed in the licensed product or technology.

In essence, if a manufacturer sees obstructions in the way of effectively and competitively building an ongoing export market for his product, or utilizing the strength of his brand name, or the international recognition and incorporation of his special process by potential users, then he should consider the opportunities to grow by licensing his product, trademark or know-how to eligible parties in the foreign markets. Generally that will be a time-consuming, but rewarding, project for a team including marketing, legal, financial and technical personnel, and, once again, should begin with considerable desk research to find the potentially suitable markets and licensees.

What can you license?

A company may seek to license the production or use of a product, business format, copyright work, process or trademark that a licensee would accept either has a use and value on its own, or would have if incorporated as part of another product.

Clearly, whatever you wish to license must be exclusive to you and not in the public domain, and that generally means protected to the fullest possible extent under patent, trademark and copyright registration laws in both the domestic and foreign markets prior to seeking a licence, or with a priority right to file such protective registrations. A potential licensee will have no reason to pay a fee or royalty if the trademark is not registered locally, because he could just go and file for it himself — similarly, if the patent is not protected, or the potential licensee finds that he could circumvent the particular patent and develop a better process or product than he already uses without actually breaching your patent. Occasionally developers of a production process will prefer not to patent it, in the belief that they actually have more security without publishing a patent. This may be very true, as a published patent may just act as an indicator to other parties of alternative research directions that could lead to circumvention of the patent. Also, if the process is expected to have a limited exclusive life before other technical developments overtake it, the developer may prefer not to stimulate competitive research by publishing patents.

The licensee must see the item being offered within the licensing agreement as giving him tangible benefit in exchange for the fees and royalties he must contract to pay out. His benefits may include:

- measurable cost savings through incorporation of the licensed process in production facilities, such as: improved yields, lower energy or input requirements, more efficient and less costly quality control, lower product return or rejection rates, less maintenance, and so on
- the acquisition of an internationally recognized brand name that may enhance his existing sales and reputation, and create additional sales of the licensed brand, which is compatible with his current product line or outlets served
- inclusion of new technology in existing or new products, which will give additional marketing strength and a tangible product advantage over competitors.

Basically, the licensee will want to satisfy himself that adoption of the licence can be expected to increase his gross profit earning through either more sales and sales opportunities or reduced costs. The amount he will be willing to pay for a product, process or brand name will directly relate to his assessment of its contribution to growth and profits.

The licensor can either sell the licence for a finite period (say, five years) either for a fixed once-only fee or, more usually, for a smaller initial *disclosure* fee with an ongoing *royalty* directly related to production or sales volumes. Alternatively, he could sell the right indefinitely without time limit, but that is often more likely if the licensor already believes that the licensed item has a limited useful life before becoming technically obsolete.

Licences can even be granted on an inter-company basis from one group member to a foreign associate or affiliate. This is commonly done to demonstrate that ownership and rights in a product, process or brand name rest with the parent company, and as a means of increasing the level of funds that may be repatriated from a market, especially where there are restrictions on such repatriation of profits or capital, or other limitations.

If the product being licensed is one requiring a particular formulation, such as a food item or perfume, then the licensing manufacturer can further protect his formula – particularly if it would be difficult to protect otherwise – by agreeing to supply only part of the formula in published format within the agreement, and by providing the 'secret' part through direct sale to the licensee of the base mix or ingredient. In this type of situation, the licensor could choose to recover his royalty fees not by a charge on units sold, but by incorporation within the sale price of the base mix, which would be used as a set proportion of the final product under the agreement terms.

In general, the licensing agreement will require the licensor to establish that the product or process being licensed complies with all relevant local laws, rules and regulations appertaining to its use and sale. In addition, the licensor should register all patents and trademarks only in his own name, not in the name of an associate or licensee, thereby having more control. He should also create such user agreements, licences or sub-licences as the transaction and agreement necessitate. The licensor is then responsible for the defence and protection of his own technological secrets or patents and trademarks, although the agreement may require the licensee to assist in defence to an agreed level.

Finding a licensee

After making the decision that the way to progress your international business is to develop a licensing programme, finding suitable licensees becomes the priority. Some guidelines for structuring research are:

- If the licence is for a specific process for treating a raw material, ingredient or waste product, then seek to identify those companies that currently produce or use the ingredient or the raw material in a related manner, or that generate the waste item.
- If a specific raw material is involved that is produced only by certain private or government ventures, then enter discussion with those ventures to identify which of their customers might have applications.
- If the licensed item is a mass-market consumer product, then identify those companies that either are already producing their own brands of similar products (say, a soft drink bottler) or have effective distribution to the suitable wholesale and retail outlets, and would see a benefit from an association with an international brand. (Note: If the potential licensee already has similar products, there is a risk that he will not adequately develop the licensed brand. This could be countered by minimum performance and royalty clauses, or by the licensor retaining a degree of marketing control, such as all advertising and promotion.)

- If the product is in a very specific market category (say, automobile components or electrical household goods), then the first approach logically would be to makers of similar items who might benefit from a range extension.
- If the product must necessarily form an integral part of another product (such as, say, a new process for coating optical lenses), then stage one would be to identify and approach the current producers of the particular item, or the persons who would beneficially incorporate it in their product.

Potential licensees need not just be those companies that are already in the market place with similar or complementary products, but could include companies that have actively been seeking an opportunity to enter a particular market category, but were without a novel idea to use as the first entry point. Possibly they were in the supply end, selling ingredients or raw materials for further processing or incorporation in products, and want to add value by producing finished consumer goods.

After considering some of these approaches to identifying potential partners, a list of names will be building up in response to the broad enquiries, describing your concept for licensing and objectives, that you have put out to your sources of information (including trade directories, banks, accounting firms, advertising agencies, embassies and chambers of commerce). Initially you could either write to these establishments or visit for discussions while in the market.

Once the potential licensee names become available, you will need to conduct studies similar to those for the selection of potential agents and distributors to elicit all available information from reliable public and private sources covering:

- size of company in terms of turnover and staffing
- current product ranges, and sales volume in various product categories
- market share data
- financial performance history
- ownership and corporate structure
- any major shareholdings
- key officers and personnel
- existing production and distribution facilities and capabilities.

Once you have built up company profiles on the basis of such relevant and comparable information, you will be in a good position to commence the process of making direct contacts with the appropriate level of company operatives to establish whether there is any degree of interest in your licensing proposal. Particular care should be taken in the case of exclusive products or processes not to reveal any technical details prior to obtaining signatures on *non-disclosure* or *secrecy agreements*, or an agreement that the party has no right to and will not use any information learned in commercial discussions with you except as part of a subsequent commercial arrangement recognizing and rewarding your company for the input.

It is fundamental to the success of any licensing arrangement that the licensee is committed to using the process, product or brand name for active marketing, sales and distribution, and any agreement should ensure that there is a time limit for the commencement of production or marketing, possibly with some form of penalty clause. The licensee must clearly have the financial standing and capital to make any necessary level of investments in plant, equipment and inventory, and in any special or supplementary distribution facilities. The licensor must be confident in the licensee's ability and willingness to honour all agreements, duties and obligations, both financially to the licensee and in respect to product, product quality and marketing.

Elements of a licensing agreement

An agreement to license a product, process or trademark will, of course, vary greatly in length and complexity, depending on the nature of the subject of the licence and on the rights, duties, obligations, commitments and programmes of the respective parties. The best person to make the first summary of the commercial terms and concepts to be incorporated in the final agreement is generally the individual manager in charge of selling licences. He may not be a lawyer, and would logically fully involve the company's lawyers at every stage, but he could beneficially put on paper his understanding of broad areas of agreement, rights, duties and responsibilities. In the appendix to this chapter I include a product licensing manager's basic first draft of the main areas needing mutual agreement to license a new food item, an instant imitation yogurt powder, which would be locally produced and marketed by the licensee from some imported and some local ingredients. These general discussion points will be incorporated, along with other finer details and definitions, in the lawyers' subsequent drafts.

The agreement, in general terms, will cover aspects of the relationship and general clauses relating to matters such as:

- what is being licensed
- fees and royalties
- timing of payments due
- audit control
- quality control

- secrecy
- patent and trademark rights and protection
- product development programmes
- supply of ingredients (if relevant)
- performance and market development
- investment
- assignment of agreements or licence
- termination of licence
- disputes and arbitration
- penalties and sanctions for non-compliance or non-performance.

These are some of the key areas to be discussed and over which agreement must be reached between the parties. The final agreement must be very specific, because many disputes arise over what a contracting party's intentions may have been rather than what was incorporated in the licensing agreement.

Specifically, to develop the general clause categories a little further, the final agreement presented for joint signature by the contracting parties should address, in appropriate detail and length, the complex issues of:

- the specifics of what is being licensed, with formulas, processes, production techniques, ingredient or component specifications, designs, plans, descriptions, plant layouts, warranties on performance, warranties on product yields
- the length of the initial agreement, and commitments to starting dates, product launch dates and any relevant dates or time spans connected with the construction or commissioning of necessary plant and equipment
- any subsequent specific or general terms or guidelines concerning the extension or renewal of the licence
- the amount of any initial disclosure or licence fee agreed between the parties to be paid by the licensee
- the amount of any ongoing fees or royalties to be earned and paid, whether unit, volume, weight or value related, or any other criterion for assessment or measurement that is quantifiable and verifiable
- the times when any fees or royalties will become due and payable, including the manner and currency of payment, and penalties for any non-payment or late payment
- identification of any geographical territorial limits to the licence to either produce or market in the licensee's home market or for export
- the licensee's rights or lack of rights in respect to any sub-licences he may wish to grant within or outside the agreed territory

- the rights of assignment of the licence to any parent, subsidiary, affiliate, purchaser of the licensee, or assignment to any other party; generally the licensor will restrict assignment to parties he may approve in advance and the licence will not automatically transfer if ownership of the licensee changes
- the audit rights of the licensor to verify any production or financial data relating to the licence and the payment of fees or royalties, including examination of production, sales and ingredient purchase records and product costings
- product quality and quality control, including the right to inspect, sample and reject product, and action and remedies to be taken by both parties in the event of quality control problems
- non-disclosure and secrecy agreements covering all exclusive product know-how, formulas and processes forming part of the agreement, including clauses to bind the licensee as to who in his company should have access to information, and subsidiary secrecy agreements with such persons to prevent disclosure for any reason subsequently
- performance clauses, which should cover any minimum production or sales or royalty matters, indicating the amount of product production, sales or value over any given time period that the licensee is expected to achieve, and any remedies in the event the licensee cannot or does not meet minimum performances
- compliance with all local laws, rules and regulations by the licensee concerning every aspect of production, plant operations or marketing, including health, labour, ingredient and labelling laws
- registration of patents and trademarks in the name of the licensor, and assistance from the licensee in the defence and protection of such registrations
- the ownership and handling of communications involving any subsequent product improvements or developments by either party
- supplies of any components or ingredients from the licensor to the licensee needed in any production-related process
- supply of any marketing materials or related matter to assist the licensee develop markets
- responsibility of the licensee for obtaining all local permissions and licences needed to construct plant, produce or market product, or for the import of components or ingredients, etc.
- investment responsibilities relating to plant and equipment, including obtaining finance
- joint marketing responsibilities and agreements, or arrangements to produce marketing programmes and plans
- insurance cover to protect the licensee against lost markets and profits in the event of a catastrophe and to protect the licensor against lost royalties

- limits upon the rights of the licensee to compete with the production of other similar products during the term of the licence or for a specific period after the termination of the licence
- the process for the handling of disputes, including an arbitration procedure, identifying the manner of selecting the arbitrators, location, limits of responsibility and commitments of the parties to accept decisions of arbitration
- causes for premature termination
- responsibilities of each party to the other if the agreement is not automatically renewed after an initial period or is terminated; this may need to cover inventories, stock in the market and returns, investment in plant and equipment, outstanding royalties
- which country's laws will be enforceable in the event of litigation, and where litigation shall take place (some countries insist it must be on their territory for a licence operating within their geographical boundaries).

Experience shows that, if the two involved parties are seriously interested in the product or subject of the licensing agreement, there will be mutual compromise until a satisfactory agreement is reached (an agreement may sometimes involve more than two companies, such as a licensor, a product manufacturer and a third party to market the product).

Summary

- A manufacturer may seek to license products, technological know-how, trademarks or patents if: he has insufficient capital to enter a market himself; import restrictions on finished products prevent further market development; freight represents an excessive proportion of costs; the product has a limited shelf life; the product does not withstand well the rigours of international shipment; the product would form a part of another manufacturer's finished item; a foreign corporation offers ready access to distribution channels; a party controls an essential ingredient needed in the process.
- A licensee will only see benefit in paying a licence fee or royalty if he could not duplicate the licensed item because of exclusive technology or patent or trademark or copyright protection, and if he has a measurable benefit in terms of cost saving, or acquires an international brand name that enhances his market position, or acquires new technology.
- Licences are generally for a specific time period with options to renew, and commonly an initial 'disclosure' fee and ongoing royalty on sales volume are paid to the licensor.

● Identifying a potential licensee needs careful research into companies that could benefit from the licence, would be capable of fulfilling the licensor's marketing objectives, and would have available capital resources to undertake the project.

● The licensing agreement will summarize rights, duties, obligations, responsibilities and commitments, and the basic programmes of the respective parties.

Appendix: Sample of the first commercial draft of a licensing agreement prepared by the product licensing manager

First Draft Agreement to License the Production of YoQuik

(1) This is an agreement between Inventive Foods, Inc., of 1 High Street, Anytown, USA (hereafter referred to as the 'licensor') and National Foods, Inc., of Suite 1000, World Trade Building, Tokyo, Japan (hereafter referred to as the 'licensee').

(2) Within the context of this agreement the following definitions shall apply.

　　(a) *YoQuik* – the product produced from the ingredients and according to the process, product specifications and formulas described in Appendix I attached.

　　(b) *Public domain* – refers to data, specifications, processes, etc. that are accessible through published literature or patents.

(3) The licensor hereby grants a licence for five years from this date to the licensee to produce, distribute and market the product known as YoQuik within the national geographical territorial boundaries of Japan in return for fees and royalties defined subsequently in this agreement.

(4) The licensee shall have no rights to offer YoQuik for sale outside the agreed territory, or to offer or arrange for any subsequent sub-licensing agreement except where the same is fully agreed in writing in advance with the licensor and where the licensor is party to all negotiations and agreements.

(5) The licensor agrees to supply full details of all formulas, specifications and technical processes required by the licensee to produce YoQuik to agreed quality standards, except where certain formulation details are not necessary to the licensee because a part of the final blend is supplied direct from the licensor as a base mix ingredient.

(6) The licensee, its shareholders, management and employees agree to be bound severally and separately by this agreement to hold all information not in the public domain relating to the specifications, processes, technology, patents of YoQuik secret and in confidence from all parties not directly needing any specific knowledge to perform their job function as part of the production, distribution or marketing of YoQuik.

　　No information may be transferred either verbally or in written form to any person not authorized in writing by the licensor to receive such information. It is the responsibility of the officers and management of the licensee to control and enforce the secrecy aspect of this agreement in all respects.

(7) (a) In return for the granting of this licence, the licensee agrees to pay to the licensor a royalty fee equal to three per cent of the gross invoiced sales value of all YoQuik in any flavoured or unflavoured form produced and sold or distributed. No royalty fee will be due on commercial samples released to customers of the licensee where these are less than 50 lbs. weight per customer.

(b) For the purpose of this agreement the gross invoiced sales value will be taken as the price a customer is invoiced at before deductions of any discounts or allowances but excluding any local sales taxes or levies that accrue to the benefit of any government agency upon product sales.

(c) Royalty fees will be calculated on the 31st March, 30th June, 30th September and 31st December in each year of this agreement.

(d) The licensor shall have the right to examine all records and accounts of the licensee to verify royalties due relative to the production, distribution and marketing of YoQuik, including but not limited to production data, inventories, sales records, invoices and other financial records. Should the management of the licensor not exercise this right directly and in person, they may appoint any independent agent including local auditors to examine any records needed to verify royalty fees, and the licensee agrees to permit full and free access all such records by the licensor and/or appointed representative or agents.

(e) All royalties due shall be paid in full to the licensor within 30 days of the end of each quarter. In the event such fees remain unpaid in full or part, the licensee agrees to pay interest on any outstanding amounts from the last day of the relevant quarter until it is received by the licensor at the higher rate of 1½ per cent per month or the local borrowing rate applicable to the licensee as established by independent data from the licensee's main bankers. In the event there is any dispute over the royalties due for any quarter, once this is resolved the licensee agrees that the same interest condition outlined above will apply to such disputed sums paid late unless the licensee has deposited with the licensor adequate funds to cover a settlement.

(f) All royalties are due in US dollars at the exchange rate applicable on the last day of each quarter, and should be remitted without deduction of any bank or other charges or taxes to the bank nominated from time to time to receive such funds for the licensor.

(g) At the time of signing this agreement the licensee shall pay the licensor a deposit of US $25,000, which shall be retained by the licensor throughout the duration of this agreement as security against subsequent payment of royalties.

(h) The licensee hereby agrees that in the event royalty payments do not exceed US $50,000 per annum, in any year of this agreement, then they shall pay a minimum royalty fee of US $50,000 per annum for each year in which the accrued royalty has not reached that figure for a calendar year.

(i) At the time of signing this agreement or disclosure of the YoQuik formula, except the base mix referred to in clause 5, the licensee shall also pay the licensor the sum of $100,000 as a once-only fee.

(8) (a) The licensor agrees to be responsible for the registration and ongoing protection of patents in the territory and the related costs of first registration and ongoing registrations. The licensee agrees to advise the licensor in writing immediately it becomes aware of any patent infringement or possible infringement. In the event of any defence of patents against infringements, the parties agree to share equally the costs of defence and any litigation to protect the patent rights.

(b) The licensee agrees not to seek to pre-empt any patent rights of the licensor in relation to instant yogurt powders based upon disclosure of knowledge of the specifications or processes for YoQuik, or to pre-empt any trademark registrations relating to YoQuik or other products the licensor may seek to market in the territory, and to advise the licensor by letter of any conflicting registrations or attempts by other parties to register conflicting trademarks immediately such conflicting information comes to the attention of the licensee. The licensee agrees to cooperate with the licensor in the registration of any trademarks and the defence of any trademark infringements.

(9) (a) As part of the ongoing relationship between the licensor and the licensee, it is apparent and likely that either or both parties will make product development improvements or agree modifications in specifications, formulations and processes.

It is hereby agreed that any costs related to product development shall be borne by the party doing the development work, but that results, information, data and improvements shall be shared freely subject to clause 9(c) below.

(b) The licensee shall be bound by the secrecy clauses of this agreement in respect of all subsequent information released to him by the licensor relating to modifications, formulas, specifications and processes for YoQuik or such other products as the licensee shows interest in.

(c) If the licensee makes any improvements or changes in formulation, specifications or processes, these should be communicated and agreed with the licensor in writing prior to incorporation in any production process, and, if any such process improvements are patentable, the licensor shall have the first right to file for patent protection in its name and at its cost and to adopt such process changes in any other territory where it markets YoQuik. Incorporation of any such product development improvements in YoQuik in the territory will not in any way change or affect the agreed payment of royalty fees on YoQuik production.

(10) (a) The licensor agrees to assist in the supply of any ingredients needed to produce YoQuik by the licensee, but the licensee will be solely responsible for obtaining all necessary import licences, foreign exchange permission or any other required authorizations to import ingredients to the territory for use in the production of YoQuik, and shall demonstrate to the licensor that all such efforts to obtain relevant documents to effect importation have been made.

(b) The licensee shall be solely responsible for payment to suppliers of ingredients for YoQuik. In the event that ingredients insufficient to manufacture sufficient product to generate minimum royalties as per clause 7(h) are available to the licensee, then the licensee shall be bound by clause 7(h) to pay the minimum US $50,000 royalty fee to the licensor for that calendar year in accordance with the payment terms of clause 7.

(c) Should the licensor be required for practical reasons or reasons of secrecy to supply any part of the YoQuik blend, then the licensee agrees to purchase such base mix at prices agreed from time to time reflecting the licensor's cost of ingredients and normal margins and costs of operation, and to pay for such base mix by irrevocable letter of credit or such other payment terms as may subsequently be agreed. The licensor shall have no obligation to disclose costing data on any base ingredients supplied by him.

(11) (a) The licensor shall work with the licensee to ensure adequate quality control procedures, and the licensee shall agree all ingredient specifications and suppliers with the licensor prior to obtaining supplies. The licensee agrees to supply such reasonable quantities of samples of YoQuik to the licensor as the licensor may from time to time request for quality analysis purposes.

(b) In the event that the licensor rejects any product as substandard or that the licensor considers the quality or quality control of YoQuik production is unsatisfactory, the licensee agrees to accept the recommendations of the licensor to improve quality control procedures and standards in a manner specified by the licensor within 30 days from notification by the licensor.

(c) In the event of failure by the licensee to operate to agreed quality control standards, this agreement to produce YoQuik may be cancelled forthwith and the licensee shall agree to pay the licensor and be liable for a compensatory sum equal to the higher of the minimum royalty of US $50,000 or the royalty of the last twelve months prorated for the number of months or years to the expired date of this agreement.

(12) (a) Pursuant to this agreement the licensee agrees to accept all

costs of installing machinery, plant and equipment for production, quality control, packaging, distribution, marketing and promotion of YoQuik produced in his facilities in the territory, and related to the training of his staff should any visits to the licensor's facility in the USA be necessary.

(b) In addition, the licensee agrees to pay the travel and subsistence expenses for one person from the licensor to visit the licensee and his production facilities once each year for duration of this agreement, and any extension thereof, for the general purpose of exchanging information, providing technical assistance, assessing quality control and any matters related to the technical elements of this agreement.

(13) The licensee agrees to promote the marketing, sale and distribution of YoQuik in the assigned territory, and to produce and agree with the licensor an annual production and marketing plan. As a further commitment to developing markets for the product, the licensee agrees to spend at least five per cent of his gross sales revenues from YoQuik on direct advertising and promotional activity, excluding any related personnel costs for employees of the licensee, and such expenditure shall be reported to the licensor each quarter with supporting documentation. All promotional and advertising plans falling within this clause should be agreed with the licensor in advance and the licensor will generally accept marketing advice of the licensee but may offer advice from experiences in other markets.

(14) The licensee will at all times maintain insurance cover in an amount agreed with the licensor and with an approved insurer to cover the replacement value of all plant and equipment and stock and which will include the provision for continuing payment of all fees and royalties at a level equal to those due over the twelve months preceding any catastrophe causing the filing of a claim for a period of at least one year thereafter.

(15) (a) This agreement shall be in force for five years from the date of signing by both parties and shall be renewable under mutually agreeable terms and conditions for further periods of five years.

(b) In the event either party wishes to terminate the agreement at the end of the first five-year period, that party shall give six full calendar months written notice to the other party.

(c) In the event the licensee is the party wishing to terminate this licensing agreement at the end of this or any subsequent contract period, the licensee agrees to return to the licensor all documents relating to formulations, specifications and processes for the production of YoQuik. The licensee also agrees immediately on termination of this agreement to cease production, marketing and distribution of YoQuik, and shall offer for sale to the licensor or its appointed agents or representatives all inventories of finished product at manufactured cost or market value, whichever is the lower.

(d) During the term of this agreement and for two years thereafter the licensee shall not produce or offer for sale any other product purporting to be an instant natural or imitation yogurt type of product.

(e) The licensee further agrees not to use his experience or knowledge gained by the production of YoQuik under licence from the licensor to produce or market any similar product that may purport to reconstitute to an instant natural or imitation yogurt or yogurt type of product with the addition of water alone or other additives within five years after the termination of this contract.

(16) (a) This agreement may be terminated forthwith by the licensor in the event of the licensee fails to pay any royalties, fees or other sums due in connection with the supply of any ingredients from the licensor. In the event of termination, the licensee agrees to pay compensation to the end of this or subsequent contract periods in the manner and amounts specified in clause 11(c).

(b) The agreement may also be terminated forthwith by the licensor if the licensee fails to operate to agreed quality control standards or to rectify quality control problems within 30 days of notification by the licensor that the product is not of suitable quality for distribution.

(c) In the event the licensee fails to produce and market YoQuik in any quarter year for any reason, the licensor shall have the right to terminate this agreement forthwith and receive compensation to the end of the contract period according to clause 11(c).

(17) (a) This agreement shall bind equally and in all respects the licensee, any parent or holding company, any subsidiaries, associate companies or joint ventures of the licensee.

(b) The licensee shall not have the right to assign this agreement in whole or part to any party except with the prior written agreement of the licensor.

(18) The licensor shall have the right to assign this agreement in whole or in part upon notification to the licensee of the name and address of the assignee, and the assignee shall have all rights, duties and responsibilities of the licensor as defined in this agreement.

(19) In the event of any dispute between the licensor and the licensee that cannot be resolved by mutual discussion, then it is agreed by both parties that the dispute shall be referred to an independent arbiter in the territory for resolution.

The independent arbiter shall be appointed by the local International Chamber of Commerce, or, if one is not in existence at the time, by the senior partners of auditors appointed by the licensor and the licensee. Both parties agree to abide by the decisions and finding of such arbiters and implement such decisions immediately they are announced.

(20) This agreement in all respects shall be interpreted and enforced according to the laws of contract of Japan, and both parties agree that these laws shall apply no matter where a dispute or interpretation is made or heard.

_____   _____
Licensor   Licensee

21

Joint Selling Organizations

External independent organizations

There are various ways manufacturers can benefit from concentrated export activity yet share the cost of operations.

Shared foreign sales offices A number of companies can combine to share the costs of a resident manager or sales office in a foreign market or region. The individual companies would need to feel that each would receive a fair proportion of time and attention. Ideally, products represented should be complementary rather than competing, so that they could possibly be marketed in a similar fashion or to similar outlets. For example, a combined foodstuffs operation could represent, say, a confectionery line, a pet food line, canned fruits and vegetables, a soup company, and so on, all marketable to the region or market's food outlets yet not conflicting.

However, it is not too common that quite independent companies can band together in this fashion commercially, possibly because of concern that they will not get a fair share of the resources, or that costs are not fairly allocated, or simply that they might just as well conduct sales and marketing matters through their own appointed distributor.

Trading companies An alternative approach is to appoint as export representative an independent trading company that has its own overseas branches or associates in a number of countries. Such trading companies have grown up mainly out of the major trading nations, including Britain, the United States, Holland, Denmark, France and Switzerland, and traditionally centred more on activities in markets where their mother country had strong traditional trading, political or colonial interests.

The trading company might require an exclusive representative agreement either for specific markets in which it operates, or across all of the covered markets, and would generally handle sales and marketing operations by buying the products through the mother country's home office and acting as exporter to the foreign market, where it would then import and distribute merchandise. The home trading office might recover costs by building in a margin to the export price, or by charging a commission. The foreign branch could incorporate in local pricing structures its requisite operating and profit margins.

The number of manufacturers operating through the major trading companies may have declined recently, but this has been a traditional way of exporting over the years, particularly for smaller companies and in times when international travel was more arduous and time-consuming.

Export management companies A variation on the export trading company with its own overseas distribution operations is the simple export trading or management company, operating only from the home market but sending its representatives to visit potential customers in the foreign markets at regular intervals. In the United States such types of exporters are more usually referred to as export management companies, and may sign a sole export agreement with a manufacturer and act rather like the manufacturer's export department in seeking to promote sales. Their operations may attempt to cover the world, or just certain regions. They may work on a commission on sales only, or charge a fee, particularly in the initial stages. Some of them will take title to goods before exporting them, and in that case will generally build their required margin in the uplifted export price to the customer. Some export management companies will also extend credit to customers and have the freight advantage of pooling shipments of different products to the one market or customer.

An export management company may provide a useful service to the smaller manufacturer, particularly supplying a specialist trade sector, such as, say, hotel supplies. The general disadvantage is that most such companies are small in staff and turnover, and do not know a manufacturer's products as well as the manufacturer. It may be that a joint arrangement could be set in operation, where the manufacturer handled the product enquiries himself but the export company could assist with desk and market research to identify potential contacts and physically handle the movement of goods and export documentation.

Trade associations Another newer development that is gaining momentum, particularly over the last decade, is the formation of trade associations of manufacturers or primary producers in an industry. Trade associations are not new. What is newer is their greater activity in marketing and promotion, particularly in generic advertising of industry products. Some such organizations from around the world have been opening foreign offices to promote their industry's products and exports in more aggressive fashion. Some of these organizations have received significant support from their government trade agencies. Examples of such organizations include: Foods and Wines from France, found in several countries; the English Country Cheese Council, which opened its first foreign office in the United States in 1980; and others such as coffee growers' associations, fruit marketing operations, and a host of others mainly geared to promoting primary producers and processors.

These associations have demonstrated considerable effectiveness in many markets, mainly concentrating on generic marketing and support programmes for a manufacturer's own export efforts. However, they do sometimes work by seeking orders and allocating these between manufacturers according to some prearranged formula considered fair by the participants. Generally such associations do not seek to take title to goods or handle export or distribution procedures, but will work to assist in distributor training and motivation, along with attention to consumer awareness programmes.

Group marketing companies

As multinational corporations become more dominant in world business, and as national companies diversify in the range of products manufactured and sold, there has been a growth in the number of companies seeking to concentrate their export effort. One approach is to set up a single group export division, which may even be a separate legal corporate entity.

As a separate corporation there may be tax benefits aimed at aiding export activity, such as deferred taxes, or taxes due only when dividends are paid out to stockholders, or even reduced taxes. Ireland, for example, for many years gave long-term tax 'holidays' on corporate profits that were exclusively the result of export activities. The USA has from 1985 introduced a system of Foreign Sales Corporations. Clearly, any company that has a significant level of export activity or international profit earnings should review the optimum corporate structure with the corporate lawyers and financial division. Additional access to government grants, aid or credit for export activities may be available.

Particular benefit to the multinational or multiproduct group with separate export management teams comes from the synergy that may result in export management activity within and between the members of a group, which can all then be concentrated with optimum use of specialist skills and reduced duplication of effort by forming a group export division. That division almost invariably will give cost savings over duplicated individual company operations. However, the initial reaction from the individual companies is that each of their product ranges needs specialist knowledge and attention, and they need to control their own destiny. That does not necessarily negate the benefit of a group operation. Individual marketing men can be assigned to concentrate on particular products or groups of complementary products, but the duplication of several shipping and administrative departments can be avoided.

If there are tangible tax benefits or other clear financial considerations, including lower interest funds or grants for export development, or a worthwhile level of cost saving from consolidation, then a group export management division or company should still be evaluated.

If there are seasonal aspects to any of the group's products in a diversified multiproduct group, it is also possible that the products may have different seasonal peaks, such as a range of summer beach accessories and a range of toys with heavy Christmas demand. In such a situation a consolidated shipping department would have a more balanced workload. While products may differ greatly, the mechanics and administration of shipping those products generally differ little, and, as each separate shipping department would be geared in staffing levels to handle peak loads, consolidation should significantly reduce supervision and clerical staff levels, and enable additional investment in computerized and other mechanical aids to be justified. The consolidation of shipping operations could produce greater negotiating strength with shipping lines on freight rates and rebates, and also with marine insurance companies.

The sales and marketing organizations could be structured either with geographical emphasis – say, each regional manager handling all the group products to a region – or with emphasis on compatible products – say, one manager is responsible for foodstuffs, another for cosmetics and toiletries, and so on. If the volume of exports in any product category is or becomes large, then many exporters' experience has led them to favour the product range specialization, with a network of regional managers for each separate product category or group, possibly with a product group export senior manager or vice-president, all reporting in to the president or general manager of the international division. When business develops to the stage of overseas branches, subsidiaries and affiliates, these also would logically report in to the international division, which would either draw on specialists from specific domestic production companies as necessary, possibly for specialist production or research matters, or have its own core management team to cover the main management disciplines.

A single group international division may also provide benefit in aspects handling imports of raw materials used in separate operating divisions. One company might be selling into a market that also supplies a raw material to a group member. If there are any currency exchange problems in obtaining payment for exports to that market, then it may be possible to use the locally accruing funds to pay for necessary raw materials. Liquor, for example, might be sold into a country that could supply fruit for a canning division. This type of arrangement might also have savings in respect to costs of letters of credit, foreign exchange transactions or other financing.

In a group where there are several companies or divisions each separately operating an export department, a chief executive might find benefits in having a group-wide study done to identify synergy and savings. Some group export organizations have even found that they could beneficially become involved in major international barter operations as a way of penetrating otherwise hard-to-enter markets, supplying their goods for barter products that could be resold in western markets.

Consortia

It is particularly common in major projects, such as building a power station in a developing country or a dairy processing plant, which might require involvement from the milk production stage right through to processing and distribution, for two or more companies to cooperate to act as a single entity or bidder in tendering for the project. Such a consortium may consist of companies from several different countries or from one nation, but each would have a specific and different contribution to make to the project. The range of skills might include architecture and design, construction and installation of plant and equipment, distribution, plant commissioning and operations, training, and even ongoing management under such a contractual obligation.

Many such consortia are formed with the active encouragement of governments at home and abroad, especially in developing countries needing aid in planning and implementing projects utilizing untapped resources, and with the blessings of international agencies and banks, which may be providing finance.

In structuring a consortium to bid for and undertake a proposal, consideration needs to be given to whether a partnership or separate corporation best suits the aims and objectives of all concerned. There must be clearly defined contribution responsibilities, obligations and duties, as well as financial structures and profit-sharing plans. If there are performance bonds to be placed, as is normal for major consortia projects, or there are liabilities in the case of failure to perform to contract, to complete on time or to agreed standards, or in respect of subsequent maintenance or faults that develop, then the risks need to be identified in advance and fairly apportioned in an agreed manner between the partners. The project will undoubtedly involve warranties, either on plant performance or resultant yields of output, and the parties in the consortium responsible for each aspect must, as part of the consortium, honour its warranties. If there is support from the government in the base country of the consortium, then there may also be some insurance or underwriting of the consortium project, costs, risks or profits available from government or international agencies, including underwriting the risk of default by the foreign party to meet its financial obligations and commitments at any stage of the project.

Generally it will be found advantageous in any major consortium project to appoint an independent chairman from outside the group of partners to maintain balance and resolve disputes that might arise between the partners. Clearly any internal disagreements should be kept from the notice of the foreign contracting party, and the independent chairman might, under the terms of the agreement binding the partners to each other, have the final say in resolving internal problems.

Consortia of partners who have previous experience working together, not necessarily in a joint bid for a project but possibly in a buyer − supplier relationship, may well operate more smoothly. Parties thinking of forming a consortium may initially benefit by seeking association with complementary skill-contributing enterprises with which they have had previous satisfactory working relationships.

Summary

- Manufacturers seeking to develop exports could work in association and open shared sales offices in key foreign markets.
- A new or small exporter may prefer to appoint a trading company with overseas branches to handle its distribution to certain regions, or to appoint a domestic export management company to accept responsibility for promoting goods to foreign markets in exchange for fees or commissions.
- Trade associations, particularly those promoting primary and agricultural products, have gained in prominence in promoting exports from their base countries, frequently opening foreign offices, and assisting their members to develop export opportunities, including providing extensive generic promotional support.
- Groups of affiliated companies should evaluate the merits of forming one single group-wide export division to reduce total costs of several separate departments and take advantage of synergistic marketing opportunities.
- Consortia of suppliers of related goods and services can generally be formed to bid for major foreign projects, particularly in construction and engineering projects. The specific responsibilities, obligations and liabilities of each consortium member must be identified in a mutually binding contract between consortium members.

22

Towards an International Strategy

This book has looked at each of the major aspects of exporting and international business transactions. It has not attempted to give the depth of subject coverage needed by the academic or functional specialist, but has tried to give breadth to and sufficient coverage of the key practical issues that an exporter or other international business executive should be familiar with. Each reader will look at the text from a different perspective. The student seeking a basic level of knowledge for courses and examinations of the professional institutes may look for a more practical insight into the realities of running an export operation. The professional seasoned exporter may simply seek to consolidate his wealth of knowledge and treat the work as something that may help him to distinguish the wood from the trees while empathizing with the problems reviewed. Non-exporters who have a line responsibility for export operations may be seeking to obtain a degree of understanding of their department's functions and role in the overall contribution and context of the company operations, so that they can conduct relevant discussion in an informed fashion with the export staff. Senior line managers and chief executives may be seeking an overview of the subject with the purpose of identifying and establishing a strategy towards international opportunities.

In this chapter I develop a scenario whereby the chief executive structures a committee or grouping of key people with relevant inputs to develop specific strategies towards international markets and business opportunities. In discussing such ideas with chief executives, I have on a number of occasions found the initial reaction to be that such attempts to formalize an approach to international opportunities could not apply or be effective within their companies. The reasons given may relate to the smallness of their key executive group, or the fact that they have a large export department, which should be fulfilling such a role. Whether a company is large or small, or part of a group of companies where an inter-company committee might be beneficial, if it has sought to formalize its international strategies and develop a planning and review system, there has invariably been benefit in expansion, through greater exports, diversification internationally, or the use of foreign products and ideas in home markets. Strategic planning should have a place in any organization seeking growth in profits and market shares or sales volumes. In making these comments prior to the discussion on some of the ways to develop strategy discussions it is my hope that the reader who feels this is inapplicable to his company will keep an open mind until he is satisfied that his organization has a satisfactory programme for developing the company's international strategy in the areas discussed.

An international strategy committee

Although I cannot attempt to set a strategy for an individual company, perhaps it would be useful to review points that may be relevant to strategic evaluations, discussions and decisions. The traditional view of international business has been just the physical export of goods from the home factories to overseas markets. In this work I attempt to take the reader into other areas of potential international profit. Modern methods and structures of businesses have put new perspectives into the conduct of international business. Multinational corporations plan and often take decisions centrally that are concerned with the maximization of global profit or such other strategy factors as may have a bearing on long-term plans. The individual unit may have large exports to a foreign market one year, and lose it within the group the next year as sourcing is switched. Here it would not be appropriate to enter a debate on multinational corporation strategy or planning. I shall instead look from the perspective of the domestic enterprise, which may or may not be part of a larger group.

In developing an international strategy I suggest that the senior line manager or chief executive give consideration to such factors as:

- his company's existing product range
- technology to develop new and modified products
- originality of know-how and technology developed within the company, particularly compared with levels of knowledge and technology considered 'public'
- management skills within the organization
- management resources
- financial, research, technical, production and other relevant resources.

Perhaps the way to start to develop a strategy to go beyond mere physical exports is to form an *international strategy committee* internally. This group might only need to meet every two or three months, or at such agreed intervals as gave the group specific developments to review and discuss. Ideally, it should probably be chaired by the chief executive. Membership would probably include the export manager or director, home sales and marketing director, research director, production director and possibly, as required, the finance and personnel directors. Other managers with specialist knowledge or skills should be co-opted as necessary. Specific projects should perhaps be delegated to committees chaired by the appropriate divisional director so that they can be the subject of detailed investigations and reports by the sub-group back to the main International Strategy Committee. Clearly I cannot attempt to suggest hard and fast rules for the membership or committee structure for any one company, if only because there can be a host of individuals who may have extremely relevant experience to contribute, such as the group purchasing director, who will have significant relevant international experience if he is travelling to buy ingredients. Such a committee is also not intended to be a duplicate of the company's main board, since in many companies the official main board consists of persons other than senior line executives. It should consist of those with relevant knowledge and experience to consider and develop international strategies, and to recommend courses of action to a higher main board.

The Strategy Committee could divide its attention, according to short-, medium- and longer-term priorities, to give consideration systematically to such broad areas as:

- direct product exports
- transfer of know-how and technology abroad
- foreign mergers, acquisitions and joint ventures
- import of foreign know-how and technology
- import of compatible/complementary foreign products
- developing of raw material and semi-processed material sources abroad.

Action under each or any of the above categories could have an effect on the company's overall earnings and profitability. Within the above general categories, I shall enumerate some of the more specific opportunities that may have a place in developing an overall strategy.

Direct product exports

The company has additional profit potential in seeking to sell from the domestic plants into foreign markets where it can competitively:

- export existing products unchanged in all respects
- modify packaging and marketing and export existing products

- modify products to meet legal, social and cultural requirements in foreign markets
- develop totally new products for the foreign markets, using existing production resources, know-how and raw materials
- develop new products that do not use existing physical resources, but where the company can develop such resources using existing or acquired technology and know-how.

Export of know-how and technology

Where it is not practical physically to export goods competitively, perhaps because of import restrictions (such as high duties, quotas, licences, unavailability of foreign exchange, regional trade association preferences, foreign government local industrialization programmes) or high levels of domestic plant utilization (and where it may be considered inadvisable because of risk or limited resources to invest in extra capacity purely or mainly for export markets), then additional earnings and profit potential may exist by:

- Licensing manufacture to foreign manufacturers with existing suitable facilities and distribution.
- Selling know-how and technology to foreign concerns that lack that resource but that have capital, management resources and skills to produce and market the products. In this respect the foreign party may well be someone not already in your product category but with his own strategic reasons for desiring to enter that category and having ruled out connections with existing local producers, such as by acquisition and merger, possibly because of local merger rules and procedures.
- Supplying consultancy services including personnel training to transfer know-how, technology and skills on a fee basis as opposed to the normal royalty system related to licensing agreements. This approach is more normal where the technology has little value in originality and the foreign party really only needs to acquire management and operational skills.
- Operational management contracts. This may be an extension of the sale of know-how, or separate, in that you would contract to run and manage all aspects of an ongoing business in return for fees or shares of revenue or profits. (This kind of contract is common to some of the major international hotel chains, and even operates in some manufacturing ventures, such as dairy plants in the developing countries.)
- Forming consortia with other interested and relevant companies providing relevant complementary input to offer total design and

construction of turnkey projects, possibly extending to management or other licensing arrangements.

Foreign mergers, acquisitions, joint ventures, branches and subsidiaries

I have earlier discussed the case for foreign branches and subsidiaries in connection with further development of exports, local control over distribution or the need to manufacture locally. Within this category of international growth opportunities, the main considerations include:

- foreign branches, where control and development of exports will benefit by being under the direction of your own personnel
- foreign distribution subsidiaries that will handle the physical distribution and marketing of products imported from the parent group
- foreign distribution subsidiaries that will organize local contract manufacture and then market and distribute finished products
- foreign joint ventures that will undertake the manufacture, marketing and distribution of an agreed product range
- foreign wholly owned subsidiaries providing manufacturing, marketing, distribution, etc.
- mergers with foreign corporations where there are compatible products and management, and the opportunity for growth, earnings and profits to increase mutually with a cross-fertilization of ideas, management and products
- acquisition of foreign corporations with an established market position complementary to your own products and objectives, and where acquisition could give you tangible 'market entry' for home products, or other know-how, technology, earnings and profit benefits.

The issues facing a company developing a strategy that includes any of the above are, I believe, more complex than those likely to arise in pursuing the more straightforward opportunities of product and know-how export. A careful audit of your own company's strengths and weaknesses, its ability to contribute to and manage any foreign venture, management and capital resources, are just a few issues in the equation. Foreign acquisitions could be the subject of a major study on its own. Factors such as the attitudes of local governments and the applicable rules on foreign ownership are paramount. Will you in practice be able to exercise the required degree of management control and authority over your assets? Or would one of the other joint arrangements in practice work more to your advantage? Is the foreign company capable of expansion or simply holding a good market share while operating close to capacity, and therefore probably needing more capital injections to develop or defend market positions? What are the capital requirements of the foreign company? Does it need major overhaul or investment in new plant and equipment? Can you repatriate profits and what restrictions apply in relation to capital invested?

All too often a home company gets involved in a foreign acquisition, frequently in an entrepreneurially owned concern, only to find that it does not have the firm business base or management team expected or portrayed, and that the home company is unable in practice to control the foreign company. Involvement and advice from bankers, merchant banks and auditors could all be most useful. Study in depth of the foreign company's performance records, consistency, market position and share, management stability, training and succession, are all important.

Import of foreign know-how and technology

Quite apart from your efforts to sell abroad, if the name of the game is overall earnings and profit growth, consideration should be given to seeking to import know-how and technology in areas in which your company is less strong but where the existing plant and equipment could be used or adapted, or where the company has capital and management resources to allocate to more sophisticated or new product areas. Some considerations are:

- obtaining foreign consultancy services to help in the design and commissioning of plant and equipment to produce new products complementary to existing items
- obtaining consultancy services to help upgrade plant and equipment for the production of existing products where such upgrading would improve quality or output, reduce costs, or in other ways improve or contribute to competitiveness in home or export markets
- obtaining licences for complementary products from foreign manufacturers who are not already locally manufacturing such products, and who may be interested in a vehicle for penetrating the market in exchange for fees or royalties
- utilizing spare capacity or developing additional capacity to contract manufacture goods for foreign concerns that may face import or other restrictions or pressures, but that may wish to control their own local marketing and distribution.

This is the converse of the domestic company seeking such opportunities abroad. Often, similar home market opportunities are simply overlooked, perhaps because the home marketing team is so busy with defensive actions against both other home producers and foreign imports that it does not consider the merits of cooperation with the foreign invaders.

Import of complementary foreign products

This is a straightforward extension of the above, and may precede any subsequent local manufacturing arrangement. If foreign products complement your own range, and fill a gap where you perhaps do not have the technology or capacity to develop your own product, then it may be beneficial to become the distributor of the foreign product, providing you can satisfy the foreign party on your intentions to develop and not stifle growth of their product. Similarly, if there is a new market sector that your strategists want to enter, but you do not yet have your own product range developed, such a product range may be available elsewhere, initially for import, and possibly for manufacture under licence, or as a market research test to facilitate own-product development.

Foreign raw material sources

This is almost an aside from the main purpose of this book, but it would be neglectful not to mention it in passing because it should form part of the overall company international strategy considerations. Most companies use some foreign raw or semi-processed materials in their production processes. Availability, price and quality are three major worries and factors in the mind of the procurement director and his staff. The overall international strategy team could give equal weight of consideration to this area as to other aspects, because a significant profit contribution can be made by effective sourcing of inputs. There are various ways of achieving this. For example:

- A foreign buying office could be set up in the source markets to control supplies, quality, etc.
- If materials need further processing before use in production processes, then either the company could set up its own processing facility in the source market, where generally labour will be cheaper and there may be other local benefits from being seen to invest, or a foreign party may be prepared to invest in the processing facility on agreeable contract terms.

Either of these approaches may reduce the involvement of middlemen, give more secure supply sources (you could go even further back in the vertical integration process to growing or mining the raw material), improve quality with reduced wastage, and overall provide marginally cheaper product.

Strategy and plans

Once all the available options have been carefully considered and evaluated, then the identified international strategy should be developed as a formal internal document, and integrated with both domestic and overall company strategies as part of the whole corporate planning process. The strategy may come from what the company would like to do under ideal conditions, or from analysis of company markets, strengths, skills, management resources and technology in relation to perceived opportunities in a global context. What often happens is that interesting and viable ideas are discarded because 'we don't have the resources to do that'. That is perhaps putting the cart before the horse, because I would always argue that the strategy should be developed initially taking the existing resources as a base but with consideration of the additional resources necessary to implement the agreed strategy in a number of planned manageable stages. Early projects may necessarily relate more to the use of existing facilities to generate additional profits for reinvestment in projects related to the longer-range objectives and opportunities. If internal resources are scarce, then there may be attractions in considering joint ventures to attract foreign capital for expansion either at home or abroad.

The broad strategies can then be allocated time-spans and priorities, enabling detailed plans to be made for the pursuit of each strategy objective. Clearly not everything can be done at once, and the approach to each market may have to be different for political and economic reasons. There will be short-range and long-range opportunities and differing risk factors. There will always be the need for change and flexibility in any plan; it cannot be cast in concrete. If an early priority is to earn income by selling consultancy and service-related skills, it will be essential to have an available pool of fully trained and competent managers to handle projects as contract opportunities arise. Clearly it would be pointless and embarrassing to send out a representative to sell your skills, and then tell him at the point of contracting, 'sorry, we do not have any engineers free just now'.

It is a traditional criticism of British businesses (although it applies equally to some other countries) that too few resources (particularly human) are allocated to the pursuit of international business opportunities. Many companies and executives approach foreign markets and international business transactions with the nervousness that comes from unfamiliarity. That is natural. But those companies that have chosen to invest in international opportunities, more usually just in the form of a small export department, have generally been surprised and delighted with the magnitude of results from few personnel. Realistic assessment of your strengths and careful consideration of the international business opportunities realistically available to your company may give you the confidence to implement a strategy and development programme, including allocating necessary management resources at the right critical points. As a final thought: if the elephant, with all his great physical strength, had the ability to assess and use that strength, would he be happy as a recluse in the jungles of the world?

Summary

- Consider establishing an internal International Strategy Committee to assess and evaluate the range of alternative international business opportunities available to your company, taking account of the range of human skills and other resources within the company, and the political, social and economic international environments.
- Major areas for consideration can include: physical export of existing products; development of modified or new products; sale or purchase of know-how and technology; sale or purchase of other consultancy services including design, training, commissioning, turnkey projects; joint ventures at home or abroad; foreign acquisitions and mergers for synergistic development; development of home markets for goods and services of foreign origin or technology; and development of raw material sources.
- Develop an international strategy and time scales, taking account of risk and resource factors, and produce a specific plan for developing the human and capital resources necessary for effectively implementing each stage of the plan.
- Conduct regular disciplined reviews of the strategy, subordinate plans and budgets, and their progress against measurable criteria.

Glossary Standard Export Terms and Abbreviations

a.a.r.: against all risks.

ad val.: *ad valorem* − freight or customs duties set at a percentage of value.

a.y.o.r.: at your own risk.

B/E: bill of exchange.

B/L or **B of L**: bill of lading − contract between shipper and carrier generally giving ownership title or right to take possession. *Clean bill of lading* refers to receipt for goods received by carrier in apparent good condition.

bonded warehouse: government-licensed warehouse where goods may be stored without duty being paid until goods are withdrawn and cleared through customs.

BOTB: British Overseas Trade Board.

B.T.N.: Brussels tariff nomenclature.

C.A.D.: cash against documents − terms of payment.

c & f.: cost and freight to agreed destination.

certificate of analysis: required by buyers of certain products, such as food ingredients, and usually certifies that product meets standards according to accepted test methods, and stating analytical composition.

certificate of free sale: required by some countries as evidence that the goods are normally sold on the open market and approved by the regulatory authorities in the country of origin.

certificate of origin: a certificate showing the country of original production of an export product. Frequently used by customs in ascertaining duties under preferential tariff programmes, or in connection with regulating imports from specific sources.

certificate of quality: a document intended to demonstrate to a buyer that goods meet a recognized and measurable international quality standard.

c.i.f.: cost, insurance and freight to agreed destination.

c.i.f.c.: cost, insurance, freight and agent's commission (possibly showing percentage commission, e.g. c.i.f.C3).

C.L.: car load.

commercial invoice: document showing commercial values of the transaction between the buyer and seller.

consular invoice: an invoice covering shipment of goods certified by a consular official of the destination country, and used normally by customs or officials concerned with foreign exchange availability to ascertain the correctness of commercial invoice values.

customs broker: person licensed to conduct business at a customs house on behalf of others.

cwt: hundredweight (100 lbs in USA, 112 lbs in Britain).

D.A.: documents against acceptance − instructions from an exporter to a bank that documents attached to a draft for collection are to be delivered against acceptance of the draft.

dead freight: freight charge paid by charterer for space left unused.

demurrage: a penalty levied for exceeding free time allowed for loading or unloading at a dock or freight terminal; charges may also be levied by a container company for delays in loading, unloading or returning a container.

D.P.: documents against payment — instructions given by an exporter to a bank that the drawee can collect documents attached to a draft only upon actual payment of the draft.

D.R.: dock receipt — normally issued by a shipping line acknowledging that goods were received for shipment; the bill of lading is issued only after goods are loaded.

drawback: repayment of any part of customs or excise duties previously collected on merchandise when those goods are exported.

ECGD: Export Credit Guarantee Department — a British agency providing government-sponsored insurance on exports.

E. & O.E.: errors and omissions excepted.

exchange rate: units of one currency exchangeable for a certain number of units of another currency.

f.a.s.: free alongside ship — price quotation term.

f.o.b.: free on board — price quotation term that, internationally, refers to free on board the vessel, but in the USA more usually refers to any agreed place where ownership transfers under terms of sale, e.g. free on board railcar; free on board plant.

f.o.r.: free on rail.

force majeure: contract clause exempting parties from performance for reasons of events beyond their control.

f.p.a.: free from particular average — 'particular average' means damage caused by marine perils to the particular interest insured.

F.T.Z.: free trade zone — area, generally near a port, where merchandise may be produced, stored, modified, pending sale or reshipment and where such activities do not require customs clearance unless entering the domestic market.

G.A.: general average — a general loss voluntarily incurred to save all interests involved in a common maritime venture from impending peril; the principle of general average applies in adjustment of all common loss, damage and expenses.

GATT: General Agreement on Tariffs and Trade — major international agreement between many of the world's nations.

Incoterms: *International Rules for the Interpretation of Trade Terms* — International Chamber of Commerce Publication No. 350.

international freight forwarder: person licensed to engage in the business of dispatching clients' goods internationally, normally by ocean vessel, but most now include air freight operations.

L.C.: letter of credit — document issued by a bank on behalf of a buyer in favour of an exporter, with the bank lending its name and support to honour the exporter's draft.

l.c.l.: less than carload, or less than container load — term used in reference to freight matters when shipment volume is insufficient to fill a railcar or container.

l.t.l.: less than truckload − term used when the quality or volume does not fill a standard truck.

marine extension clause: clause extending insurance coverage during transit delays until goods reach the final destination.

marine insurance policy: contract between an insurance company and the person having an insurable interest in merchandise.

mate's receipt: issued by the mate of the vessel acknowledging cargo receipt, particularly in the charter trade; not a negotiable document.

metric tonne: European measure of 2,204 pounds weight, or 1,000 kilograms.

pro forma invoice: draft invoice sent to an importer by the exporter prior to order confirmation and shipment to assist in matters relating to obtaining import licences or foreign exchange allocations, or simply to advise the value of a consignment so that letters of credit can be opened.

S.E.D.: Shipper's Export Declaration − a US customs form to be completed for all exports to assist the government in compiling export statistics.

S.I.C.: Standard Industrial Classification.

sight draft: draft payable on first presentation through a bank.

SITPRO: Simplification of International Trade Procedures Board.

S.L. & C.: shipper's load and count

T.T.: telegraphic transfer of funds.

transshipment: the transfer of goods from one carrier to another.

VAT: value added tax.

W.A.: with average − an insurance term meaning that the shipment is protected against partial damage whenever the damage exceeds a stated percentage.

war risk: normally used in relation to insurance coverage concerning action against a vessel or goods by a hostile government.

warehouse receipt: receipt for products deposited in a warehouse; a non-negotiable document if delivery is specified to only one party.

weight − gross: weight of goods including all packing materials.

      net: weight of goods excluding packaging materials.

      tare: weight of packaging or container.

Recommended Reading

To supplement this general introduction to the management and practice of exporting and international business, I would recommend the reader to additional selective study from the following works.

Marketing

International Marketing, L. S. Walsh (Plymouth: MacDonald & Evans, 1981)
Introduction to Marketing, Dr J. Frain (Plymouth: MacDonald & Evans, 1983)
Marketing Today, Gordon Oliver (Hemel Hempstead: Prentice Hall, 1980)
Export Strategy: Markets and Competition, Nigel Piercy (London: Allen & Unwin, 1982)
International Marketing, Simon Majaro (London: Allen & Unwin, 1982)

Legal

The Export Trade, C. M. Schmittoff (London: Stevens & Sons, 1980)
Charlesworth's Mercantile Law, C. M. Schmittoff and D. A. G. Sarre (London: Stevens & Sons, 1977)
Legal Aspects of Export Sales, C. M. Schmittoff (London: Institute of Export, 1980)
Agency Agreements in the Export Trade, C. M. Schmittoff (London: Institute of Export, 1980)
Patents, Trade Marks, Copyright and Industrial Designs, T. A. Blanco White, R. Jacob and J. D. Davies (London: Sweet & Maxwell, 1978)

Finance and payments

Finance of International Trade, A. Watson (London: Institute of Bankers, 1981)
Uniform Rules for Collections, International Chamber of Commerce, No. 322 (Paris, 1983)
Uniform Customs and Practice for Documentary Credits (1983), International Chamber of Commerce, No. 400 (Paris, 1983)
Modern Managerial Finance, J. R. Franks and J. E. Broyles (Chichester: Wiley, 1979)
Finance for the Non-Accountant, L. E. Rockley (London: Business Books, 1979)
Incoterms [International Rules for the Interpretation of Trade Terms], International Chamber of Commerce, No. 350 (Paris, 1980)

Documentation and transport

The Elements of Export Practice, A. Branch (London: Chapman & Hall, 1979)
Elements of Shipping, A. Branch (London: Chapman & Hall, 1981)
Marine Insurance – Principles Vol. I, R. H. Brown (London: Witherby, 1978)
Systematic Export Documentation, 2 vols, SITPRO (London: Simplification of International Trade Procedures Board, 1976 and 1979)
The Effective Export Department, SITPRO (London: Simplification of International Trade Procedures Board, 1982)

Government services

Export Handbook, British Overseas Trade Board/HMSO (London, 1982)

Market research

International Directory of Published Market Research, British Overseas Trade Board/HMSO (London, 1984)
The Practice of Marketing Research, Anthony H. Davies (London: Heinemann, 1973)
Marketing Research: An Applied Approach, T. C. Vinnear and J. Taylor (Maidenhead: McGraw-Hill, 1979)

Statistics

Statistics in Theory and Practice, L. R. Connor and A. J. H. Morrell (London: Pitman, 1977)
Applied Statistics for Management Studies, David Croft (Plymouth: MacDonald & Evans, 1983)
Statistics for Business, Finance and Accounting, J. P. Dickinson (Plymouth: MacDonald & Evans, 1976)
Statistics for Management, John Ashford (London: Institute of Personnel Management, 1980)
Essentials of Statistics in Marketing, C. S. Greensted, A. K. S. Jardine and J. D. MacFarlane (London: Heinemann, 1978)

General

Exporting Made Simple, H. Deschampneufs (London: Allen, 1977)
Hints to Exporters, British Overseas Trade Board (London)
Doing Business in . . . , Price Waterhouse (London), free series of guidebooks
Investment in . . . , Peat Marwick, Mitchell & Co. (London), free series of guidebooks
Croner's Reference Book for Exporters (periodical)

Index

International Chamber of Commerce 153 222
International Convention for the Protection of Industrial Property 208–9, 210–11
International Directory of Published Market Research 13
International Strategy Committee 259–60, 266
introductory letters 21–2, 34, 36
inventories 33, 83, 121
investment grants 234
invoices 128; certified 128, 137; commercial 128, 136; consular 128, 136; pro-forma 128, 130, 131, 132
irrevocable letters of credit 49, 152 156–7

Japan 28, 39, 51
joint selling organizations **252–7**
joint ventures 38, 42, 227, 232–6, 237, 260, 262, 265; partners 232 jurisdiction on agreements 54

know-how: export of 260, 261–2; import of 260, 263–4
Kompass 13

labelling, product 88–9; approvals 85; declaration 89; information 84, 88; and language 84, 90, 95; regulations 14, 17, 18, 19, 84–6
'landed duty paid' 79
language and product labelling 84, 90
lawyers 217; legal costs 221; patent and trademark 208
leaflets, promotion 98
leasing plant/capital equipment 161
legal costs 221
letters of credit 14, 49, 65, 88, 131, 132, 141, 144, 145, 149, 151–7, 165, 193, 201, 256; confirmed 152–3, 156–7; documentary 151–2; irrevocable 51, 153, 156–7; revocable 153; revolving 154; standby 154; transferable 154–5 unconfirmed 153; validity of 152
libraries 7
licences, export 138, 194, 197–8, 206, 216
licences, import 15–16, 18, 42, 92, 261; basis of allocation 15
licensing **237–51**, 261, 263–4; agreements 16, 239–40, 242–5, 246–51, 261; assignment rights 244; audit rights 244; fees 237; licensee 237, 238, 240–1; licensor 237, 239–40; sub-licences 240, 243, 246
licensing regulations 216; *see also* export licences; import licences
lien on goods 193
lifestyle advertising 94, 105
limitations of liability, seller's 130
literature, product 88

litigation over contracts 219, 221
loans 164
lobbyists 217
local manufacturing/distribution arrangements 16, 26, 121
London Chamber of Commerce 222

management contracts 261
management fees 235
management structure 235
manufacturing, local 16, 121
marginal cost 39, 69–72, 79–80
margins 26–7
marine insurance policy 128, 135–6, 165–6
market information 32, 48
market positioning 75
market research: agencies 13; as data source 13, 16
market returns 73
market share: of distributors 120–1; of export sales 119–20
market visits **21–36**
marketing programme 32
media 25, 38
meetings, exploratory market visit 24
mergers, foreign 260, 262
Middle East 37
minimum wage laws 235
modification, product 41–2; checklist 42; design 41; function 41; packaging 41
multilingual labels 84
multinational corporations 259

nationalism 84
negotiable document 132
negotiable drafts 141
non-conference shipping lines 178
non-disclosure agreements 242
non-durable consumer products 95–6
non-performance penalties 189
non-tariff barrier 84

ocean freight 175
open account 147, 156
open cover policies 168
order 112–13; acceptance 113; confirmation 128, 130–1, 136; planning system 122, 124–5; progress record 112–13; requirements 88–9; right of rejection 52
organization charts 31
outlet surveys 97–8
ownership rights, seller's 191, 192–4

packaging **81–91**; colour in 86–7; design 81, 83–4, 91; freight and 90; modification 41; physical protection 81–2; regulations 14, 17, 18, 19, 47, 84–6; scientists 82; specifications 88
packing list 129, 138
parallel exports/imports 66–7, 211
patents 87, 232; conventions 208; infringements of 213–14, 248; licensing